Praise for GRIZZLY HEART

"With clear respect for the many bears that surround them, Russell and Enns offer deep insights into the bear psyche and eventually prove that it is possible for humans and bears to live together, even to trust one another. More an adventure narrative than a scientific study, the thrilling events of their story should not diminish the importance of what Russell and Enns have shown: humans are the aggressors here, not bears. Their message is strong, at times shocking, and eloquently told."

—*Quill & Quire*

"The account of the three orphaned cubs is rich in detail and insight."

—*Winnipeg Free Press*

"The value of his work is clear. During their time in Kamchatka, Russell pitted his instincts and beliefs about grizzly behaviour against the views of the "experts," and emerged enlightened. Through hundreds of encounters with grizzlies and the experience of raising three orphaned cubs, he and Enns paint a picture of bears as intelligent, emotional, reasonable and predictable, yet forever on the receiving end of all things nasty in human-bear encounters gone wrong…. It's an uphill battle, not without its risks and disappointments, but *Grizzly Heart* shines a light on what's possible."

—*The Calgary Herald*

"It's a compelling read about their effort to prove a peaceful coexistence isn't reserved for fairy tales."

—*The Edmonton Sun*

GRIZZLY

HEART

LIVING WITHOUT FEAR AMONG
THE BROWN BEARS OF KAMCHATKA

CHARLIE RUSSELL
and MAUREEN ENNS

with FRED STENSON

VINTAGE CANADA

VINTAGE CANADA EDITION, 2003

Published in Canada by Vintage Canada, a division of Random House of Canada Limited, Toronto. Originally published in hardcover in Canada by Random House Canada, a division of Random House of Canada Limited, Toronto.

www.randomhouse.ca

Vintage Canada and colophon are registered trademarks of Random House of Canada Limited.

National Library of Canada Cataloguing in Publication

Russell, Charles
Grizzly heart : living without fear among the brown bears of Kamchatka/
Charlie Russell and Maureen Enns with Fred Stenson

ISBN 0-679-31195-5

1. Grizzly bear—Russia—Kamchatka Peninsula. 2. Human-animal relationships.
3. Russell, Charles. 4. Enns, Maureen.
I. Enns, Maureen II. Stenson, Fred, 1951– III. Title.

QL737.C27R87 2003   599.784   C2003-900904-1

The authors wish to acknowledge the assistance of the Canada Council
and the Alberta Foundation for the Arts.

The excerpts on page 111 and 112–113 are from *Explorations of Kamchatka 1735–1741*, by Stepan Krasheninnikov, translated by E. A. P. Crownhart-Vaughan. Copyright © 1972 by the Oregon Historical Society.
The excerpt on page 236 is from *The Adventures of James Capen Adams*, by Theodore H. Hittell. Copyright © 1911 by Charles Scribner's Sons.

Text design: Sue Thomas/Digital Zone
Cover design: Daniel Cullen

Printed and bound in Canada

10 9 8 7 6 5 4 3 2

To my son, Anthony, who at age eleven saved my life in the only physical altercation I ever had with a bear.
—Charlie Russell

Contents

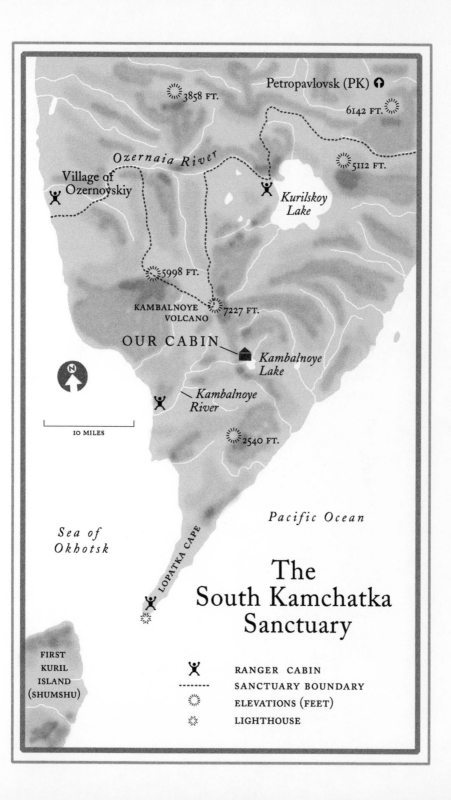

3858 FT.

Petropavlovsk (PK)

6142 FT.

Ozernaia River

5112 FT.

Village of
Ozernovskiy

*Kurilskoy
Lake*

5998 FT.

KAMBALNOYE
VOLCANO   7227 FT.

OUR CABIN   *Kambalnoye
Lake*

N

*Kambalnoye
River*

10 MILES

2540 FT.

Pacific Ocean

*Sea of
Okhotsk*

LOPATKA CAPE

The
South Kamchatka
Sanctuary

FIRST
KURIL
ISLAND
(SHUMSHU)

RANGER CABIN
- - - - - - - -   SANCTUARY BOUNDARY
ELEVATIONS (FEET)
LIGHTHOUSE

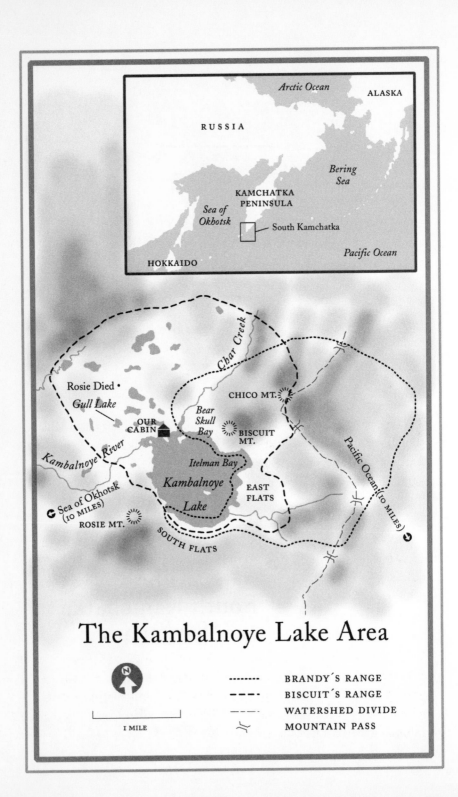

The Kambalnoye Lake Area

Arctic Ocean

ALASKA

RUSSIA

Bering
Sea

KAMCHATKA
PENINSULA

Sea of
Okhotsk

South Kamchatka

HOKKAIDO

Pacific Ocean

Char Creek

Rosie Died

Gull Lake

CHICO MT.

Bear
Skull
Bay

OUR
CABIN

BISCUIT
MT.

Kambalnoye River

Itelman Bay

Kambalnoye
Lake

Pacific Ocean (10 MILES)

Sea of Okhotsk
(10 MILES)

EAST
FLATS

ROSIE MT.

SOUTH FLATS

N

1 MILE

- - - - - - - BRANDY'S RANGE
- - - - - BISCUIT'S RANGE
- - - WATERSHED DIVIDE
MOUNTAIN PASS

Prologue

In the spring of 1994, in the rain forest along the Khutzeymateen Inlet of British Columbia, I sat on a moss-covered Sitka spruce log as a female grizzly bear walked down the log towards me. I knew if I did not move, she would keep coming. I had decided to let her come as close as she wanted.

Occasional slivers of sunlight penetrated the high spruce canopy. I was in a moss and jade world that, until that moment, I had only fantasized sharing with a grizzly bear. This bear and I were not strangers. For five years I had been guiding bear watchers into the Khutzeymateen and, being uncommonly friendly, she had been one of the main attractions. Now, looking into her eyes, it seemed she wanted to push the frontiers of her experience with humans, just as I wanted to embark on something new with bears.

As she made her way down the log, she moved with a swaying nonchalance. I am certain she was trying to set me at ease. I tried to accomplish the same thing in reverse by talking to her in the calmest voice I could muster. There was an uncertain look on the bear's face, and a similar look must have been on my own.

Finally, she sat down beside me. After a time, she moved her paw along the log towards my hand and touched it very gently. I reached out and ran my finger along her nose, feeling her well-muscled upper lip, which she pronated to explore my fingers. She let me feel her teeth, and then, without understanding why I was driven to do so, I slipped my fingers into her mouth and slid them along the tops of her square grinding teeth. I ran my index finger back along the ribbed roof of her palate. She could have had my hand (and the rest of me) for dinner, but she did not.

Even as it happened, I knew I was experiencing something that would likely change the course of my life. If I could build on this moment, correctly and ambitiously, the significance of what had just happened might have the power to change the relationship between humankind and bears. I know how that must sound—like advanced megalomania—but I still believe it is true. So much of the reputation of bears, and people's fear-dominated, love-hate relationship with them, is based on the belief that the experience I enjoyed is not possible. If I could prove that it was not a fluke, not an anomaly particular to this time and this bear, a huge shift in perception might flow from it. People might learn to live with bears in a way that would not lead to collision, violence, and the ongoing destruction of a threatened species.

I also knew in that moment that I could not back away. What was happening was something my life had been moving towards for decades, and from which I must not swerve. I had to follow where it led.

Where it led was to Kamchatka, to the most remote and wild part of Russia, to the least despoiled grizzly bear habitat in the world.

PART ONE

(1994–1995)

I

Bear as Friend:
How Bears Taught Me to
Believe

Each year, for a month straddling May and June, the bears of British Columbia's Khutzeymateen Inlet gather to eat fresh sedge grass on the estuary and at the mouths of several creeks along it. This inlet, Canada's only grizzly bear sanctuary, slices through imposing granite mountains for twenty miles. When the bears come down to feed, the tops of the mountains are still draped in winter snow. Beyond the wet sedge meadows, the valleys are filled with rain forest.

For seven years, 1990 through 1996, I guided eco-adventurers to this magical spot in the employ of Tom Ellison and Jenny Broom, owners of the *Ocean Light*, a fifty-five-foot, gaff-rigged cutter from which the tours were staged. Tom is a tall, good-looking man who once supplemented his university funds modelling for the Eaton's catalogue, and he takes his captain's responsibilities seriously. Through thirty years working along the notorious west coast, from Panama to Yakutat, Alaska, Tom and his boat have escaped serious mishap. Tom admits to only one major lapse of judgment in his career, and that was the day he gave me free rein to work with the bears and his eco-tourists.

When we took clients out into the deep and steep-sided Khutzeymateen Inlet, we were able to sail within a few feet of shore. Most bear sightings were made from the deck of the boat. To explore the tidal channels, we used an inflatable boat that held eight tourists at a time.

Most of the bears in the valley were afraid of us. In the country outside the bear sanctuary, both to the north and south, bear hunting was still big business and completely legal.[1] Some bears had enough experience with hunters to be extremely wary. We were lucky to get a glimpse of them. But there were other bears that did not fit that mould; the most striking example was the bear I described in the prologue. We called her the Mouse Creek Bear because that was where she was most often found. Mouse Creek was the spot where her mother and brother had been killed by a male cannibal bear when she was a yearling.

Now an adult, this orphaned female was wild in every way, but had decided she liked people. If we had a group on shore, she liked to come near and perform some antic. She would balance on a small log, or bend a tree and let it snap back up. When we were in the inflatable boat, she would wade out near it and grope around in the water until she found some object to her liking, a stick or a rock, then, lying on her back, she would play with it, rolling it around on her belly, flipping it in the air. She also liked to thrash around, creating a turmoil of flying water.

Most often, when we watch animals in the wild, we are voyeurs, sneaking peeks. But this was different—a mutual experience—and much more enjoyable. This grizzly wanted an audience. We were happy to provide her with one.

The Mouse Creek Bear had something in her nature I have never read about, not in any of the shelves of books I have collected about her kind. She allowed me to set the limit on how close she could be to my clients. If I firmly said *no* and stepped towards her when she approached, she

---

[1]   In February 2001, a three-year moratorium was placed on all hunting of grizzly bears in British Columbia. Though a 1996 Angus Reid poll showed that 91 per cent of the people in that province opposed the trophy hunting of bears, and 77 per cent wanted it banned altogether, the official reason for the moratorium was to give scientists time to do a population study. When the Liberals were elected in B.C. in May 2001, the new premier said his government would overturn the decision and allow grizzly bears to be hunted.

would stop—and stay at that distance. The bear was so well mannered that I often let her come quite near. She had a way of setting everyone at ease. She radiated respect and what you might even call love for those of us who gave her a few weeks' company each spring.

The moments our guests had with this bear were often the first they had spent with a grizzly in the wild. Many described the experience as the most profound of their lives. Once I had to almost physically restrain a woman about to walk up to the bear and give her a hug. This same woman had been so full of fear that she hadn't wanted to leave the security of the boat. But after an hour with the Mouse Creek Bear, she had abandoned all sense. So strong was the magnetism of this special bear, I could understand the woman's impulse. If she had slipped by me and actually hugged her, it seemed possible that the bear would have allowed it.

Trustworthiness is not a quality often attributed to grizzlies, but the more I observed this bear, the more I came to believe that trust might be possible with her. In our long history of conflict with bears, grizzlies in particular, no one has much considered the possibility of working out a truce. The more I was around the Mouse Creek Bear, the more I felt it was time.

While our guests were learning to fraternize with grizzly bears as though they were dolphins, the reality beyond the sanctuary could not have contrasted more. Up and down the west coast of British Columbia, hunters were paying US$10,000 for the opportunity to shoot a grizzly bear, the animal they regard as the ultimate prize. The hunting outfitter nearest to the Khutzeymateen operated off a big boat called the *Smuggler*. From ship to shore, their hunting parties travelled by Zodiac. Occasionally, the *Smuggler* showed up in our inlet and anchored nearby for the night. It did not happen often, but when it did, a mood of depression always settled over us.

Twice, Tom Ellison and I accepted invitations to drink whisky aboard the *Smuggler*. It was definitely a form of masochism, but we did it thinking we could learn more about the outfitter's reasons for coming into the grizzly sanctuary. Maybe the hunters had so thoroughly overshot their hunting territory, they had to come to the sanctuary to show their clients live bears.

Each time, across a table full of whisky glasses, we talked bears, and I was treated afresh to the anthropological puzzle of how two groups from

one society can talk about the same animal in such a contradictory fashion. Hunting guides describe bears as ferocious, unpredictable, and savage
predators. They tell one horrifying story after another about people being
torn apart. The victims are always those who approached the encounter poorly
armed. Then the guides move on to recount countless acts of sportsman
bravery: tales of real men stopping huge angry bears just short of the
barrel of their guns. They keep it up until their clients are shaking in their
boots, barely able to muster the courage to face the dreadful foe. I suppose
when these hunting clients actually do kill a bear, they feel tremendously
powerful, as if they have collected all the formidable power of the bear
into themselves.

What keeps me from hating these people is that I was raised in a hunting family—a hunting and outfitting family to boot. Dad bought me my
first gun before I was ten years old, as he did my three brothers and my
sister. In my late teens I became a hunting guide for so-called "big game."
The first clue that I wasn't cut out for it was when I started wondering
how my clients would like the chase if they were the ones being hunted.
I told Dad that I liked animals more than wealthy hunters, and ended my
career as a professional guide after one year.

Although my entire family crossed the great divide to become naturalists and protectors of wildlife, I can still remember what it was like to be
trained as a hunter, and to be a hunter. That background keeps me humble
and grounded, and allows me to be patient with the process of change.
Until gentler ways of getting pleasure from nature catch on, enough to
become meaningful in the overall economy, we will have to go slowly.

As I guided the bear watchers into the Khutzeymateen, often to within
feet of the Mouse Creek Bear and other friendly grizzlies, I knew how far
I was exceeding normal wildlife viewing protocols. In fact, what we were
doing was so far outside the guidelines set by the park, it wasn't funny.
Eventually, inevitably, it led to trouble—with the authorities rather than
with the bears—and, frankly, I had wanted it to. For what we were doing
to have a greater meaning, to have a chance at changing society's opinion
of bears, our encounters had to be seen, discussed, and believed.

The key incident happened on a day when I was taking a group to see
the Mouse Creek Bear. We landed the inflatable boat near where she was

eating and I allowed her to come to within a few yards. She was foraging on the sedge grasses when she started to play with a section of log. She lay on her back and balanced the log with all her feet. Then she began to twirl it around. The bear was unmistakably having fun and the tourists and I were laughing, which in turn egged on the bear. None of us had any inkling that a wildlife biologist was watching through a spotting scope from the far side of the inlet.

The local ranger station was built on a large steel raft anchored off shore and, next morning, I was called there to account for myself. The wildlife biologist for the area (including the sanctuary) was studying the effect of tourism on bears and he described what he had seen across the inlet as "something from a Las Vegas circus act." Running our eco-tours in the newly formed park was an experiment, and a shaky one at that, and I was worried that I might cost Tom and Jenny their licence. At the same time, though, I knew that these were the very wildlife officials who were in charge of the regional hunting of grizzlies.

Although I felt the biologist misunderstood what he had seen, I took my responsibility in the matter seriously. I have never believed that bears are harmless and that people should be turned loose on them. That would be terrible. Rather, I believed there needed to be protocols for the meeting of the two species, and I was trying to gather evidence upon which those protocols could be based. What I was starting to understand was that it was wrong of me to use my eco-clients as a means of accomplishing that research. Somehow, I had to find a way to have my own experiences with bears, at my own risk and on my own schedule.

My curiosity about grizzlies had grown to an obsession, a powerful need to explore and answer an array of questions about bears. That, combined with a lucky group cancellation, allowed for that amazing day when the Mouse Creek grizzly and I discovered that trust between a grizzly and a human is not a fairy tale after all.

I had to get away and do a long-term study of grizzlies. The big question was where. With so little absolute wilderness left, and so few bears, and so many wildlife managers who did not share my views, where would I ever find the opportunity to do what I was desperate to try?

During two of those years guiding in the Khutzeymateen, I was involved in a second bear project, also on B.C.'s west coast. In 1992 and 1993, I worked with filmmakers Jeff and Sue Turner on a documentary for the BBC about a rare white phase of the black bear, called the kermode. Nearly one in ten bears on Princess Royal Island off the north coast of British Columbia are of the beautiful kermode type, presumably because the gene responsible for that colouration is more concentrated in that remote place. The island has not been inhabited by humans for many years. The original goals of the documentary were to make people aware of the kermode bear and, with luck, stop plans for logging the old-growth forest of the island. My role was to show Jeff and Sue ways of being safe around bears that would enable them to shoot film without having to hide or to work from tall stands.

Right from the start, the bears on Princess Royal were curious, friendly, and unaggressive. Putting a nose-print on the lens or rubbing the tripod became commonplace events. One of the white black bears wanted to be around humans, much like the Mouse Creek Bear. We called him the Spirit Bear, which would eventually become the title of the book I wrote about the experience.

I don't want to repeat too much of what I wrote in *Spirit Bear*, but suffice it to say that the bear became our friend in ways none of us imagined possible. A good fisher but small, the Spirit Bear used us shamelessly as human shields to protect his catch from a stronger bear who preferred stealing to fishing. "Don't follow bears" is a sound principle, but eventually I did go inland with the Spirit Bear to learn about the rest of his life. I found his cave and even entered it to photograph the bear at home. We played tug-of-war with a stick, and I was also allowed to scratch him with it. The Spirit Bear became so comfortable around us that we could step right over him while he slept. For that matter, we could lie down beside him and have a snooze of our own. During these two years, the Turners and I lived in a tent camp right in a key part of the bears' habitat. We were literally living with bears.

It was after the first year of filming on Princess Royal Island that I met Maureen Enns, a photographer and painter who had her own bear project going—part of it was a documentary film for which she hoped to interview me. When she called, it was early spring 1993. I was at home in Twin Butte,

Alberta, sharing the house we call the Hawk's Nest with my father, Andy Russell, a naturalist and author himself. I was up to my eyeballs in my winter's project: building an ultralight airplane, equipped with a float, for the second year of the kermode project. We wanted to gain access to difficult locations on the island and get aerial views of the bears' habitat.

MAUREEN: Two years before I met Charlie, I had been granted permission by Parks Canada to ride the back country of Banff National Park to do an artistic study of the grizzly as a symbol of Canada's disappearing wilderness. I was terrified of bears at that time, but was determined to apply my artistic talents to saving wilderness. Near the end of that season of study, I had a moment a bit like those Charlie describes with the Spirit Bear and the Mouse Creek Bear. Leading my pack horse, I was riding out of the Cascade Valley towards Lake Minnewanka north of Banff when, going around a blind curve in the trail, my horses jerked up their heads. I looked where their ears were pointing, and there was a silver-tip grizzly, digging roots beside her year-old cub. The two bears were no more than twenty feet away. The mother looked up. I stopped the horses. She calmly resumed foraging as I filmed her from horseback. The horses actually fell asleep during the process and, when the cub started towards them, I nudged them awake. With the cub literally at their feet, the horses stepped back a bit, but calmly, and the young bear returned to her mother.

That moment exploded two myths that had been on my mind all summer. Myth one was that horses are instinctually terrified of bears. The second was that bears who are unafraid of humans are dangerous. Not as far as these two grizzlies were concerned. I was ecstatic. It made me want to learn a lot more.

Out of the first year of the project came paintings that were framed in red and set against red backgrounds: reflections of my fear. The following winter saw a lot of change. When I painted the female grizzly I had met with my horses, she was beautiful and triumphant. I called her "The Queen of the Rockies." If there was red in these newer paintings, it no longer made you think of blood. By the second summer, the project was less about the "great Canadian wilderness" and more about bears. I had several more interesting encounters and was well on my way to concluding that the bear is a much misunderstood species when I arrived at Charlie's door.

To be honest, when Maureen called, I was in no mood to talk. I had been piecing the new Kolb airplane together for months and the skeleton had grown to completely occupy the already small living space I was sharing with my father. Somewhat impatiently, I took Maureen and her crew down the hill to my brother's place so we'd have enough room to set up the camera and lights. But the more we talked, the more we had to talk about. By her own means, and in a much shorter period of time than I, Maureen had come to question a great deal of the accepted wisdom surrounding bears. On that plateau, we met and became interested in one another.

Several months after the interview, when I was back on Princess Royal Island, Maureen came to visit. In addition to hobnobbing with the kermodes, we did some flying in the now-completed Kolb. In a particularly magical moment, we flew above a pod of humpback whales in water so clear we could see down a hundred feet. The whales, unbothered by the plane, began as indistinct forms in the deep that grew in size and detail until they breached below us.

Though Maureen and I have not been the most successful people on the planet at forming lasting relationships (I have had three marriages; she, one), faced with one another, we found we were willing to try again.

Our first winter together was the winter of 1993–4, and we spent a good deal of it writing. I was working on *Spirit Bear*, trying to find words for the Eden-like experience I had enjoyed on Princess Royal Island. That kind of connection with bears was something I'd dreamt of since childhood. Now that it had happened, I wanted to tell people about it in hopes of changing the relationship between humans and bears to something less hostile and rigid. I had to almost invent a new language to describe the human-wild animal relationship in ways that were not about conflict and fear.

By definition, a wild animal is one that is fearful of humans. Simply by enjoying the company of a human, a wild animal becomes something that can no longer be accurately described that way. I struggled with this anthropocentric view because of the negative twist it put on the possibility of kinship with wild animals. Humankind believes it no longer fits into the wild, or even needs to fit. We have spent centuries perfecting a rhetoric that distances us from the idea that we are also animals, a rhetoric that closes the door to understanding what we have in common with our fellow mammals and other fauna.

Scientists, attempting to invent a word that describes the human influence on wildness, have come up with "habituation," which is defined as an absence of response after repeated benign stimulus. For example, if a bear is initially frightened by people and runs away, and the next time still runs but not as far, and finally, because his experiences with humans no longer feel threatening, doesn't run at all, we say the bear is habituated. There is a great deal wrong with this term from my point of view. First, it refers only to how animals respond to people. Second, the connotation is negative; that is, a habituated bear is a problem bear. My experience on Princess Royal suggested that bears were neither naturally fearful nor naturally aggressive towards people. What this left was human fear. I began to believe that human fear was the true obstacle to coexistence.

I struggled to infuse *Spirit Bear* with these ideas and it turned out to be a widely read book. The bear's whiteness enables it to stand out against its dark green world and beg protection. In British Columbia, the kermode bear and Princess Royal Island debate captured the public's attention more powerfully than any other environmental issue that I had ever seen. As for my other agenda, the possibility of reducing man's conflict with bears, the book left a great deal undone. For one thing, *Spirit Bear* was about a white variety of the black bear and did little to improve the reputation of the grizzly. Black bears have fared better than grizzlies and have managed to survive in higher numbers because they reproduce more quickly and do not inspire as much fear in humans. From my experience with the grizzlies in the Khutzeymateen, I was increasingly confident that improved relations with humans was possible for grizzlies too. But how was I going to prove that?

Maureen's project, meanwhile, had also come to an end, but she realized that her unfamiliarity with, and fear of, bears had left her with that unfinished-business feeling. She began thinking about exploring the emotions bears might feel towards her. Given the right circumstances, she could also explore creatively the connection grizzlies have with the land.

All in all, when Maureen and I looked forward to the kind of work we wanted to do next, we were at an apparent impasse. What we both wanted was to live with grizzlies that were as new to the encounter with humans as the white black bears of Princess Royal had been.

Where on earth was that place?

Even if we *could* find it, was it likely that a visual artist and an ex-rancher would be able to persuade the local wildlife authorities to let them do a prolonged study of one of the world's most scientifically sought-after animals? There wasn't much chance a study of the possibility of human-bear coexistence would be approved by anyone in North America because it ran counter to the prevailing wisdom that mutual fear was the only sensible relationship between humans and bears. No one in the wildlife management world was interested in changing that attitude. A major stumbling block was that, as my ideas conflicted with the status quo, I was often viewed as a danger to bears rather than as their guardian. I've been involved with bears all my life and know many of the people who study and manage them in North America. Out of this group, even close friends begged me to reconsider my up-close-and-personal approach, worried that if Maureen or I, or some influenced member of the public, came to harm at the claws or teeth of a bear, the whole enterprise of protecting wilderness and bears would be compromised.

I never dismissed these arguments as unreasonable, but because so much of my experience with bears had been positive, I couldn't help but disagree with a bear management system based on the impossibility of peaceful coexistence. That animals so capable of complex emotion and so forgiving of human rudeness had to be perceived as dangerous in order to survive did not, and does not, seem morally right. If the mutual-fear policy had been hugely successful at protecting bears, I might have buttoned my lip. But that was hardly the case. You simply cannot make the general public enthusiastic about the beauty and the right to life and habitat of an animal they are being told is a psychopathic killer of humans.

In my view, it is much better to win people over to protecting bears by showing them what fascinating beings bears are and by supplying a simple, practical means of living peacefully with them. Both Maureen and I believed then, and still do, that peaceful coexistence is a realistic goal. We were willing to give ourselves to the venture, if only we could get it off the ground—or, more precisely, find ground to get it on to.

The story of how that search for a project home finally led to Russia goes all the way back to 1961, the year I took my first job outside the family guiding business. Eighteen years old and tired of my wars with the Alberta school system, I bolted all the way to Pasadena, California. I found an incredible job helping the soon-to-be-famous inventor Ted Heyer work on the discovery of the "shunt" valve, the device that changed the fate of children with hydrocephalus, a condition that prevents the brain from draining fluid. The shunt provided an outlet for the fluid and a solution to a tragic condition, and remains in use today.

Working on such a groundbreaking project was heady stuff for a backwoods wrangler from Alberta, and so was 1960s California. Solving difficult problems and manipulating new materials like silicon rubber helped me gain back much of the confidence I had lost in my tug-of-war with formal schooling. My apprenticeship convinced me that I had ability as a builder and a troubleshooter and allowed me, in time, to take on projects like teaching myself to fly and building my own airplanes.

At the same time, California gave me an intense homesick hunger for wilderness. Our ranch borders the mountain wilderness in the Waterton National Park area of southwest Alberta, and, throughout my childhood, Dad had made our living by giving wealthy families the chance to take a month off and live like nomads wandering the mountains on horseback. They could not bring along anything that wouldn't fit on a pack horse. Each summer, Dad allowed us children to go on these trips, one child per trip, and my first experience of the pack-train had been when I was six.

Our family was full of people eminently capable of teaching my four siblings and me about that environment. At the head of the list was our maternal grandfather, Bert Riggall, a well-respected botanist, naturalist, photographer, and hunting guide. Then there was my father, Andy Russell, who worked for Bert as a wrangler before marrying the boss's daughter and, in time, taking over the business. My mother, Kay Riggall

Russell, had grown up even more backwoods than we had (she was born in a tent!) and she too taught us much about how to live with nature. I saw my first grizzly from the back of a horse when I was seven. So however delightful Pasadena and my work there were, I had nary a second thought when my mother phoned to say that Dad wanted me to come home and work on a movie about grizzlies for which he had been successful in scaring up funds.

To say that my father underwent a conversion from being a hunter to being a naturalist and writer at about this time is a considerable over-simplification. As he put it in his first book, *Grizzly Country*, he had "joined the grizzly in retreat" from their common enemy, the bulldozer. The bulldozer and the chainsaw were destroying our beloved wilderness so rapidly that Dad's livelihood was literally cut out from under him and from under our family. Like the grizzly bear, my father was cornered inside a shrinking habitat, and his response was to become a film producer and writer. Starting with *Grizzly Country*, he has written twelve books and has earned a great deal of respect and recognition as an authority on bears and as a guardian of wilderness. He is still writing at the age of eighty-six.

In 1961, the project Dad had in mind was to film grizzly bears in the wild. This was a time when sentimental animal films made by producers like Disney were at the peak of their popularity. We knew that, contrary to appearances, the films were made with animals in captivity. If any of the animals were considered dangerous, they were rendered harmless by having their teeth and claws removed. Some predators were allowed to keep their teeth because it was their job to be ferocious. These animals were coerced into violence by being starved, then placed in tight enclosures with other animals they were meant, for film purposes, to fight and feed on.

Dad had the idea of a film depicting grizzly bears as they really were, something that had not been done before. The money came from the Frank Taplin Foundation, Frank being one of Dad's hunting clients from New Jersey. With some of the money, Dad bought a pair of Bolex movie cameras, which he promptly put into the hands of my older brother Dick and me. We were twenty-two and twenty. Though Dick and I had been well trained in photography by our grandfather (who left 8,000 photographs in his estate when he died), film photography was new to us.

The three of us began our search for grizzlies in the Selkirk Mountains in southeastern British Columbia and in our own Waterton backyard. Then we planned to take the Alaska Highway to the Yukon, where we would travel the Bates River, in what is now Kluane National Park. It didn't take us long to discover how hard it was going to be to get good film footage of grizzlies. There was little protection in those days for bears or wolves, even in the national parks. Nor did anyone much care, for it was a common belief that Canada was a place of inexhaustible wilderness and innumerable bears. As a result, the bears we did find had come to expect gunfire when they saw people, so we couldn't get anywhere near them. Despite all the stealth in the world, what we saw through our camera was usually bears disappearing into the bush or running at top speed over a distant mountain ridge.

As we delved deeper into the project, and went farther afield in search of less flighty bears, we eventually dispensed with our rifles—at first simply to lighten our load. But going into the wilderness without guns seemed to soften our approach to the bears and eventually helped us succeed. Dad, Dick, and I came to the conclusion that bears could somehow fathom our intent, even beyond the nature of the hardware in our hands. Without guns, our motives no longer included the possibility of harm to a bear, and, as if they could smell that difference, the bears let us come closer.

When we were driving north to pursue our quest in the Yukon, we took a side trip to Haines Junction west of Whitehorse to visit friends at a forestry cabin. As we got closer, we could see a column of smoke rising out of a long sweep of forest in front of us. Dad said, "Let's dig out our boots. Someday you can tell your grandchildren you drove 1,800 miles to fight a forest fire in the Yukon."

Before the crew arrived to fight the fire, a fall of rain began to put it out. As Dad drove around in a pickup truck, already elevated to some management job, Dick and I were given cold backpacks full of water. Our instructions: to put out the live embers in dead logs and mounds of peat.

Our crew had been press-ganged out of a Whitehorse tavern. For Dick and me, one American fellow stood out from the rest. He seemed at home in the bush, and the way he shouldered his pack and got on with the job implied he was no stranger to hard work. Nature had this fire well under control, so the three of us got out of sight and made a fire of our own to warm up by.

If I ever knew the man's name, I have long forgotten it. He was planning to walk all the way to Kamchatka, Russia, and was biding his time until the Bering Strait froze over. Dick and I perked up to hear a plan so absurdly more daring than any of our own. The fellow was dead serious and had done his homework. As he talked, eastern Russia grew in both our minds. I had always believed that the Yukon was about as wild a place as there was, but I knew almost nothing of Siberia and Kamchatka. Cold War cartoon images of Russian people and landscape had kept me from knowing how lightly populated it was by humans or how well populated by bears.

The American went his way, presumably to Kamchatka, and we went ours, into the backwoods of the Yukon. We soon discovered that Yukon bears were just as frightened of humans as bears in Alberta and B.C. After two years, we finished the film with the aid of the Alaskan brown bears of McKinley Park. I turned twenty-one in a camp on the Toklat River and marked the day by climbing a mountain and meeting face-to-face with a three-year-old grizzly.

Meeting the wandering American in 1961 cemented Kamchatka and Siberia in my imagination. In 1993, when I went looking for a home for Maureen's and my bear project, Kamchatka came to mind.

That winter, I started to make phone calls in search of information about Russia. One inquiry led to an unexpected offer from the Great Bear foundation in Montana. The foundation's director, Matt Reid, thought Maureen and I could do a study of the extent of brown bear poaching in Kamchatka on their behalf. It wasn't quite what we had in mind, but it was an excellent chance to convert the Russia of my imagination into a Russia on the ground.

2

Scouting Kamchatka

Soon Maureen and I were on our way to Russia. Officially we were investigating bear poaching in that country. Unofficially, we were scouting to see if Russia would suit our own project. The trip to Kamchatka from Seattle took us up the British Columbia coastline. By pleasing coincidence, we passed over both Princess Royal Island, home of the kermodes, and Glacier Bay, home of the blue glacier bears, another exotic colour phase of the American black bear. These bears live in preserved jewels of habitat, but we saw a lot of destroyed country too. As naturalists, we spend much time struggling to preserve bears in their habitat against the inexorable tide of economy and industry, and because we lose more often than we win, it is inevitable that we spend much time feeling negative and doomed. Now, by a magic akin to the reversal of time, Maureen and I were about to enter a country with more brown bears than the rest of the world's countries combined.

The Bering Sea is the storm generator for much of North America, and, not surprisingly, was obscured by dark cloud. With the help of a crude map in the in-flight magazine, I estimated that we crossed the Chukotka coast into Russia a few miles north of the town of Anadyr. Once we were over land again, the clouds opened on hundreds of miles of tundra, mountains, and huge, braided rivers. There were no roads and not even any survey lines. My bit of knowledge told me the big rivers were salmon rivers, and that meant bears. It was a long time before we started seeing marks in the forest, vehicle tracks and such, and, when they came, they signalled the approach to Magadan, a remote port city on the northeastern edge of the Sea of Okhotsk.

Magadan was a scheduled stop and our first ground-level experience in Siberia. It was a dreary-looking place, located on a flat landscape of scrub bush and muddy streams. The city was founded in the 1930s after a gold discovery in the region and had been used by the Communists as a gulag, or forced-labour camp. In fact, it had been the administrative centre for all the Siberian gulags and was a closed city until 1989. The runway was so rough that it kept bouncing our jet back into the air. Finally, we slowed enough to stay on the ground. The large wheels and heavy-duty underpinnings of the Russian planes that lined the runway suddenly made sense. Many of the military planes and worn-out passenger carriers had been cannibalized for engines and other parts.

After dropping off a few passengers, we bounced into the air again and headed southwest. Such is the size of Russia and the convolutions of its air travel that we had already flown well past our real destination of Kamchatka. Getting there would mean backtracking a couple thousand miles after a change from Alaska Airlines to Aeroflot in the city of Khabarovsk near the Manchurian border of China. Because Khabarovsk is near a Russian nature preserve and is home to an important natural science institute, the Great Bear Foundation had scheduled a meeting for us there with some Russian scientists. We were about to make our debut as foreign investigators of Russia's bear poaching situation. And whether it was the glimpse of the gulag city of Magadan or the approach of our first assigned meeting, every negative preconception we had about Russia came alive in our heads.

Khabarovsk is surrounded by the meandering wetlands of the Amur River where it flows east to the Sea of Okhotsk. The flat terrain, unmarked by roads or power lines, was rich in various washes of intense green. The glassy water, in graceful loops and oxbow lakes, reflected the blue of the sky and a few puffy clouds. As we landed, we saw only one barge on the water and the odd village linked by river to the rest of the world.

Once past customs, we met the interpreter and driver our hosts had arranged for us. Oxana, the interpreter, cured some of our paranoia instantly. She was a young college woman, formidably well educated, beautiful, and stylish. The drive to the offices of the Wildlife Foundation took about a half-hour, a good chance to see the city. The second to last stop on the trans-Siberian railroad, Khabarovsk had a cosmopolitan air, the feel of a place that connects much territory and many cultures. It had an enormous market full of flowers, food, and dry goods from all over the far east.

By the time we pulled up in front of the Wildlife Foundation's building on a street of overhanging trees, we had been travelling for thirteen hours. We had journeyed six thousand miles through three countries and over an ocean. Looking who knows how bedraggled, we trudged up the steps and into our meeting with biologists Dr. Yuri Dunishenko and Dr. Alexander Khulikov.

Our Russian hosts took it easy on us. Instead of talking business, which we would have time for the next day, they toured us through the foundation's collections. My bleary state reduced the tour to endless shelves of dusty brown bear and Siberian tiger skulls. We compared skulls, and though the brown bear's was bigger, it was not that much bigger than the tiger's. I had never imagined a cat that size. I also remember thinking there must be more Siberian tiger skulls in the foundation than there were live Siberian tigers in the wild (about 400 at that time).

Oxana met us the next morning and escorted us back to the foundation. It was pouring rain, and the streets were rivers we had to wade, ankle deep. It was also hot. The meeting itself was disappointing. About all that we learned was that due to the great number of Russian bears there was a lack of interest in working with them. Why would you study them when you could be studying something *really* endangered, like the Siberian tiger?

The visit did eliminate some possible locations I had been considering. I had been told that the Shantar Islands in the Sea of Okhotsk might have the required combination of remoteness and high bear population, but the Russian scientists informed me the Shantars were a bear Eden no more. Poachers had all but erased the bear populations.

Another possibility was Primorskiy Kri, a huge wilderness south of Khabarovsk and east of Vladivostok. Again, the two scientists had knowledge to the contrary. This lush mainland area was slated for logging by Canadian, Korean, and U.S. timber companies. As we needed a wilderness that was going to stay a wilderness for a few years, that was the end of that. We pinned our hopes on Kamchatka.

We continued our journey with Aeroflot. Travellers of backwoods Russia often say that Aeroflot combines air travel with elements of Mexican bus travel. Pets are common cabin companions and, as we winged our way from Khabarovsk to Petropavlovsk in Kamchatka, one traveller was holding onto an enormous box which, according to its label, held a Hitachi TV. Apparently the carry-on rule on Aeroflot isn't how much you can stuff under the seat but how much you can fit on your lap.

Since 1961, I had been trying to picture Kamchatka. Now, I was about to see it. After two hours above the clouds, the pilot began to come down through the high overcast. Once beneath it, a long line of snow-capped volcanoes appeared, stretching north as far as the eye could see. The valley forests gave way to alpine meadows at about two thousand feet. We banked around Avacha Bay, with Petropavlovsk built among the hills on its north side. I could tell by the way the pilot was lining up that the airport was still some distance away. In fact, it was near an entirely different city, called Yelizovo.

As we landed, both sides of the runway were lined with bunkers, each with a MiG fighter parked beside it. In clearings cut into the birch forest were dozens of other aircraft, all relics of the war that was never fought. It was the most incredible collection of flying hardware I had ever seen.

Because we had already been through customs in Khabarovsk, we were free to stand around for a while on the airport tarmac and soak up the sights: mainly the incredible ring of volcanoes in which Petropavlovsk and Yelizovo are set. The overcast was burning off fast and it was becoming a beautiful summer day.

Igor Revenko, our guide, was supposed to meet us at the airport, but so far there was no sign of him. Finally, we went on our own to collect our luggage from a galvanized metal shed, and it was then that a pleasant-looking young man strode up and introduced himself in good English as Igor. He was about five feet ten inches tall with thick black hair that tended to flop down over his eyes. From the start I could tell that he liked to appear calm and that he expected that quality in others.

In the parking lot, he led us to a little red Datsun, and for a while it was a puzzle how he would stuff us and our luggage into it. With a resourcefulness we would soon take for granted, Igor produced a roof rack that attached with four big suction cups, and soon had our mountain of luggage clamped onto it. Each time we hit a pothole, I expected to see our stuff raining down, but it stayed put.

Yelizovo and Petropavlovsk are about twenty-five miles apart, and the two cities contain eighty-four per cent of the population of Kamchatka—about 350,000 people. This was very good news. It meant that most of Kamchatka, which has a land area similar to California, was almost empty of people. Igor also told us that the population of the two cities was rapidly shrinking. The biggest employer had always been the military, and as the military had been scaling back since 1989, people were leaving in droves.

He took us to a small hotel where we got a room and dropped off our luggage. Then we went to his home for lunch. He lived on the third floor of a concrete apartment building built on a steep hillside, with a view of three towering volcanoes from the kitchen window. There was a sharp contrast between the building's dreary concrete exterior and stairwells and the beautifully kept, carefully decorated apartment Igor and his family lived in. As it was Saturday, his wife Irina was home with their two children, Katya and Egor, six and nine. Irina was a dental surgeon, in great demand for her knowledge and skill. Come September, Igor would be home looking after the kids while Irina took in a conference in Minsk. They seemed to have worked out a pretty comfortable life in this forgotten part of their country, and I was eager to get to know them better.

Igor had been researching brown bears in the southern part of Kamchatka since 1985. Perestroika had opened up entrepreneurial opportunities for him, so that his work was slowly changing from scientific study to organizing foreign parties like us. If people wanted to make a film about bears or other wildlife, or simply have a look at a place that had been off limits for so long, Igor was their man.

It was Igor's plan that we should first see the Valley of the Geysers in the Kronotskiy State Preserve. It was a spectacular place and a key destination of most foreign travellers. Igor thought it would be best if a man named Vitaly Nikolaenko guided us while there. Vitaly was another student of bears, and we got the sense that there was a territorial understanding between Igor and Vitaly about who should guide where.

But before we could fly off to see the geysers, we had to face up to some realities of Russian bureaucracy. Russian state preserves were not created for public use the way North American ones have been. In the Soviet era, preserves were purely scientific and had nothing to do with tourism. For a foreign person to be allowed into them was a new thing and, naturally, there was quite a bit of negotiation and paperwork involved.

The following day, Igor took us to the Kronotskiy Preserve office in Yelizovo and introduced us to its director, Sergei Alexeev. The price of a trip into Kronotskiy was steep. Per day, it was about equivalent to the price of a good hotel at home, plus the cost of our guide, our interpreter, our helicopter, and food for everyone. Even at that, it seemed fair, as long as the money went to offset the costs of administering the preserve and not into someone's pocket. Sergei asked that we give him the money for Vitaly and the interpreter, but we insisted on paying them directly, which he finally accepted. We decided on a ten-day trip, leaving as soon as the weather allowed. Three days later we set off.

The Valley of the Geysers was as fascinating a thermal area as I have ever seen; every bit as amazing as Yellowstone. The most active part of the valley is a half mile of spouting geysers, some intermittent, some steady; some hot-water, some steam. Where the hot water isn't scalding, lush grasses grow. It is the first place to green up in spring, and is a popular grazing place for bears in late April and May. Even in July, when the whole country was green, we saw a bear near the geysers and many bear tracks in the mud at the edges of the bubbling mud pots.

When we left the Valley of the Geysers, we hiked with Vitaly between a series of cabins strung out for many miles through the preserve. There were bears everywhere and in settings I had never seen them in before, like black sand beaches. On the wide coastal plains they ate vetch while they waited for the salmon to arrive.

Our final destination was Vitaly's own cabin at the foot of the Kronotskiy volcano. Once there, Vitaly almost exhausted Stas, our interpreter on the trip, telling us about bear behaviour he had observed over the years. He said the bears were wary of people and admitted that he had seen evidence of poaching in the preserve. He rolled up his pantleg and showed us a scar from a bullet hole in his leg, his permanent reminder of the dangers of dealing with poachers. Despite the old wound, he insisted that poaching was not a big factor within the preserve at that time.

Near the end of our week together, I tried to explain to Vitaly, with Stas's help, what I wanted to study. No matter how I struggled to be clear, he did not see it as a scientific pursuit and insisted that only scientists would be allowed to study in the preserve. Even though he was not a scientist himself, I did not argue. It was obvious that the Kronotskiy Preserve was Vitaly Nikolaenko's territory and, big as it was, he didn't feel there was room for us.

Our 150-mile trip back to Petropavlovsk turned out to be a milk run that doubled the distance as the pilot dodged weather systems and went up and down to drop things off at hunters' cabins along the way. In Russia, a hunter is a person who has the right to use a certain allotment of land to make a living by trapping or shooting. What the hunter does is supposedly legal, but often it is not. Poaching bears for their gallbladders and salmon for their caviar are common black market activities in which hunters are involved. Learning the legal and illegal practices of the licenced hunters was important in understanding why bears are poached, in what numbers, and for what price.

From Petropavlosk, we flew with Igor into south Kamchatka, his true domain. The immense peninsula was more than we could have imagined and everything we had hoped for: a land untouched by roads and survey lines, rich in tundra and crystal-clear salmon rivers. We flew down the peninsula's mountainous spine and the farther south we went, the more we began to see a mosaic of deep trails in the tundra that had been worn exclusively by the feet of brown bears. Eventually, we arrived at Kurilskoy Lake, a body of water cupped in an ancient volcanic caldera, where hundreds of bears lived off prodigious spawning salmon and many species of berries.

Here, for eight years, Igor had worked as a bear biologist, trying to count the bears and understand how they might be protected. Until 1984, when the lake became part of the newly-created South Kamchatka Sanctuary, sixty to eighty bears were killed there for meat each year. The level of protection afforded in a sanctuary is less than in a preserve like Kronotskiy—and it was not patrolled by rangers—but the activity and presence of scientists, fishery inspectors, and film crews made it awkward for poachers to operate. Still, on our hikes along the rivers, we did find a couple of cable snares.

We travelled in Igor's boat to the mouths of many streams where huge schools of sockeye salmon were massing for their surge upstream to spawn. Many bears had staked out the stream mouths and were having an easy time gorging themselves. Igor said that the bears would soon be on the berry fields south of his cabin in great numbers. The beaches were the bears' highways and we almost always saw bears along them. The number of bears was stunning. In a single day at Kurilskoy Lake, I saw more bears than existed in the entire Khutzeymateen Inlet.

It was a different twist for me to be guided, but Igor was both skilled and thoughtful. He had built a cabin on a point of land jutting out into Kurilskoy Lake and, over the three weeks we spent there, we often sat around a campfire trading stories into the early morning hours. Igor had been raised in the Ukraine during Communist times, when great importance had been placed on education. Children with special aptitudes were encouraged to pursue their interests as far as they could. Igor's genius was mathematics and physics, combined with a keen interest in nature. To the consternation of his teachers who had dreamt for him a future in the national space program, Igor had chosen to pursue his interest in natural science when he got to university.

When Igor was getting his education, Kamchatka was still an almost mystical place to Russians and Eastern Europeans; a place so far from Moscow that it could take years of travel just to get there. As soon as Igor got his degree in biology in 1985, he was offered a job as a ranger and biologist in the newly created South Kamchatka Sanctuary. His family was horrified when he accepted, thinking of how far away from them he would be—nine time zones! There were some perks, however, such as getting to fly out to civilization once every two years, at mostly the state's expense.

Maureen and I plied Igor with questions regarding our bear study. I told him in detail the kind of location we were looking for, and that I understood it might not even exist in the world anymore: a place with many brown bears; a place where no people lived; a place where there had been little or no human interference. We would, of course, need the acceptance of those whose jurisdiction we were in. Kurilskoy Lake itself almost fit the bill, except that there was a small village of about twenty people nearby who conducted research on salmon, and some foreign film-makers had come there to make documentaries about Russian bears.

On one of those nights around the campfire, Igor told us about a place farther south that might be what we were searching for. Kambalnoye Lake was like Kurilskoy, he said, but more the way it had been decades before. No one lived there except for the bears who fished the plentiful salmon and denned in the depths of snow come winter. A few days later, Alexei Maslov, the manager of the salmon research station, came to visit. He had been doing some recent surveys to determine the extent of the salmon runs in various rivers. One of his last trips was an aerial survey down the Kambalnoye River, a steeply descending stream that ran from Kambalnoye Lake to the Sea of Okhotsk. In a stretch of ten miles, he had counted eighty bears, most of them fishing close to the lake. He called the area "Kamchatka's forgotten place."

Maureen and I made plans to rent a helicopter for a detour there on the way back to Petropavlovsk. But, when the time came, bad weather hung over the southern tip of Kamchatka. We had to leave without seeing the place that seemed the most promising of all.

3

The Bear Project Is Born— and Airborne

After our scouting trip to Kamchatka, I hit the ground running. Almost immediately, I was off on a thirty-two-city North American tour for *Spirit Bear*. In every city, I gave a slide show and spoke about turning Princess Royal Island into Spirit Bear Park. The effort resulted in thousands of letters to the premier of British Columbia and his environment minister.[2] During the tour, the things audiences said to me, positive and negative, had an enormous effect. The more I heard, the more I was convinced that the North American approach to wildlife management was often based on untested prejudice, particularly against grizzlies, but also against bears in general. Science has the highest standards for most animals, but resorts to myth when it comes to bears. Bears are killers, scientists tell us. Bears are dangerous. Bears cannot live calmly and safely in proximity to humans. It was imperative that Maureen and I get somewhere and start

---

[2] I am delighted to say that a park did result. In April 2001, after ten years of struggle, an agreement was reached between loggers, environmentalists, First Nations, and government, and a sanctuary was created for the Spirit Bear.

testing these propositions against their opposite: that bears, treated with respect, might not be killers; that bears might only be as dangerous as we make them; that bears can live in proximity with people, if people observe some rules that make the bears feel secure. We didn't know the answers either, but we were willing to search for them.

In September 1995, I flew home in my Kolb from a wolf-spotting mission in Alberta's boreal forest to find a very promising e-mail from Igor awaiting me. He had a rough plan for our first year in Kamchatka, based on our being at Kambalnoye Lake, the "forgotten place" we had missed seeing.

Another piece of news was that Igor was coming to North America to attend a meeting of bear-viewing guides in Juneau, Alaska. Not too surprisingly, I wound up involved in the bear conference too. Being the only guide present from a Canadian grizzly-viewing area (the Khutzeymateen), I was asked to give a slide show on my guiding techniques. I threw in a couple of slides of our eco-clients at close range with the Mouse Creek Bear. This move was tactical, as I wanted to know if anyone else out there was beginning to relax about the danger of bears, due to benign experiences as a guide.

I should have known not to expect much. The group as a whole was putting forth the message that bear viewing is a dangerous business requiring fully competent guides with heavy rifles. A heavy rifle, in their view, was a large part of what qualified a person as a professional. In the last four years of guiding in the Khutzeymateen, I hadn't carried a gun. I relied on pepper spray, which in many official and accidental trials had proven it could stop a charging bear. So far, I'd never had to use it. In Alaska, most of the good viewing spots, while protected, were very close to country that was open to hunting. In other words, the same bears who stood quietly in places like McNeil Falls while hundreds of people took their picture were also being shot at twice a year. Is it any wonder the truce between bears and humans seems shaky at times?

The reaction to my talk wasn't entirely negative. Larry Aumiller and his wife Colleen Matt, who had been in charge of bear viewing at McNeil Falls for twenty years—with a perfect safety record—were delighted that I had brought up the question of trusting bears. They told me that they had several bears at McNeil Falls that behaved like the Mouse Creek

Bear—bears who liked people so much that Colleen and Larry had given up on trying to discourage the friendship. But they did have an area from which people could observe and photograph, and the bears understood they were not to enter that space.

Larry and Colleen worked for the Alaska Department of Fish and Game. Most of the others who worked for that department held more traditional views. It was evident they considered the hunting part of their mandate the most important use of bears in Alaska, the giveaway being their frequent use of the word "harvest." I can't imagine using that word as a synonym for killing an animal you actually care about. I suppose that harvesting an animal feels different than killing it. Many were also using the words "sow" and "boar" for female and male grizzlies, which bothered me as well. The comparison of bears to pigs, far-fetched to begin with, has always been popular with people who want to classify the bear as something to be killed, for sport or through necessity.

Igor Revenko was a big hit with his video about the bears of Kurilskoy Lake. Many of the Alaskans present, who had been around bears all their lives, were only beginning to realize that their huge neighbour to the west might have more brown bears than they had. As well as trading ideas about bear safety, Igor was feeling out the prospects for serious eco-tourism in his country. If the enthusiasm of the resource people present was any indication, he was in business. There wasn't one person there who wouldn't have jumped at a chance to see Kamchatka.

Next morning, in a coffee bar on a steep Juneau street, Igor and I finally had our talk. For all I was pleased with Igor's effort, I had to be convinced that the plan was practical. It was very important we be allowed to build a cabin in the sanctuary. In a place where we didn't understand the weather, or how bad the mosquitoes might be, I didn't want to commit to living in a tent for several years. If we were allowed to build a cabin, what materials were available to build it with?

Then there was the question of the Kolb. Would I really be allowed to bring my plane into Kamchatka and fly it? During one of our campfire talks at Kurilskoy Lake, I had told Igor that I very much wanted my ultralight plane with me in Russia. I had used it on two wilderness projects to date, and I knew its value for keeping track of wildlife in road-free country. Also,

with the plane, we would be much less dependent on others for our main-
tenance. At the same time, as I said it, I had scant hope of it happening.
Getting a plane to southern Kamchatka and through the layers of red tape
I imagined would be involved seemed hopeless.

Igor, to my amazement, said he was quite optimistic that I would be able
to do it. In search of permission, Igor had been talking to Sergei Alexeev, the
director of Kronotskiy Preserve and also of the South Kamchatka Sanctuary.
Sergei told Igor that we should bring US$10,000 as a fee for each year we
would conduct our study in his territory. Igor assumed the money would buy
us the right to build the cabin and fly the plane, though Sergei hadn't spelled
it out.

Hearing this, I could imagine all kinds of problems with potential
funders. Giving the Russian authorities cash and not knowing where it
was ultimately going would not look good on the kind of budget one pres-
ents when raising funds.

I asked Igor to tell me everything he knew about Sergei. How committed was he to his job? What were his personal interests? Particularly,
I wanted Igor to think of something tangible that we could give Sergei in
lieu of cash that would be of obvious and significant use to him in his protection of the preserve, something he could not acquire in Russia.

We completed our meeting on that note. Igor would try to find some
of the answers, and I would go home and talk things over with Maureen.
If we were both truly ready to commit to the project, we would start raising funds.

Back at home, Maureen and I carefully went over every piece of information we had. We considered every outcome, every implication. For one
thing, I seriously wondered if I was tough enough. In my prime, I had
been rugged and strong. Now, at 54, I was living inside a body that had
taken a lot pounding. On the other hand, Kamchatka promised to answer
the questions that obsessed me. I did not want to lounge around for the
rest of my life knowing I had not taken up the challenge. I had to do it.

Maureen was also inspiring. Whereas my approach tended to be sitting
in the hot tub with a beer, contemplating the future, she chose to work
out and get ready physically.

MAUREEN: I wanted to be fit enough to hike out of South Kamchatka if I had to, in the event of something happening to Charlie. My exercise highs did not last all day though. I rewrote my will for the third time. I contacted friends and relatives with endless instructions for care of my animals. But, due to financial concerns, the question of whether we were going was still not absolutely settled.

I thought long and hard about the use of my ultralight airplane in Russia. I had built it myself and thoroughly tested it, but it was still a small and fragile craft. Airplanes require a lot of attention and, in South Kamchatka, I would be far from any technical support, not just a few days away but possibly years.

Then there was the weather. In flying, weather is everything, and my vague impression of the weather in southern Kamchatka was that it would be similar to the notorious necklace of Aleutian Islands associated with Alaska. The Aleutians are famous for their high winds and fog, the two things that should be avoided like the plague in a light aircraft. There was no doubt that I wanted to fly in Russia, but I didn't want my enthusiasm to get too far ahead of common sense.

At the point when I was very close to committing to the project, I ordered a topographical map of the Kambalnoye Lake area from the U.S. Department of Defense. I studied the map carefully. Kambalnoye Lake was much smaller than Kurilskoy Lake, where Igor had done his own research. It was also 1,000 feet higher. It looked like it could be exactly the remote, bear-populous and human-free place we wanted, but we had never personally seen it so it remained a pig in a poke.

Finally, Maureen and I could look each other in the eye and say that we were committed to going to Russia. That left the small matter of raising US$90,000.

Maureen and I told funders that within our isolated study area we intended to live by rules quite different than the ones people normally followed in bear country. We would let the bears live as close to us as they wanted. We would try to coexist peacefully with them, in such a way that we would all be undistracted and safe. We discovered we were not as desirable funding prospects as we might have thought. Most granting foundations prefer to work with organizations or university-backed groups, with the rationale that individuals are too risky. If a person were to break a leg in the middle of a project, everything would have to be scrapped and the money would be wasted. Considering where we were going, we could hardly argue with them.

But we continued to peck away and, amazingly, we got somewhere. By the end of March 1996, we had enough of the budget to start provisioning the project. The biggest outlay was what we'd come up with as an alternative to paying Sergei Alexeev US$10,000 in cash. Sergei liked the idea of using an ultralight for ranger duty and poaching patrols in his preserves, so we decided to give him an unassembled Kolb with a Full Lotus float system as the equivalent of two years' payment. The plane looked great on our budget. Its end use would help bears, plus it had the advantage of being too big to fit into anyone's pocket.

In early April, Igor e-mailed us with a plan to transport our cabin-building materials and aircraft fuel to Kambalnoye Lake. First, he would use a truck, taking it to the west coast on the only road in south Kamchatka. Then he would load it all onto a gigantic all-terrain vehicle that was used to supply a fishing village on the Sea of Okhotsk. In April the snow would be very deep, but the ATV had enough power to take our fourteen tons of material overland to Kambalnoye Lake.

The rub was that Igor needed cash to buy the lumber and other materials, and to pay for the transport. If we couldn't get him the money fast, the opportunity would be lost. Igor had a friend coming back to Petropavlovsk from Seattle whom he was certain we could trust to hand-deliver the cash. If we wired the money to another friend of Igor's, an American, he would pick it up at the bank and give it to the Russian. "Send US$14,000" was the final line of the note.

We had struggled so hard to persuade people to trust us, and now we were supposed to give an unknown American fourteen thousand dollars so he could give it to an unknown Russian. We thought of each of our funders in turn and imagined their response. The ones who already thought we were on the weird side would now be completely certain. Others *might* pass it off as the kind of risk you take to get a difficult thing done. But if we waited and took the money ourselves in June, we would wind up buying lumber that had already been picked over by every dacha owner on the peninsula. We would be late getting into the field and would pay twice as much for transport.

Finally, we wired the money to Seattle. Igor's American friend sounded very put out about having to interrupt his busy schedule to chase down our international bank draft. Then, the Russian failed to show up to collect it. We still don't know what happened to him. It took us two more very trying days to get the American friend to return the money to us.

We barely had the cash back when another e-mail came from Igor with a new plan involving a different receiver and Russian runner, located in Homer, Alaska. This time, things worked reasonably well—at least until Russian customs seized the cash from our courier at the Petropavlovsk airport. Somehow, Igor talked his way through that problem and took possession of every dollar we sent.

The irony is that, after all this international intrigue involving money, Igor changed plans and did not use the ATV to freight our building supplies to Kambalnoye Lake. An even better method opened up to him, involving a giant Mi-26 military helicopter. In any case, Igor had our money in his hands to pay for the purchases and plans he made on our behalf.

In early May, I took my Kolb to Doug Murray, a friend who lived not far from my ranch, and entrusted him with the installation of a new motor. Doug had built a Kolb a couple years before and was an ace mechanic. The new Rotax 912 engine was a key part of the strategy for the whole venture. It was much more powerful than the engine I had been flying with, and I was counting on it to pull me through the bad weather and the long hauls in Russia.

In mid-June, we loaded all our gear, plus the planes, on a truck and onto Doug's trailer and headed for Seattle. We crossed the mountains safely and were soon packing my Kolb and Sergei's unassembled one into a shipping container that was supposed to arrive in Petropavlovsk the same day we did, June 20.

As the container ship pulled out of Seattle, one thing niggled at the back of my mind: I had not had time to test the new engine. I would have to do that over strange wilderness in a foreign country.

PART TWO

(1996)

4

To Russia with Love

Our second journey to Russia was a piece of cake compared to the first. Air Alaska's new direct flight to Petropavlovsk cut off thousands of miles and days of travelling. Twelve hours after leaving home, we dropped into Avacha Bay and took in the welcome sight of Petropavlovsk nestled in the hills and almost surrounded by volcanic mountains.

This time around, I knew a little more about the city that would be our main provisioning centre for the life of the project. Avacha Bay, 180 miles north of the south tip of Kamchatka on the ocean side, is the most secure harbour in the Russian far east. Fishers and mariners have sought the protection of its natural breakwater for centuries. Over the winter I had read *Where the Sea Breaks Its Back*, Corey Ford's book about the exploration of Alaska, which includes an account of Vitus Bering's voyage of discovery. In 1740, after crossing the whole of Russia by land, Bering stopped on the north shore of the Sea of Okhotsk to build his two ships. Then he sailed south around Lopatka Point and up to Avacha Bay where he stopped to provision for the historic crossing to Alaska. He and most of his men did not survive the discovery of Alaska and the search for the Bering Strait, but the few who did brought back tales of bountiful sea otter, which sparked Russia's commercial interest in the west coast of North America.

Petropavlovsk takes its name from the Bering voyage, or more precisely from the names of Vitus Bering's two ships: *St. Peter* and *St. Paul* (or Pavel). During the Russian fur-trading exploitation of the North American west coast Petropavlovsk served as Russia's north Pacific seaport, the staging place for North America–bound ships.

By 1930, Petropavlovsk was a fishing town, with a population of around 20,000, and had been officially renamed Petropavlovsk-Kamchatsky to differentiate it from another Petropavlovsk in Kazakhstan. People started calling the city PK, and still do. At the start of the Cold War, the Soviet Union capitalized on Avacha Bay's natural concealment and proximity to North America by turning it into both a nuclear submarine harbour and an air force installation. As a result, the population rose to over 400,000. As far as the outside world was concerned, Soviet Petropavlovsk was a secret and dangerous place, best known as the city where a Korean airliner was shot down for entering its air space in 1983.

Under the Soviets, residency in PK was never permanent. It was an isolated assignment and people didn't stay a day longer than they had to. Rather than investing in the city, residents hoarded their isolation pay for the day they could return to civilization, much as southerners do in the towns of Canada's far north. Even today, the city has the untidiness of a place that people don't care much about. The cement-bunker look of most of the buildings is also of Soviet origin. Because of the area's history of destruction by earthquake, the Soviets constructed every building to resist great seismic assault, resulting in architecture that is repetitive, far from pretty, and very unlike the fine architecture of Moscow and St. Petersburg.

The city might as well have been situated on an island or enclosed by high walls for all the importance the surrounding countryside was given. Even at the height of the Cold War, there was never enough funding to build a road network or a railway to connect Kamchatka to the rest of Russia. This isolation turned out to be fortunate for both the land and its bears. Right next to the city, wilderness and wildlife flourished. Igor showed us a recently occupied bear den on a ridge separating two neighbourhoods, a demonstration of how little the city was disturbing the animal population.

There had been some exploration into harnessing thermal power for electricity, but other than that, PK's surroundings resembled a wilderness park.

In 1996, seven years beyond the Cold War, Petropavlovsk was both better and worse off. Without the paranoia and military budgets, the city was shrinking at a remarkable rate. On the other hand, the people still there were there by choice. The greatest virtue of Petropavlovsk is its stunning location: its beautiful bay surrounded by active volcanoes soaring to 12,000 feet, and its wilderness—wilder than the wildest place in Europe.

The ship containing the two Kolbs had made it too. Clearing ourselves and then the airplanes through customs was the first dreary but necessary task. The extraordinary thing was that it was easier to get the Kolbs through customs than it was the special coffee and the few bottles of wine we had tucked in with our supplies.

The plan was to purchase the last supplies and prepare my plane to leave for the south on June 27. The first step was to load the Kolbs on a flatbed truck and take them on a terrifying trip through the potholes to the Krechet Helicopter Company aerodrome on the edge of the city of Yelizovo. The 40-minute high-speed drive caused more damage to the planes than the previous 5,000 miles of transport.

The aerodrome was a strange combination of hangars and houses inside a high-security compound owned by Anatoly Kovolenkov, a keen-eyed and cunning man who also manufactured elaborate log buildings there. Our arrival at his aerodrome caused a stir. Russians are justifiably proud of their aviation and space exploration history, and they take flying very seriously. A small and simple personal aircraft was of considerable interest because few Russians can actually afford to own one.

So, with everyone helping, or at least watching, we lifted my Kolb and the crates containing the other plane off the truck. As the news spread of what I intended to do, you could almost feel the gathering skepticism. Anatoly in particular suggested taking such a fragile piece of equipment into Russia's most forbidding wilderness was lunacy. (I later learned that he predicted I would survive for a few weeks at most.)

I test-started the Kolb for the first time on Russian soil. It had barely fired when there was a loud bang and it died. One of the three propeller blades had flexed, probably because of the hesitant combustion of Russian gasoline, and had clipped the fuselage. The blade had shattered and was completely ruined. It was not a glamorous debut, but luckily I had spare propeller blades. Over the next couple of days, I got on with installing a new one. I also sawed a piece off the fuselage frame to create more propeller clearance. On the second test, things worked fine.

Around the same time, Maureen and I let ourselves loose in the markets of the city. We needed to buy enough food for the next four months. One of the things for sale was beef canned during the Soviet era. It was actually pretty good and reminded me of when Dad would kill a moose and Mom would can the meat because we didn't have a freezer. Many Russians do not own freezers, and those who do have to contend with power outages that can last for months. They tend to preserve everything. We were able to buy vegetables in huge canning jars that were in themselves very attractive. Our favourite item, this time and every time since, was Russian chocolate. We've always made sure not to head for Kambalnoye Lake without a goodly supply of it.

Igor arranged for a helicopter that would fly our supplies to our site on Kambalnoye Lake. The plan was for Maureen to go with the helicopter while Igor and I flew in the Kolb. We would leave about the same time in hopes of getting to the lake the same day.

When June 27 arrived, the weather to the south was not good. We stood by and waited in hope that it would clear, and, by early evening, it began to do so. Knowing that it would be light out until about 11 p.m., we decided to give it a shot.

In the helicopter, stuffed to the limit of its three-ton capacity, Maureen and the crew lifted away. The chopper could fly twice as fast as the Kolb, and soon it was just a dot in the sky. Within twenty minutes of our own takeoff, Igor and I were beyond the last of the roads, soaring among the snowfields and the high volcanoes. Then, like a sentinel ushering me on my way, a lone bear appeared on a horizon of snow, standing on the shoulder of a volcano and looking down at the green valley floor, two thousand feet below.

One of the many things I did not understand was to what extent our being up in this sky was known and accepted. I knew that Igor had arranged to have us approved by some authorities, but probably not by all.

In the chaos that was 1990s Russia, it was almost certain there were some who did not know about us and were being kept in the dark deliberately. Early in the flight Igor told me to stay behind a ridge that would keep us out of sight of the "Secret City," the nuclear submarine base tucked into the folds of Avacha Bay. Whether there was a real need to do so or if it was just force of habit left over from the Cold War, I still don't know.

Igor also told us that we were not allowed to bring a two-way radio. English-speaking voices on the airwaves of Russian Kamchatka would not be good. To be in such a remote place without a radio wasn't good either but we went along with that too. We were truly here on our own, without any of the customary safety nets that accompany modern wilderness adventurers in most parts of the world. Our only defence was to take no risk that wasn't necessary.

I landed on Kurilskoy Lake, not far from the salmon research station. One of the people who greeted us was an American scientist named Bill Leacock, a lightly built, angular man in his forties who was also about to start a bear study. His work involved radio-collaring bears and might, if things went well, earn him a doctorate. He had worked in Laos and Thailand, for the Peace Corps and UNESCO. His wife, Tip, was from Thailand. They had two daughters, Nina and Grace, aged five and eight, and the whole family was at Kurilskoy, living in a metal box not unlike a ship's container. Someone in Europe was fabricating these boxes as living quarters.

While I transferred gas from a jerry can into the Kolb's tank, I asked Bill if he had seen Maureen's helicopter go by. He had, about an hour earlier. That made me anxious to get back in the air. I was pretty sure the helicopter crew would not stick around after they had unloaded at Kambalnoye. They would want to get back to PK and would need the remaining daylight to do it. That meant Maureen would be on her own, standing guard over the food supplies, until we got there.

When I told Igor I was worried about Maureen being there alone with our food, he joked, "Why? Is she the kind who might eat it all?"

As soon as we took off, I started to relax—we only had twenty-five miles to go and one more mountain pass to surmount to get to Kambalnoye Lake. As we topped the pass, a sea of fog lay dead ahead. A cloud had pushed up the slope from the Sea of Okhotsk, completely filling the

Kambalnoye basin. The easiest thing, and the smartest, would have been to turn tail and head back to Kurilskoy for the night. But, if the helicopter crew had also come upon the fog over the lake, it would have been just as logical for them to return to Kurilskoy, and I knew they had not. I had to assume that they had arrived at Kambalnoye ahead of the fog, unloaded everything, including Maureen, and left. That would mean Maureen was down there, enveloped in fog and all alone. I pictured her seated on top of the pile, pepper spray at the ready.

It was now 10:15 p.m. and the sun was setting over the cloud-covered sea. The mountaintops poking through the fog were brilliant pink. We flew down the ridge that forms the spine over the peninsula's final few miles and saw a family of three cubs and their mother on the tundra near one of the peaks. When they saw us coming, they loped down into the refuge of clouds.

It was easy to see where Kambalnoye Lake was situated because of the way the tops of the mountains stood out of the fog in a semicircle. If Maureen was down there beneath the wool, she would hear our motor and at least know we were in the vicinity.

I crossed the east side of the divide into the next valley, which was cloud-free. Then I turned the plane around and approached the ridge from that direction. Tucked under the leading edge of the cloud that was spilling over the divide from the west, I saw a small lake, better described as a puddle. Igor said it was three, maybe four, miles from the cabin site. If I could land, we could climb over a mountain pass on foot and descend to the lake.

The decision had to be made in an instant. If I messed up or chickened out, we would be into the murk that was quickly taking over the pothole lake. Using every bit of the available water, I skidded across the pond in an instant. I manoeuvred between a couple of boulders and up onto the tundra on the far side.

The dark was gathering fast now, and I was full of trepidation about leaving the plane to the mercy of curious bears. We had a little food with us, and some warm clothing, but no tent or sleeping bags. I made a mental note never to make another Kamchatkan flying foray without them.

The vision of Maureen defending the food pile helped me unscramble my priorities. We secured the plane with corkscrew ground ties and charged off into the gathering gloom. Before long, we came to a deeply worn bear trail that headed towards the pass, which was somewhere ahead in the smother of fog. If we kept to this trail, Igor thought it would take us over the ridge and down to the lake.

The snow in the pass was deep, and our vision was very limited as we fought our way over the wet drifts. Then darkness, made even more black by the fog, completely overtook us. We slowed to a crawl. We came to a creek and this was a good sign. We reasoned that it must flow down to the lake, and for the next two hours we felt our way along it. When we finally came to the lakeshore, Igor made his best guess and we continued west. Eventually we stumbled upon the lumber pile.

Only then did we find out that Maureen had never landed. Her helicopter had turned back from the thick fog and gone somewhere other than Kurilskoy Lake for the night. Igor's guess was that she ended up in a fishing village called Ozernovskiy, sixty miles to the northwest.

Knowing even that much was a relief. Igor and I got on with making a fire and huddled beside it. When it started to rain towards morning, we dug beneath the lumber pile for the hammer and nails Igor had put there in April and cobbled together a shelter, overlapping some boards for a roof that would keep us dry as long as the wind didn't blow.

Not knowing anything about the country, it seemed logical to me that the sky would soon clear, but it did not. Around one o'clock the next afternoon, we heard a helicopter to the west. The pilot was feeling his way through the fog at low elevation. Then the direction changed. He had turned up a wrong tributary of the river and it took him some time to sort that out and return.

Then the engine was very close. Visibility was no more than seventy yards, and we each picked up the longest boards we could find and began to wag them back and forth. Out of the mist squarely in front of us, the machine materialized, looking massive. The rotor blast picked our shelter up off the ground and scattered it. The pilot set the chopper down beside us.

There was Maureen, and I was damn glad to see her. I applauded the pilot for his skill and his courage. To find our camp in such a mess of fog was extraordinary flying. Within ten minutes, we'd unloaded the chopper. Straight up into the fog, the helicopter rose and disappeared.

MAUREEN: Sergei, the helicopter pilot, grew troubled, as small clouds began merging into a thick fog as we flew south. Finally, only the volcano tops were visible. He dropped the chopper straight down to see if he had visibility below. There was none. When he climbed back out of the cloud, I thought we would have to go back. Sergei, his co-pilot (also namd Sergei), and the engineer spoke no English, so I couldn't ask. A while later, the helicopter started another vertical descent. This time when we broke through the ceiling, I could see cows and muddy tracks. Sergei landed, and as soon as the rotors were turned off, a big army truck zoomed up and uniformed men came on board. These were coast guard, and they wanted to see my passport and permits. Finally everyone smiled and I was encouraged to join the helicopter crew for the walk into town. I had no idea where we were, but found out later we were in Ozernovskiy. Together, we slogged down the village's muddy main street. Though it was almost dark, no lights were on in the buildings. I heard the word *hotel* as we approached a grey, sprawling building. Sergei (pilot) carried a briefcase inside while Sergei (co-pilot) carried a pail. I had my camera pack, my makeup, and a can of bear spray I'd grabbed just before leaving the helicopter. I had no idea whether I could trust my companions. At that moment it seemed possible our summer supplies might be sold to the villagers while I was abandoned.

I started to calm down when we entered the hotel. Carrying candles, we went to two rooms with a toilet between them. In their room, the crew started heating the pail over a small gas stove they'd borrowed from the kitchen. The pail turned out to be full of layers of food. The engineer disappeared for a while and came back with a big crab. Sergei (pilot) opened his briefcase, and voilà!—it was full of vodka. With lots of laughter and gesturing, they informed me that we were going to wait until the weather cleared, they hoped by the next morning. Given the speed with which four bottles of vodka were disappearing, I was relieved to know we weren't leaving right away.

As we "spoke" in this fashion, I came to understand that they were intent on seeing me safely to Kambalnoye Lake, but were concerned about whether Charlie and Igor would be there by the time we arrived. They were afraid to leave me at the lake with our provisions. As to the dangers I would face, big bears were pantomimed, with an expression of horror at my potential fate if left alone on the tundra. That night, I slept fitfully with my bear spray under my pillow. While Charlie was at Kambalnoye worrying about me, I was safe and dry, full of fresh crab, and worrying about him.

Next day, we left the village at noon and headed south down the west coast. I had already resolved to talk them into leaving me at Kambalnoye with our gear, whether Charlie and Igor were there or not. I was certain I could take care of everything. Flying close to the ground under the thickening fog, we followed a creek inland and returned to the ocean. An old cabin at the coast appeared and, from there, we followed what looked like a river, the ground just twenty feet below and visibility reduced to 200 yards. As we moved along, I could barely make anything out ahead. Suddenly, out the side window, I spotted something waving. It was Igor waving a board with a very wet Charlie nearby, doing the same.

If this were a book of fiction, the fog would have risen shortly after Maureen landed. And, as the fog rose and burned off in the sunshine, I would have given a stirring description of all that my eyes could see. Reality being less co-operative, the day kept on as it had started: rain and fog and more rain. We could see into the mist about fifty yards.

What we could make out at that distance were a few deeply worn bear trails and an impressive amount of bear scat. We knew that the bears were out there, and much of our conversation that day was about how many there were and how close they might be. We also wondered how many bears it took, over what length of time, to wear trails that deep.

Then the rain let up and the fog thickened. We covered our food and gear with tarps and set up our two backpacking tents. Igor grabbed a bite and immediately retired to his tent. Maureen and I saw the sense in this and did likewise, certain that the weather would improve soon.

Having our food close by and unprotected from the bears might strike some as dangerous, but I wasn't worried on that score. Igor said the valley hadn't been occupied by humans for a long time. My experience is that, given that degree of isolation, bears are quite reluctant to approach and ransack human food. If that kind of behaviour had been successful for them recently, they might have had a go at it, but, under the circumstances, I was sure they were more likely to shy away. I counted on that being discouragement enough until we built an electric fence around our camp. The only other precaution we took in the first few days was not to cook anything terribly aromatic.

We hadn't planned on a big sleep, but exhaustion overruled intention. We didn't wake until evening, when Maureen got up to make us tea and a small meal. Even after we had eaten, Igor was still not stirring, so we decided to leave him and go for a walk. We wandered into the dense fog, going slow and being extra cautious lest we lose our bearings. We were deep in cloud when, above a nearby stretch of dwarf pine, we saw our first Kambalnoye bear: a dark form ambling through veils of mist as if walking in mid-air. He was very close, but we were camouflaged in shadows and our scent was blowing away from him. We watched as he followed one of the deeply incised paths. He entered a tundra corridor between two solid walls of stunted alder and, rounding a corner, disappeared. We followed for a short distance until the trail opened into a shrouded meadow dotted with lakes.

During our first tentative probe into our new surroundings, I could feel Maureen's uncertainty. She was wondering how she would fit into a landscape so short on visibility and long on bears. Maureen is a very independent person, but some of her questions showed me how unsure she was of ever being able to wander this labyrinth alone. I had my own fears, and the way I sought to calm them was to remind myself of how comfortable I was in the presence of bears. However unfamiliar the landscape might feel, the bears were bound to have a lot in common with the bears I had lived among in other places. Bears would be my balance and my centre until the land itself ceased to feel alien.

The fear I could not calm was about my plane. The longer the fog persisted, the longer it would be until I could retrieve it. I kept imagining bears, powered by intense curiosity, dispassionately dismantling the Kolb with tooth and claw. If our time in Russia was to be fruitful, we had to avoid the usual mishaps of bears eating our food and destroying our equipment.

We needed to navigate skilfully around those clumsy interactions, and we also needed Maureen to achieve confidence and comfort here. And while I was afraid for my plane, I was much more confident about Maureen.

As for myself, I had entered the Kambalnoye basin with only one conviction: that so-called "delinquent" bears were the product of human mismanagement. It would do no good just to survive, or for Maureen and me to learn tricks for living around bears that others couldn't replicate. For the relationship between bears and people to improve generally, we had to come up with a diplomatic protocol and some simple procedures that other people could easily and reliably follow when living around bears.

When we got back from our walk, Igor was still sleeping. I took a turn around the immediate area and began to plot where our cabin should go. Maureen and I also decided on some priorities for the next few days. First off, we would build the floor and frame for the wall tent and get it erected so some of our stuff would be under cover. This would be home until the cabin was complete enough to move into.

Assuming the Kolb was in one piece and flyable, I gave some thought to where I could safely moor it. The most protected place was a hollow near the beach, 150 feet from the cabin site, but the spot was currently full of snow and looked like the last place where the snow would melt. I decided I would tether the plane to an anchor in the bay and let it pivot in the wind for a few days. In time, I would build a slippery ramp up the beach so the plane could climb by its own power out of the lake and up the tundra slope. The final line of defence would be an electric fence—a small pen where the Kolb would be safe when it wasn't in the air.

That evening Maureen and I made an inventory of building materials. Igor had somehow managed to acquire the finest pile of lumber available in Kamchatka. The wood was from the river valley to the north, the only heavily forested place on the peninsula. It wasn't planed and didn't need to be. The boards and studs were more precisely cut than any lumber I had ever seen.

Eventually, Maureen and I had to call it a day as darkness called it for us. We climbed back into our tent and I was tired enough that even concern over the fate of my plane could not keep me awake.

Sometime during the night, the rain stopped, but the morning was as foggy as ever. It had now been eighteen hours since Igor had entered his tent—I had almost begun to worry, when he poked his head out, grinning broadly. In just a few hectic weeks, he had sorted out both our and Bill Leacock's various problems, had made arrangements for a Japanese crew to come film bears at Kurilskoy in three weeks, and had made his own plans to take his family across Russia to see relatives in Ukraine. Now, after his monumental night's sleep, he was himself again, ready to take on the world.

My plan to fly him back to Petropavlovsk was still deeply smothered in fog, and there wasn't much of a time cushion before his family's departure for the Ukraine. This didn't seem to faze him. Neither did the possibility that my Kolb might be in tatters. "Don't worry," Igor told me. "You have been good to the bears. They will be good to you." Unless I were to climb to the pass and sit beside the plane for the duration of the bad weather, there was nothing to be done. We got on with building the wall tent.

The heavy canvas was already sewn into panels, and we carefully measured its inside seams. With those measurements we could build the floor and frame. For the ten-foot-wide floor, we used two-inch by ten-inch planks nailed to beams and set on pillars of stone. It was so stout you could have parked a bus on it.

We worked quickly and were soon sliding the tent over the frame. We secured it to the base and proceeded to make a table and a double bed. We built the bed high so we'd have space underneath for storage.

We weren't quite done when the clouds started to lift. At about six in the evening, Igor and I left camp, which gave us five hours of daylight to hike up to the pass, find the plane, and fly back. We left as Maureen was mounting our spotting scope on a tripod to look out over her new home for the first time. I envied her that.

The pass was to the northeast and, by the time we had hiked the two miles up to it, the clouds had risen above the saddle. Climbing over the pass, we bumped into two bears coming from the other direction. They ran away, but I made the last of the journey with my heart in my mouth, wondering what they might have been up to with my plane.

But there it was, completely unmolested beside the puddle where we'd left it. I felt enormously grateful, both to the place and to the bears for, at the very least, not using the tail as a handy rubbing post. There was no way to take off from the puddle on which I had landed, but the quasi-amphibious float allowed us to lift off from a bog close by.

When Igor and I flew over the divide, it was the first time I had really seen the place that was to become my second home. The lake was at the bottom of a big basin that Igor described as a caldera, an ancient volcano that had collapsed into itself. I found out later that although this was how Kurilskoy Lake was formed, it was not the same for Kambalnoye. A renowned geologist, Vera Ponomareva, who had spent many years sorting out the geology of the area, explained to me that the lake was created when a landslide came off the top of the Kambalnoye volcano 6,900 years ago, probably during an eruption. It came with such force that it swept over a small mountain ridge and continued south for several miles across the valley, eventually forming a dam across Kambalnoye River. The lake it created was 1,100 feet higher than Kurilskoy Lake, and the mountains rose smoothly another 2,000 feet on three sides. I say smoothly because they were not rugged or craggy like the mountains back home in Alberta. Except for a few cliffs, the edges were softened by layers of volcanic ash and eroding lava flows.

In the bottom of the basin, beside the lake, were two large grass meadows, lushly, almost tropically, green where several bears were grazing. The complex shoreline of the lake had sandy beaches and stretches of boulders where the waves broke. In still other places, tundra ledges overhung the water. Between the meadows, a ridge of dwarf Siberian pine sloped and fell into the lake. Several of the shallow bays contained boulder islands. There were still many deep snowdrifts in the gullies and on the windward sides of ridges. Every depression would have been completely full of drifted snow in the winter, to a depth of fifty feet or more. The remnant drifts were twisted patches of gleaming white, sometimes snaking from the top of a mountain to its base. Surrounding the snow was brilliant green.

The basin was without the high trees and shady canopies of the Kurilskoy Lake area. Here on the west side of the divide, and all the way south to Lopatka Point, the country had no forest, only dense mats of dwarf pine and alder. Over time I figured out why the tree growth was that way. Every part of a tree has to be under the snow during the severest part of winter. Any living thing above the snow from December to April would be too severely blasted by winter to survive. Snow crystals driven by 100 mile-per-hour winds would carve the bark off a taller tree, guaranteeing its death. Thus, the dense mats of dwarf pine and alder are shaped to the contour of winter snow. In summer, the thickets are contoured to that invisible snowscape, and every vista is smooth.

Swooping in to land at the cabin site, where our big white tent now perched on the hill, I felt that I was truly arriving. Everything felt under control—a rare mood.

As Igor and I walked up the bear trail from the anchored plane, Maureen bounded down to meet us, grinning and talking fast about what a paradise we had come to. She pointed out the bears on the slopes all around the lake and, at that exact moment, a blond female with two dark cubs jumped onto a sheer slope of snow and came tobogganing down a twisted ravine, a distance of at least half a mile. She slowed to a stop with her cubs tumbling down beside her.

The whole basin was alive with bear play, bear courtship and bear breeding. The cubs and non-breeding females passed on romance in favour of the succulent grasses and bountiful wildflowers upon which they rely for post-den sustenance, until the first run of salmon climbs the river from the Sea of Okhotsk.

Paradise indeed and, for that day at least, all uncertainty melted with the snow.

5

Shelter

On the morning of June 30, the mountaintops were again lost in cloud. But we could delay no longer. If Igor was going to make his flight to the Ukraine, I had to get him to Petropavlovsk. I felt uneasy about leaving Maureen so early in the game, but she said she would be fine.

I filled the main tanks of the plane from one of the fifteen gas drums that arrived in April along with the lumber, and I still had a full jerry can strapped to the side of the Kolb from the flight in. Igor and I taxied into the lake. As soon as the engine was warm, we took off.

We hadn't been in the air more than five minutes when I knew I had trouble. The engine was running rough, and, by the time I had crossed the 3,000-foot pass out of the valley, I was afraid to throttle back for the entire descent into Kurilskoy Lake lest my engine die altogether. Igor said he'd bought the gas from two different places, and that he was more confident of the quality of ten of the drums than of the other five. I had likely filled up from one of the questionable five. The gas probably had too much moisture in it, which was freezing in the throat of the carburetor at high altitude.

We managed a safe landing at Kurilskoy, and I topped up my gas tank with good gas from the jerry can. Then we were up in the air again, and the combination of warmer air and better gas smoothed out the engine considerably. Twice more I landed the Kolb and topped up the tank.

Our route north was longer than the trip south had been, owing to the low cloud. Igor directed me through a confusing sequence of valleys to the flying school at Nikolayevka. Knowing I would have to make the reverse journey on my own, I tried to remember every loop and turn. We landed in a flooded gravel pit, and Igor headed into the village on foot to find better gas. I stayed with the plane, entertained by a bunch of local kids, until Igor returned two hours later with gas and some friendly folks from the flying school. While they helped me gas up, I was grilled about how the flying was going. Before long I was airborne again, making my first solo journey to Kambalnoye Lake.

If anything, the clouds were lower now, and I barely squeezed through the low pass we had traversed earlier in the day. Some of the valleys west of the divide were dead ends now, shut off by cloud, and I had to jog west into unfamiliar country. A couple of times I landed on a lake and studied my map. The final pass into the Kambalnoye basin was lost in cloud, so I looped south all the way to the Sea of Okhotsk and approached camp along Kambalnoye River, the same method used by Maureen's helicopter pilot when he found us in the fog. By the time I landed, I had only a few feet beneath the clouds in which to navigate.

Maureen had spent her day watching bears, building shelves in the wall tent, and organizing our gear against the storm that seemed to be gathering. With the weather in mind, I brought the Kolb ashore onto a bare patch of sand at the edge of the snow and cinched it down tight with ground screws.

The storm struck in the middle of the night, with sudden blasts of wind from the northeast that shook the tent so hard all the cans and gear rained down off Maureen's shelves. The pots and pans we'd hung from nails swung out and clanged against the cross braces. The tent was like a drum beaten by giants.

By morning it was pouring rain and, if anything, the wind had increased. Our extra clothes were soaking wet from flapping against the tent walls, and a fine spray was coming off the heavy canvas roof. Both of us were afraid the tent would tear and put us directly into the teeth of the storm. We arranged things as best we could and busied ourselves at note writing and making cabin drawings. It was too noisy to talk. For a time, I contemplated getting the helmets and intercom out of the Kolb, but decided it was too ridiculous a plan.

The storm lasted three days and, by the end of it, we were a wiser pair. We went at building the cabin with maximum dispatch, so we would not have to endure any more cyclones under canvas.

The little beach where I anchored the Kolb was our best source of clean sand for a foundation. We had brought a few cardboard sauna tubes, eight inches in diameter, stuffed with fishing poles, electric fence rods, and spare aluminum tubing for the plane. Now, the same tubes could be used as forms for the concrete pillars on which one end of our cabin would rest.

We began the back-breaking work of hauling beach sand in buckets, mixing it with water and cement on a plastic tarp, and pouring the slurry into the partially buried tubes. The tall pillars would allow us to hang one end of the cabin over the edge of the hill, thus conserving the bit of flat ground we had for a yard. We rolled cardboard from boxes to make shorter pillars for the cabin's other end.

The procedure took a full two days, and, looking up from our work, we would sometimes see a bear watching us in seeming amazement. It gave us a feeling of great self-sufficiency to be creating this home from a heap of materials on the ground. While the cement was hardening, we got the electric fence set up. We had lots of battery power to fuel the fence, enough for several months, stored in two 80-pound solar cells. I decided I didn't need to set up the solar panels until the cabin was built.

I measured out a perimeter around the foundation and the wall tent, with a little extra room for a human guest to pitch a tent. We had enough fence for more space than that but we didn't want to invade any more of the bears' territory than necessary. As much as possible, we wanted to stay off their trails. Since our objective was to get along with the local bears, not impeding their movement seemed a good start. I pounded two-by-fours at the four corners of an area surrounding the tent and cabin site, then inserted fibreglass rods into the ground between the posts. Onto these, we clipped four strands of aluminum wire. Once I had them hooked to the storage cells, our living quarters had all the protection we'd ever need.

If you're not familiar with electric fences, they get their shocking power from an energizer that converts twelve-volt battery power into millisecond pulses of several thousand volts, each one second apart. Very low amperage keeps the shock from being dangerous. Dangerous or not, it was good and startling, which we discovered every time we got careless. I already knew it would work to keep bears out of camp, because I had used the system at my camp on Princess Royal Island during the filming of *Spirit Bear.*

The next step on the cabin was to build the floor out of six-inch by six-inch beams. We made it twenty-five feet long and thirteen feet wide. The cabin interior was designed to be nineteen feet long, so that left six feet outside the front door for a porch. For now, at least, the porch would have no roof.

When we had the four walls framed on top of the floor, we started on the rafters, building each of the ten on a template nailed to the floor. Because we had an extra pair of small windows in the lumber supply, we decided on a clerestory roof design. The east pitch of the roof was steep. It passed the roof's centre line by about a foot. The west pitch started out almost flat. At the point where the higher pitch passed over the lower, we built a vertical wall the length of the cabin, within which we fitted the two small windows. They let in the afternoon sun, which reflected down through the open rafters into our living area. They gave the interior a cheery brightness, even on foggy days. Building wall frames and rafters took a week, with several of the days obscured in a wet fog.

When all was ready and there was no wind, we hoisted and braced our walls. We slapped on boards and moved on to raising and bracing rafters. After closing in the roof with boards, we added tarpaper, held in place with battens. Doors and windows came next. In addition to the two small windows in the clerestory roof, Igor had provided a pre-built window for each wall. Some fellows from the flying school near Yelizovo were in the automobile glass business, and they had supplied the panes: sturdy five-millimeter tempered glass. The glass was strong but had not been carefully packed. One pane was broken, and it was remarkable the other three had made it intact.

Frightened by the spectre of future storms, Maureen and I kept our heads down over the work of building through most of the first three weeks of July. By then we had a cabin we could live in. Perhaps it was lucky we'd had the storm to scare us into such industry, because the temptation to slack off and go exploring might have been irresistible otherwise.

When we lifted our heads from building, Maureen and I acknowledged that we had never seen anything like the numbers of bears that lived in this basin. By mid-July, the snow was mostly gone and the mountainsides were lush. The bears ranged up the slopes, eating and breeding. One female bear had three older cubs, almost the size of herself, and we were able to watch one day as she left those cubs to join up with a big male whose coat was almost black. He was an amazing creature, the size of a buffalo, and was always easy to spot. The cubs, who were probably three years old, were also easy to keep track of because they were so noisy. They roared at each other and at times sounded very angry. Even on the foggy days, we could hear their brawling roars echoing across the lake, amplified by the fog. In three days, after she was bred, the mother returned to her big cubs. We watched the group throughout the summer and they were still together come fall. About fifteen per cent of bear mothers stay with their cubs into a fourth summer; the others separate in the third summer when the cubs are two. This bear must have really liked her cubs, and we often wondered if she would den with them again.

Our cabin-building kept most of the bears from venturing along the nearest shoreline, at least until we stopped pounding nails and using the chainsaw. However, the noise did not prevent a steady parade along the opposite shore of the lake. In the morning we would sometimes see tracks along the beach in front of the Kolb. I was pretty sure the bears were smart enough to know that our commotion was not directed at them.

Beyond the bears, there didn't seem to be much wildlife, except for birds. There were Steller's sea eagles, peregrine falcons, and several kinds of hawks, as well as a few different owls. There were also several species of ducks, gulls, and terns on the lake. In the bushes around the cabin were strange little birds we could not identify, though I eventually learned the names of most. They gave us no less pleasure that summer for being nameless. One had a fluorescent red throat and would sit in the top of a mountain ash, singing its heart out. They must have been hardy creatures to raise their young in the savagery of the local storms.

Maureen and I often compared what we were seeing to our North American experience, thinking how far, wide, and long we'd had to travel on our home continent to see and be around bears. Here, it was impossible to go for a walk without encountering bears, and, while that might not be every person's cup of tea, it was what we had come for.

The building campaign was not entirely without reprieves. The first, on July 11, was the result of me wrenching my back while constructing the roof. I decided to take the day off and go exploring. I fired up the Kolb and flew south towards Lopatka Cape. I was gone an hour and saw forty-three bears. I also saw the cabin Maureen had told me about on the west coast near the mouth of the Kambalnoye River. The fog started lowering again, and I just made it back to camp before the sky dropped to the ground for the night.

It was soon apparent that Maureen was going to be a reluctant flyer, even on the best of days. On July 12, I persuaded her to come look at the bears I had seen in the river the day before. The problem was that there was enough of a breeze heating in the morning sun to create sharp turbulence. On the return trip from the river mouth, I suggested we continue on to Maslov's research station, but Maureen begged to be let off at the cabin. After that, she did go on the odd foray, but the intervals between her flights grew longer.

MAUREEN: When we arrived at Kambalnoye Lake I was reluctant to fly in the Kolb, but eventually my better judgment was weakened by my need to see more of what Charlie was raving about. On one of those early flights, we flew in for a landing at the cabin under a low cloud layer. I have very bad depth perception and begged Charlie to land far out on the lake and taxi into shore at a comfortable speed. Charlie has low tolerance for other people's fears, particularly mine, and he landed as he ordinarily would, as close to the shore as he thought safe. But he also miscalculated due to a tailwind, and we didn't stop until we were ten feet up the bank with the nose of the Kolb touching dense alders. Given that the lake was a mile wide and he had tried to make do with the last 200 feet of it, and misjudged the tailwind, Charlie was quite sheepish. But I felt downright angry and swore I would never fly with him again.

I have tried to fly with Charlie several times since. But I always feel the same fear, and beyond this deeply rooted dread there is always the personal humiliation, after being bounced around in turbulence, of sensing Charlie's impatience at my discomfort. When it is calm I do love to go up and count the bears along the river and see the land from the air, but I can't imagine how my fear of this kind of flying is ever going to completely subside, given the frequency of less-than-perfect conditions and a pilot who doesn't understand what I am experiencing.

I continued on alone to the salmon research station at Kurilskoy to have tea with the resident co-managers, scientists Katya (Ekaterina Lepskaya) and her husband Alexei Maslov. I already knew them slightly, from the scouting trip in 1994 and from having stopped there while passing through on the way to and from Petropavlovsk. Katya and Alexei's children, Lisa and Viktor, live there with them.

The research station is located where the Ozernaia River starts out of Kurilskoy Lake for the Sea of Okhotsk, twenty-five miles to the west. It was built in 1940, making the salmon fishery of Kurilskoy Lake one of the most studied in the world. Depending on the run, between 400,000 and 6,000,000 sockeye come there to spawn each year. Katya and Alexei's responsibility is to assess, as closely as possible, what the current year's salmon return might be. The commercial take allowed at the ocean mouth of the Ozernaia River is set each season based on their evaluation. Katya also studies the life cycle of freshwater plankton, the food source of young salmon in the lake for the two years before they become adults and leave for the ocean. The salmon numbers are ultimately determined by the amount of plankton available.

On top of his managerial duties, Alexei does an annual aerial survey of hundreds of salmon rivers in the province of Kamchatka, an area roughly

the size of California. It's a gruelling job because of the time spent aloft
in a noisy helicopter, but he loves it.

Over time, Katya, Alexei, and I would develop a mutually satisfactory
barter system. I would do various chores for them with my plane, and, in
return, Maureen and I would benefit from their bountiful vegetable
garden. There was often a fresh sockeye salmon to take home as well. On
July 15, near the end of cabin construction, Maureen and I decided to take
a break together. We left camp at 5:30 in the afternoon and hiked down
the river. By now, we had discovered that the only way to travel in this
soggy country was in hip waders. The impenetrable dwarf pine and alder
stands were often tight to the rivers, and the only way to get around was
to cross and cross again. Maureen loved her hip waders and had decided
to turn them into a fashion statement. I was less enamoured with mine,
but they were better than being constantly wet.

In the several hours of that hike, we saw thirty-three bears, many grazing the mountain sides and some hanging along the river, waiting for the
salmon to come. Every bear that detected our presence ran from us. We
looped back along the north edge of the valley and got back to our tent
and cabin in the last light at 11 p.m. After two weeks of carpentry work,
the hike had exhausted us.

I was troubled by what I saw that day. My theory, on which so many of
our hopes and plans were based, was that fear of people is not a natural
response in bears. The way these bears ran from us meant one of two things.
Either I was completely wrong, and it was natural for even the most innocent bears to fear humans, or else the Kambalnoye area was not a violence-
free paradise for bears as we had been led to believe. The latter seemed more
likely. The quick fear displayed by the bears, along with the remote location
and relative closeness to the grotesque Asian markets for bear gall and bear
parts, suggested to me that poachers had been active here recently, and
perhaps still were. If so, we had a problem. We needed an area free of human
influence, except our own. It was not fair to teach bears that people were
non-threatening if it meant they could be killed because of their trust.

Two days later, we finished the cabin, the final touch being to cover it with
sheet metal to protect it from bears in the months we would not be present.

The added benefit would be additional shelter from the onslaught of wind and rain. With that done, we moved in.

Come evening, we left our labours to sit out on the roofless porch and celebrate the product of three weeks' hard work. I retrieved two bottles of beer that I had tucked away in a makeshift cooler. A local brew with no preservatives, the beer was well beyond its expiry date and had gone skunky, but it was cold and wet, and we toasted each other as though it were champagne in crystal.

We were happily admiring our surroundings and watching a family of bears across the lake when the stillness erupted. The floor beneath our feet heaved and the pines around the lake jogged before our eyes. For the first time, I witnessed the strange phenomenon of a lake lying still, almost without ripple, as the surrounding scenery danced. When the earthquake subsided, I checked the narrow pillars of concrete that supported the rear of the cabin. They had survived. It would have been embarrassing to have our cabin tilt twenty degrees on the day we moved into it.

Kamchatka is perched on the unstable rim of the Pacific, an area of active volcanoes, and all that summer and fall, earthquakes of various strengths hit us so regularly we grew accustomed to them. Often the shaking was preceded by a disturbing noise, like a powerful motor coming up the river. These earthly intestinal rumblings usually stopped with the first bump of the quake. From that day forward, we began to keep watch on the nearby 7,000-foot Kambalnoye volcano for any sign that it might be coming to life. We could see where the last eruption in 1922 had blasted out the side of the crater and spilled lava into the valley. Even after eighty years it looked fresh, and very little grew there.

After our first earthquake, the sky was mirrored in the calm surface of the lake. High to the north, above the remnant ribbons of fog, the peak of Kambalnoye volcano shone. The valley was patched with tropical green and shimmering snow white. We had taken little time to enjoy these spectacular views so far, but that night, with a roof over our heads, we could afford the luxury and indulged ourselves thoroughly. We had risked everything for the experience of this moment. All that remained was to see how our hopes of living harmoniously with bears would take shape.

6

Smoked Out

The tempered glass windows of the cabin pointed in the cardinal directions, like a viewing room for bears. On a clear day, with the naked eye, binoculars, or the spotting scope, we could see bears through every one of our floor-level windows.

On July 18, the day after moving indoors, we had promised ourselves a voyage of discovery, but got caught up in improving our habitation. Maureen went to work on the new kitchen, and transformed the wall tent into a place of storage. Meanwhile, I tried to achieve fingertip electricity. I installed the two solar panels and hooked them to the storage cells, then set about wiring an inverter into the system. The inverter converts 12-volt battery power into 110-volt current, and was the secret to powering the North American conveniences we had brought from home. Tops on that list was the electric coffee grinder; as soon as we had a darkroom built, the inverter would also power Maureen's photo enlarger.

By the time we were finished, it was six o'clock in the evening. With the sun lowering in the west, we took to the air in "the butterfly," Maureen's sometimes affectionate name for the Kolb. We flew down the river ten miles and landed near its ocean mouth. We fetched out our fishing rods and caught a silvery sockeye, so fresh from the ocean it still wore a necklace of the tiny shrimp called sea lice. It was a beautiful evening on the beach, and, watching the sun sink into that strange sea, it had the same unusual effect on both of us. Like the sun into the ocean, the fact of where we were sank into us. We felt the thrill of this adventure and the aloneness of it, the deep chill of its vast unknowns.

In the next few days, we divided our time between building Maureen's darkroom and exploring. Sometimes, when I was making notes about what we did each day, I would neglect to mention how many bears we saw, because bears were so unavoidable, so reliably a part of every vista. It was common to see fifty of them in four hours of hiking.

The size of these Kamchatkan bears took some getting used to. The bears with which I worked in British Columbia's Khutzeymateen Valley were big compared to the grizzlies I was raised with in the Rockies, but the 300-foot Sitka spruce around them often made them seem smaller. The tundra in south Kamchatka had the opposite effect. Already twice the size of Canada's inland bears, the Siberian grizzlies looked even larger against the low vegetation of tundra country. I never weighed one, but, from what I understand, a big Kamchatka female can weigh 800 pounds and a male 1,500 pounds. The upward limits for bear weight in the Rockies would be 400 for females and 850 for males.

The goodly supply of fish in most years was what enabled these bears to reach the top size for their species. Around the middle of July, the first sockeye salmon were beginning to arrive in Kambalnoye Lake. While it's not a major run or easy to fish—due to the high water caused by the snow run-off—it put the bears in a fishing mood. The adults, especially the rangy, muscular, younger males, have worn off all of their fat by the time the salmon come. They look long-legged and gaunt, tucked up in the belly like greyhounds. These empty frames made them appear very athletic, especially when in full pursuit of salmon in the river shallows. I had never seen bears in Alberta that looked like this.

The colour variation among Kamchatkan bears is dramatic: from almost black to bleached straw. The silver tip that is the hallmark of bears in southwestern Alberta is found here as well, but is not quite as striking because the ends of the hair are cream-coloured instead of pure white. Russian bear cubs tend to have a pronounced white collar, called a chevron, which they sometimes keep until their third year.

Are the Kamchatkan bears grizzlies? people ask. Aren't they, in truth, Asian brown bears, and, if so, how do they differ from Alaskan browns? In the past, taxonomists separated brown bears into forty species. Now all of them are considered to be one: *Ursus arctos*—and the grizzly is referred to as a brown bear like all the rest. There are some big differences in size and colour among brown bears in different areas, but such variations can be found among humans, who are also classed as one species. Because of the amount and quality of food available to them, our children are giants compared to our own ancestors. Some people have tried to tell me that Kamchatkan bears are genetically docile compared to the Rocky Mountain grizzlies. We would sadly discover for ourselves how untrue that is.

There are several levels on which I know I am not a scientist. One is that I like to start my explorations with the assumption that a wild animal is more intelligent than I am, regardless of its inability to talk to me. I also assume that they have a broader emotional range than I do. Scientists like to work from the other direction, assuming the animals are limited, and grudgingly crediting them with capabilities after much evidence.

Another difference is the amount of wonder I bring to my work. I find that when I look up a plant or a bird or an animal, and commit its Latin name to memory, I feel proud of myself, but I also lose some of the amazement I had about that living thing. Once it has a category, I hardly look at it again. I guess I prefer to live with my wonderment intact, and that makes me stay away from hairsplitting methods of study.

The scientists can, of course, do as they like and think of my work what they will, but I feel I can learn more of what I want to know by resisting the urge to swiftly capture what I see in the amber of categorization. For my work, I need my open-mindedness and capacity for wonder in full working order.

In those early days at Kambalonoye Lake, we were always aware of our need for safety, and how maintaining our safety and our credibility were virtually the same thing. Nothing would cost us credibility faster than if either of us was injured by a bear. One of our rules was never to go anywhere

outside the fence without pepper spray. On our early walks, I began to
understand the degree to which Maureen was still afraid of bears. Most of
her solo experience had been on horseback in Banff National Park, and at
Kambalnoye, she was reluctant at first to leave the cabin without me. I saw
this as totally understandable, something she would get over in the longer
run. She was going to be a tremendous asset to the project, precisely
because of her fear. If Maureen could overcome her fear, it would be solid
proof of the usefulness of our results.

North of the lake, between the cabin and the 600-foot ridge that forms
the rim of the basin, is a mosaic of dwarf pine and alder, little lakes, and
corridors of open tundra: a labyrinth several square miles in size. Because
the natural corridors are dictated by water and the impenetrability of the
pine and alder thickets, it was inevitable that Maureen and I would come
face to face with bears as we explored. Surprising bears at close quarters,
especially fearful bears, was a great concern.

At the beginning, when Maureen was still quite frightened, we
approached blind corners with trepidation and noise. We whooped and
we hollered, although making loud noise goes against my principles of
bush travel. I like peace and quiet as much as I assume the animals do, and
wanted to cut down on our noise-making as soon as possible. I tried out
various ways of announcing my presence that weren't so obnoxious, and
the experimentation led to several close encounters. What I found, to my
delight, was that I was able to soothe each bear we surprised by talking to
it softly. Even if my heart was in my mouth, I had to be able to sound as
though I were perfectly calm.

I had discovered in my experience with bears before Russia that I could
use my voice effectively this way. Nonetheless, I was astounded by how well
it worked for us in Kamchatka. Bears don't speak Russian or English, as far
as I know, so it was definitely a matter of tone rather than content.

From the start Maureen had an ability to project her voice in a cheerful way. It was not long before she too was turning tense situations into
mellow ones, just by saying things like, "It's okay. We aren't going to hurt
you. We like you. What gorgeous cubs you have." This was very good for
her confidence, and it clearly showed that the talking technique was not
some aberration particular to me. It could be developed.

Wilderness guidebooks sometimes recommend that you play dead in a bear encounter. This is something I would never do. I see it as a last resort to be tried when all other options are used up, including pepper spray. The reason playing dead often does work is because lying on the ground demonstrates that you are not a threat. But I know of instances when this technique has not worked—with young, brash, food-conditioned brown bears. Also, it doesn't work with black bears, which attack to kill you. You must fight an attacking black bear if you hope to survive.

Female bears with their cubs were our greatest concern when we were walking. We were both fully up-to-date on the many statistics about how dangerous mother bears can be in protecting their young. We also knew that we would inevitably encounter such a bear. Luckily, we had a stretch of time to experiment with our techniques before it happened.

On July 21, in the midst of construction on Maureen's darkroom, we ran out of nails. I knew this would happen. Igor had done wonderfully well at finding us quality wood, but had, for some reason, been parsimonious with nails. After we hammered in the last one, we were stuck. The hardware store was 160 miles away.

Another problem was looming—a shortage of firewood. I had assumed that, in a place so devoid of human fire-builders, there would be tons of deadwood. What I hadn't reckoned on was the incredible longevity and health of the pine and alder thickets. They simply did not create much deadfall, and what was there was locked in the depths of the heavy-branched and tightly woven brush and I couldn't get at it without half killing myself. For now, we were able to burn the odds and ends of construction wood, but we would soon run out of that.

Happy to fly at any time, I now had excellent excuses. Firewood. Nails.

The two coasts, the North Pacific to the east and the Sea of Okhotsk to the west, were equidistant (within ten miles). The Okhotsk side had tundra flats that reminded me of the prairie at home. Lopatka Cape, the southern tip of the peninsula, was a bit farther away at twenty-five miles, and I stayed away from there for two reasons. First, the weather at the cape was even wilder than at Kambalnoye. Second, the area was still a strategic military zone and Igor had told me not to fly where I could be seen from its lighthouse.

In my search for wood and nails, I flew west towards the abandoned cabin above the ocean mouth of the Kambalnoye River. A mile north of it, I spotted a considerable log jam, years worth of firewood, on a small creek. Winter storms and high tides had been pushing drift logs through a gap in the grassy dunes until there was a great pile. The problem was landing close enough to make use of it. The nearest lake was tiny, and, though I could probably land, I would never get off again with 200 pounds of wood aboard.

I continued to the cabin and landed on the river nearby. The sea itself is never calm enough for landing a plane like mine. Even on this day, which was totally without wind, the ocean swell was over eight feet.

At a glance, it looked like there was plenty of driftwood on the beach. Before I went for it, I decided to search the cabin for nails. Alexei and Katya had told me that it was built as a patrol cabin when the southern end of the peninsula became a nature sanctuary in 1984. Not long after, the resident ranger died of a heart attack and was not replaced. Since then, the place had served as a stopover for the lighthouse crews at Lopatka Cape and the military border patrols on their way south from the fishing village of Ozernovskiy. If poachers were active in the area, the cabin was probably useful to them as well. The road between Ozernovskiy and the cape was no more than a pair of ruts in the tundra.

The cabin was roomy inside and in fairly good condition. I searched it carefully and was rewarded with a box of rusty nails I found tucked in a corner under a bench in the porch.

I put the nails in the plane, grabbed my chainsaw and my canvas wood bag, and went to the beach. The canvas bag, which the wall tent had come in, could hold 200 pounds of cut wood—exactly the weight and size I could carry, strapped down in the passenger seat of the Kolb. The bag also kept the wood together, which was absolutely necessary, given what a bunch of stove lengths could do to me and my plane if we hit rough air.

As I set to work with my chainsaw on the beach, I noticed the drift-wood itself. A thirty-four-foot log, four feet in diameter, was a Sitka spruce, the giant rain-forest species that once dominated the west coast of North America from Alaska to the southern tip of Vancouver Island. That log had drifted all the way across the Pacific. It even might have come from Princess Royal Island. Other logs had an exotic feel to them. I imagined them riding the currents from the Sea of Japan or even more distant tropical coastlines.

With the tent bag full and tied securely in the Kolb, I couldn't quite make myself leave. I wanted to know how the bears used these broad, green coastal flats. Several bears were out foraging on the tundra, and a few more were jumping around in the thundering breakers, miles from any cover. The combination of ocean and plain made me think of California in the days before the stockmen waged war on bears to make the frontier safe for themselves and their cattle. Here were bears digging and eating, and standing for a better look, just the way it would have been in that far distant time before people took charge.

Earlier in the afternoon, I had noticed a dark blue line way out to sea. While I watched the bears and explored the beach, that line had been drawing closer, but I had failed to notice. The air was completely still and the sky cloudless, except for a few wispy mare's tails. The very things I found reassuring should have been scaring the hell out of me, but I didn't have sense enough yet to be alarmed.

I went and sat on a big grass-covered dune, a vantage I liked because I could see my plane on the river and a pair of young bears in the breakers in the opposite direction. A school of salmon was trying to make its way into the shallow river mouth, and, every time the waves surged in, more salmon were caught and rolled onto the sand. The salmon flipping in the ebbing surf were easy meat for the excited young bears.

I looked up from what the bears were doing and suddenly became aware of what was going on. A long line of exploding whitecaps on the dark sea marked the leading edge of a high wind coming at me with incredible speed. The Kolb was several hundred yards behind me, and I ran for it as fast as I could. By the time I was there and had the engine started, the first gusts were rocking the plane hard.

Taking off into that rising storm, over the angry boiling sea, with my load of wood weighing me down, was frightening. I U-turned as soon as I could and hightailed it for home. At Kambalnoye Lake, I landed the

Kolb and scooted it up onto the mooring spot below the cabin. I tied it down solidly, knowing the wind could hit at any moment. I warned Maureen and we prepared to be slammed. But the storm, when it came, lacked the ferocity with which it had hit the coast. It was powerful enough, however, to reveal a severe design flaw in our cabin.

The instant we made a fire the southwest wind caused the cabin to fill with smoke. This was a problem of possibly disastrous proportions. If we couldn't light a fire during a storm, we were in trouble.

After twenty years of ranching, of building everything from barns to houses to airplanes, I considered myself a practical person and felt confident on my initial approach to the chimney problem. For one thing, I had lots of spare stove pipe with which to fashion a solution. Out into the wind and rain I went, and I kept at it until I had an elaborate extension built onto the chimney, twice the height of the cabin and tied down in three directions with wire.

But it didn't work. The smoke kept driving down instead of escaping up and out.

Next, I built baffles along the ridges and the eaves. The wind had by now died back to a breeze, and I thought I had the problem licked. But, when another storm rose, and just when we needed heat the most, we were again driven out on the porch, coughing and rubbing our eyes. Maureen poured yet another bucket of water on yet another fire.

I was humbled, and Maureen's confidence in my abilities had declined considerably. She was coming up with her own theories now and conducting her own experiments. We dressed more and more warmly and argued about what to try next.

On top of the smoke problem, we discovered that our roof leaked. A straight-down rainfall was no problem, but, when the wind accelerated to eighty miles per hour, the rain was driven horizontally under the battens that held our tarpaper roofing down. The water travelled to the nail holes and through, dripping on us from many spots at once. During the brunt of a storm, we were forced to erect the fly from our travel tent over top of the bed. Without the luxury of a concrete foundation, the gale also affected us from below. Enough air was forced through the cracks between the floorboards to walk the carpet across the room. Since Maureen is smaller than I am by quite a margin, she was nominated to wriggle under the cabin and seal the underside of the floor.

When not repairing the cabin, I was out in the wind and rain, trying new methods of mooring my aircraft. The search for a way to protect the control surfaces from damage by the salt wind was more or less unending. By the control surfaces I mean all the hinged parts (ailerons, flaps, rudder, and elevators) that control the aircraft in flight. As long as the wind hits from the front, everything is okay; that's what they're designed for. But when the wind comes from behind, the parts get flipped up and down and back and forth against their stops. It took a while to learn how to restrain them so they didn't get damaged.

It often seems that fate has a sense of humour—a bad one. You come to what many would regard as the end of the earth to live among 400 brown bears, who by their mythical reputation are supposed to be raring to kill and devour you, and you wind up plagued by weather and smoke. Even now, my instinct when referring to the smoke problem or the bad weather is to make a joke, but both problems were far from funny then. Given the frequency and ferocity of the storms, smoke inhalation or its alternative, bone-chilling cold, threatened to defeat us. We began to wonder if we really were tough enough to endure in this amazingly harsh country.

The day after Maureen had been under the cabin plugging gaps between the floor planks, it was finally pleasant enough for a walk. We struck off in a new direction and came upon a group of depressions that we recognized as pit houses from an Itelman village. We knew they were the remains of dwellings hundreds of years old because we had already been introduced to such an Itelman village at Kurilskoy Lake. Igor's cabin, built on a spit that juts into the lake, is surrounded by several of these pit house depressions. The pit houses were even more obvious and easy to see at Kambalnoye because of the elevation. For some reason of climate and altitude, the alpine alder and pine had not re-established around the houses where the Itelman people must have cut the trees for firewood.

I knew very little at the time about these early inhabitants, but I wanted badly to know more. Since their time, no one else has found a good reason to withstand the fierce climate and live here. What fascinated me as well was that the Itelman had obviously found a way of sharing this place with bears, with likely as many bears as currently live in the region. What's more, they had shared a food source with the bears: fish, the salmon and the char. Modern wildlife managers would shudder at this situation: people competing with *Ursus arctos* for food, the ultimate formula for disaster. Though I had no way of knowing how things had been between the Itelman and the bears, the fact remained that, long before firearms, the Itelman had been able to live here, and long enough to establish several villages and to chop down a considerable area of the rugged forest for their fires. In other words, they had not been wiped out; nor had they suffered so much injury and loss that the lake had been placed off limits to their people.

At that time I didn't know what had become of the Itelman, and to some extent I still don't. I did learn that they occupied the area for at least 6,000 years, until the Russians began demanding that the natives of Kamchatka pay *iasak*, a tax in sable pelts. The Itelman living at Kambalnoye Lake and Kurilskoy Lake had to move north into forested areas to find sable to pay the tax. Otherwise they would have been killed.

I also thought about smoke. With no more than a smoke hole above an open fire, these people had probably been able to make their fires draw. I, with all kinds of technological advantages, could not do the same. I was buffaloed by the chimney problem, and to be honest, I don't think I ever really solved it. To this day, when a real doozer of a storm blows in out of the southwest, we still get smoked out on occasion. I once asked Igor why the hell he had not warned us of the incredible extremes of weather when he was talking us into working at Kambalnoye. His reply was: "All you asked about were the bears."

MAUREEN: While Charlie fought with the chimney and the smoke problem, I was trying desperately to get my artistic work underway. First it had been the cabin-building that kept me from it. Then I had had to build a darkroom. When that was done, I finally got down to work— or at least tried to. I had already taken some photographs, and the moment the darkroom was completed, I was in it making prints and enlargements. The painting side of things came on less quickly.

The biggest obstacle so far was the bears' instinct to run from us. I wanted to photograph and paint bears in ways that portrayed their personalities and thoughts, not just as depictions of wildlife on landscape. How could I expand my own understanding and portray that understanding in paint if all I ever saw on bears' faces was wariness and fear? There were certainly all kinds of bears around to paint, but that wasn't what I'd come to do. I wasn't at Kambalnoye Lake to be a "wildlife artist" any more than Charlie was there to slap on radio collars. Eventually, I would understand that my instinctual efforts the first year did lay the groundwork for three future series of work, but I had no way of knowing it yet. Charlie seemed a lot more clear about his goals at the outset, and I envied him the security of that.

A lot of people believed we would fail. Some even laughed at our goals. At the stage we were at in late July 1996, I don't think either of us knew if we were proving them wrong or proving them right.

The one gain I could honestly claim to have made was in my confidence around bears. I felt more at ease with them every day and was exploring more on my own. Charlie felt some guilt about leaving me alone while he went exploring in his Kolb, but I think we both knew this was more of an old, paternalistic pattern than a real need on my behalf to be protected.

7

Meeting Michio

Maureen and I flew to Kurilskoy together in late July, hoping to talk to Igor, who was back from the Ukraine with his brother Andrei in tow. Igor was already up to his ears in his next project, making arrangements for a Japanese crew shooting a documentary about the renowned Japanese-American photographer Michio Hoshino. I had studied three of Michio's books and greatly admired him, and both Maureen and I were hoping to meet him. But the trip turned out to be a bust. Instead of meeting Michio, who was out working on the lake, we wound up visiting with a Petropavlovsk television person who had flown down in a helicopter to do a TV news piece about the shoot. He was up in a tower that had been built for the film cameramen, and he was avidly videotaping an adult male brown bear that had gotten into some food near the foot of the tower.

It was a situation neither Maureen nor I liked, and it went from bad to worse. It was believed that this same bear had broken into Igor's cabin while he was away, to get at food there. Confident in his ability to get food in human areas, the bear was becoming increasingly bold. Since the weather was closing in on us, we had to leave quickly, and just barely made it home.

Two days later, while Maureen got on with her own work, I flew to Kurilskoy for another attempt at connecting with Igor and meeting Michio. I spotted Michio and the film crew from the air and carefully guided my plane down onto the glassy lake surface near where they were scooting along in a motorboat. They swooped over for a chat.

They told me that the bear problem was escalating. The big male had ransacked the film crew's food supply while they were away working. Igor believed the bear's boldness was due in part to the slow spawning of the salmon at Kurilskoy that season. The bear was looking for an alternative food source, and, given his considerable success at scrounging, had gone to that strategy to cover the salmon shortfall. Igor had already resorted to throwing rocks and pepper-spraying the bear, his method of showing dominance over the bear in hopes of driving him away. Clearly, it wasn't working very well.

While having this conversation, plane to boat, I was also getting some first impressions of Michio Hoshino. He contributed to our conversation in a quiet way, but I was interested to see how many other things he seemed to be taking in at the same time. He gave my ultralight a careful and appreciative going-over, then shifted from one view of the beautiful morning and exotic surroundings to another—an observant man.

I returned home to Kambalnoye later that day, preoccupied and depressed by the Kurilskoy bear situation and how badly it was being handled. Ironically, my arrival sparked an unexpected breakthrough in Maureen's efforts to paint. As I circled, preparing to land, Maureen noticed a bear on shore watching me. Every move the plane made was echoed by a movement of the bear's head. As the plane descended, the bear didn't run away or even move. He continued his study of the plane, even as I taxied to shore.

When I pulled up, Maureen was greatly excited. Here was a bear who was more interested in us than afraid, who was behaving as we had hoped all the bears here might. Maureen took many pictures and immediately began a series of charcoal drawings. It was great to see her so fired up.

That night, we sat and discussed what was happening at Kurilskoy. Our own situation was so dramatically different. Our electric fence and our disciplined care not to leave food or garbage outside the perimeter had prevented the problems that were plaguing Igor and his film crew. We wished that we had brought a second electric fence kit to give to Igor.

By now, the second run of fish up the river was well underway. This was a run of char and, though there were ten miles of river along which to fish, the bears were concentrated along the two miles closest to the lake. The first mile below the lake flowed over the rubble of the ancient landslide that had dammed the valley. It was not easy for us to travel, and we had recently scouted out an alternative route. We made a path that cut off the first big loop in the river and rejoined the river where the country opened up into gorgeous meadows that allowed easy viewing of animals on either river bank.

The new cut-off crossed several bear trails at right angles, and, as Maureen and I walked down to watch the bears fish, a big female suddenly stepped from behind a pine bush twenty yards from where we stood. The bear was startled and took off running across a swampy meadow. Then she stopped. It made me cringe to realize why. Out of the same pine bush stepped two small cubs, both plainly confused by the situation. When their mother ran, they had not followed. Now, what she saw looking back was her cubs a great deal closer to two humans than she was to them. It was the situation everybody fears and which we had always known we were fated to experience.

The mother bear came running. She pounded towards us, plumes of water flying from her feet in the wet grass, a look of great ferocity on her face. Seeing their mother running at them so fast and so full of anger confused and frightened the cubs even more. They moved away from her, closer to us.

From the moment the female stepped from the bush, I had been talking to her in a calm voice. Even as she charged, fierce and huge, I kept it up. Talking, talking, forcing myself to sound calm. I also turned my body sideways to her and nonchalantly reached down to pluck some goldenrod, another method of looking as non-threatening as possible.

Beside me, Maureen was talking too, but not in the language we had decided would calm a bear. "Oh shit," she said. "Christ Charlie, get out your pepper spray!"

As the mother bear got closer, we saw the panic begin to leave her. She slowed, and when she reached her cubs she stopped. The three bears were now no more than a dozen yards from us. We had all calmed down considerably in that short time. Maureen's voice had lost its fear and she took over from me, talking in the cheerful way she had been practising earlier. The big female began to lead her cubs away, continuing on the path towards her original destination. She did stop once to look back—as if to decipher what Maureen was saying so sweetly about her beautiful cubs.

Maureen and I were thoroughly shaken, but exhilarated too. The moment had been a major test of our ability to defuse a dangerous situation: the biggest test yet. Thanks to remaining calm and to using our voices well, and to maintaining non-threatening postures and not succumbing to the desire to flee—and thanks to the good sense of the mother bear—we had passed the test with no harm done. We hadn't even used the pepper spray.

Two days after that meeting with the mother bear and cubs, I decided to go flying again. I wanted to explore beyond the sanctuary's boundary to the north, so I flew sixty miles in that direction. It was on this trip that I saw, for the first time in my life, a bear with four cubs. I was to eventually see four cubs that survived to the time their mother weaned them, and began to realize that four at birth must be quite common in Kamchatka—in North America it is a very rare event. I was well on my way back home, within a couple of miles of the cabin in fact, when a sudden wind hit my plane so hard from the front that I was all but stopped in the air. Trying to gain height, I shoved the throttle on full—only to be blown backward in relation to the ground, which appeared to be heading in the wrong direction. The wind was so strong and turbulent that I couldn't seem to turn around inside of it.

It was like falling into a wild, swift river and trying to get back to shore again. While I struggled to turn towards the still air, some unseen force had hold of my plane and was trying to roll it upside down. Normally, the controls have enough authority to counter such a force, but this spiralling air was trying to make me do tricks I was not capable of performing. I was hanging almost upside down, and everything loose was falling on the canopy or flinging around the cockpit. Something hit me in the face and almost knocked my glasses off. Maybe I should have let the plane roll in the direction the turbulence was trying to flip me, but habit made me resist.

I was losing altitude fast during this struggle, so when I finally did turn end for end, I was only a hundred feet off the ground. But then, all was smooth again, outside me if not inside. Under control, I realized that my vision was blurred. As quickly as possible, I backtracked and looked for a place to land. I needed to get on the ground before anything got worse. After the third pass over my chosen spot, an alpine basin, I regained enough composure to land on the grass.

I sat for several minutes, savouring being alive. I reached up and touched my face and glasses, and only then did I realize, with another wave of relief, that the problem with my sight wasn't my eyes but my glasses. Whatever had hit me in the eggbeater turbulence had knocked out the right lens. The rear of the cockpit was wide open above the seat back, so at first I assumed that the lens was lost. But after much careful groping, I located the lens and was able to press it back into the frame.

The basin where I sat in my plane held a few small ponds. I watched a black-throated loon that had been disturbed when my much bigger bird had come in to land. Gradually, the loon made its way back to a nest on a mound in the middle of its pond. Carpets of bright gold globeflowers and mats of vivid pink rhododendrons hung from dripping ledges of moss. The world looks especially good when you've almost lost your life.

It was eight in the evening, and the sun was still well above the horizon. There was no breeze in the basin, nor a cloud in the sky. The wind, like a river, was contained by its banks, and the closest bank remained south of the pass. Remembering that eggbeater hell, I forced myself to stay put for an hour and a half before making another attempt to fly home.

At sunset, I took off on the wet grass and flew the pass. This time I was vigilant, watching for any sign of where the edge of the wind might be. There is a subtly different look to fast-moving air, perhaps because of the moisture it picks up over the sea. Sure enough, just beyond that invisible barrier, the alder bushes on the ground were shaking violently. "Good judgment comes from experience. Experience comes from bad judgment," the saying goes. A few hours older, and distinctly wiser, I headed back to Kurilskoy Lake. I didn't like leaving Maureen trapped in the wind and possibly unable to use the stove because of the chimney problem, but I also knew better than to try to cross that river of wind a second time.

Earlier that day I had made a brief stop at Kurilskoy, hoping to talk to Igor, but he was off with the film crew. What I found instead were sixteen American tourists and correspondents, along with a Russian camp crew. The group, sponsored by the environmental society Friends of the Earth, had been dropped in by helicopter that morning. Some were busily making camp; others wandered the lakeshore. I didn't stop to visit them. When I landed at Kurilskoy the second time that day, it was nearly dark and the group was milling around a big campfire near Igor's cabin. I flew the plane down a steep slope of trees and landed on a pond near the lake. With two nylon ropes, I tied the plane to trees on opposite sides of the pond, to centre it on the water for the night. I parked it there with the problem bear in mind.

Igor and his brother were busy rearranging the camp, and he introduced me around to the Friends of the Earth group. I think he wanted to free himself up so that he and Andrei could get the camp the way they wanted it. I knew he was worried about the bear, though he was at pains not to admit it. He and Andrei were moving tents to get them as close to the cabin as possible, so none were any farther out than the rest. At any rate, I was soon besieged by questioners, eager to learn more about this foreigner flying around the Kamchatkan wilderness in such a small plane.

Shortly after dark, I got a look at the worrisome bear. He was making his rounds, looking for something to eat. In preparation for the evening meal, someone had caught a few char and the heads and innards had been thrown into the lake, fifteen yards from the cooking fire. Now the bear was in the water, retrieving the tidbits off the lake bottom, while one of the campers trained a flashlight on him.

I could feel myself tensing as this scene developed. The group was laughing now, hooting and hollering, all within a few yards of the big bear. Then a rock arced out from the onlookers' direction and landed a couple of feet from the bear. The person who threw it ran laughing for the cabin.

Luckily for everyone, the bear chose to ignore the rock, as though it were just another spawning salmon flipping in the water.

This last act of foolishness got me motivated to intervene, but as I made my way over to the taunting merrymakers the bear walked down the shore beyond the beam of the flashlight and disappeared.

I didn't feel as superior as this account might make it sound. When I was a teenager, I went through a period of disrupting black bears "for fun." My brothers and I used to sic Dad's hunting dog on well-meaning bears when they showed up near our house to eat saskatoon berries. We didn't kill them or hurt them, but I cringe now to think of how we put those poor bears out, getting our dog to tree them for our amusement. We never thought then about the seriousness of their quest for food, their entirely unhumorous need to gain weight prior to hibernation, and how our games were keeping them from doing it. To our credit, our adolescent notions were supplanted by a stronger wish to observe animals at peace.

These people, the Friends of the Earth group and the Russian camp crew, did not have the excuse of youthful stupidity. They were grown-ups, just not acting that way.

The bear eventually disappeared into the darkness, and I went to sit where I could see my fragile airplane reflecting the fire's glow. An American journalist stationed in Moscow joined me. He asked if I'd mind doing an interview. I was very disturbed by what I had seen and welcomed a chance to talk about it.

The American's first question was what had brought me so far from home. I explained it was a desire to find out if people could live with grizzly bears. "I'm aware of the depressing possibility," I said, "that we may never be civilized enough to act any better than the people here tonight."

Next, he wanted to know why I couldn't pursue my quest back home. Even though I sensed considerable skepticism, I went ahead and explained that Maureen and I wanted to let bears become friendly towards us if they would. It was the only way we could find out if closeness without mutual fear was possible. "No jurisdiction in either Canada or the U.S. wants me to persuade bears that it's okay not to fear people. So here we are."

The reporter wanted to talk about what had happened that night with the problem bear, and I knew he wanted to link it to what I was saying about the potential for a new relationship with bears. I asked him to consider the poor bear. First he gets offered food, and then, when he comes to eat it, everyone goes bughouse. "That bear's only interest is building up fat for the winter."

All Maureen and I were trying to do, I said, was demonstrate that we could live and work at close quarters with bears while they were going about their business of survival. The only trick was not to disturb them, and not to let them get messed up in our food and garbage.

When he asked why we wanted these things, I told him it was so that bears and people could share the same territory, which I believe is the only real hope for bears. I told him about being a rancher in southern Alberta's grizzly country for eighteen years. In all that time, the grizzlies had been frequent visitors and I did absolutely nothing to discourage them. Nor did I ever lose a cow or a calf to a bear. The bears and cattle got on with their business and left one another alone. There was nothing peculiar about my approach, or my cattle, or the country, or the bears, so I believed my success could be replicated anywhere people were willing. There were hundreds of square miles of semi-wilderness ranches in Alberta. If people would bother to understand bears, it could all be viable grizzly habitat.

The journalist herded me back to the here and now, to the problem bear. He wanted to know what I would do to salvage the situation. I explained that it wasn't my department, that I was more interested in preventing situations like this one than solving them after they'd started. In North America, where they had the drugs and expertise, they would try to relocate the bear. If he flunked relocation and returned to people, they would shoot him. In Russia, where everything is scarce, the cheapest alternative, the bullet, is the solution of choice.

"The sad thing is that it was preventable. It's just not that hard to keep a bear out of your food."

My final word on the subject was that he should come back here in a few years and I would show him what could be done. "I expect to be alive."

Our interview ended when two Russians stripped to their shorts and jumped in the lake at the exact spot where the bear had been fishing for salmon parts. Someone on shore threw a soccer ball–sized rock at them, and when it hit and bounced quickly up again everyone had a good laugh. It was a pumice stone.

About then, I decided I was more than ready for bed. There had been some confusion earlier about where I would sleep, given the congestion in camp. The Friends of the Earth group would sleep in their tent village close to the cabin. The cabin itself was full to the rafters with Japanese filmmakers, who didn't want to sleep outside on account of the bear. The exception was Michio Hoshino, who had chosen not to sleep in the cabin or within the tent town. He had a roomy tent, and he pitched it a little distance away. Igor had warned him that this might be dangerous, but hadn't pushed it. Michio was a legend and was well-known for his independent approach to being around bears. He did as he liked.

When Michio heard Igor and me discussing where I might sleep, he offered a billet in his tent. I thought about the bear, and wished I had returned to the alpine meadow to camp for the night. Now I found myself in a situation I was not completely comfortable with—spending the night in the vicinity of the problem bear—but given the choice of sleeping jammed in the cabin or in Michio's big tent, I went for the latter. Perhaps the overall numbers of us sleeping outside that night gave all of us a false sense of security.

Michio and I retired around one in the morning. I was so worn out I assumed I would fall asleep immediately. Instead I found myself immersed in a conversation about my favourite subject: everything and anything bear. It was a pleasure to find out how much Michio knew, and also how broadly his interests ranged. His goal was to show people, through photography, how to become part of the natural world again.

Michio also paid me the compliment of being interested in what I was doing. We were polite to a fault, each trying to get the other to talk the most. Michio's style was to resist telling any of his own anecdotes until he had satisfied his curiosity about his guest. Michio had a lot of friends in the world—I had met a number of them—and it was easy to see why.

Michio's current book project, to which he would return after this filming session, was set in Chukotka, the northern Russian province that lies between Kamchatka and the Bering Strait. It would be his twelfth book and it focused on the way of life of the natives there. He told me a few stories about the reindeer herders' harsh life and how much he respected them. I had a selfish interest in Chukotka because, whenever this project of ours ended, I wanted to fly my Kolb all the way back to Alberta, and I had heard that air clearance was difficult to get. He promised to keep in touch about any intricacies of Chukotkan bureaucracy he came across.

On and on we talked. I chased him all the way back through his life with my questions. He was living in Fairbanks, Alaska, but much of his work was written in Japanese. It had all begun for him twenty-five years before, when, at eighteen, he had seen a photograph of an Alaskan village called Shishmaref in *National Geographic*. He had written to the mayors of several Arctic villages, asking if it would be possible for him to come and live with a family there for a month. Only the mayor of Shishmaref answered. Michio's stay there grew to three months and his life's ambition was changed by it.

Until then, Michio had been directed towards a corporate life, but when his family saw that he was drawn to and moved by wild places, they gave him their support. He switched to the study of photography and returned to Alaska to live in 1978.

Through our long conversation, I kept one ear tuned to the night sounds. When I asked Michio if he could hear anything in the direction of the lake, he laughed and told me a story about camping with his wife in Katmai National Park. He awoke in the night and was aware of a strange wheezing outside. A bear had fallen asleep next to their tent, and he didn't know if he should wake his wife so she could hear the breathing inches from her ear. He decided not to. Michio was laughing so hard by the time he got to this part of the story he could hardly continue.

This story led him to talk about how he enjoyed the fear bears caused in him. In Japan and much of North America, nature was being tamed, but here in Kamchatka, where there was so much wilderness, he could still feel an instinctual fear. "The wariness forces upon us a valuable humility," he said.

Despite my enjoyment of these stories, I had to interrupt twice because of a sound my imagination interpreted as a bear splashing out to a plane. I had to go out and check. On my second return, I could hear by his breathing that Michio was asleep. I followed him to that destination, clutching my bear spray all through the night.

The following morning, the sky looked promising. I was sure I could go home. The Friends of the Earth group were packing up to move somewhere north of us, and I wasn't sorry to see them go. As everybody mobilized, it was discovered that the problem bear had tipped over the only gas barrel the film crew had, leaving them with less than ten gallons for the remainder of the shoot. I volunteered to bring back a few jerry cans from the barrels I'd found too unreliable for my plane. As the crew needed the gas only for their generator and boat, there was no great risk to their using it, beyond the odd stall. With that, Michio, Igor, and I said a brief farewell, thinking we'd be visiting again within hours.

But in Kamchatka, things often do not happen as you anticipate them. The morning calm lasted just long enough for me to return home to Kambalnoye. Then the wind resumed with a vengeance.

I had been concerned that Maureen would worry about my not coming back the night before, but she was fine. We had discussed this situation before, and she had told me never to fly back on account of her when it would be smarter to find a place to land and camp. Exhausted, I hit the sack, needing badly to get the sleep I'd missed out on. I slept all afternoon and was slightly alarmed to wake and find that Maureen was still away. She had left as I was falling asleep and several hours had passed. With my binoculars, I scanned each surrounding hill and valley, and eventually found her on a promontory overlooking the lake about a half mile east of the cabin.

Maureen was painting, and I could see what she was looking at: the afternoon light slanting into the basin under dark clouds, each stringer of cloud illuminated as it spilled over the mountains from the south. Then I saw a mother bear with two spring cubs rounding a point along the lakeshore. Their path would take them right to the foot of the slope where Maureen was painting.

I set up the powerful spotting scope so I could see Maureen's reaction. As the bears came to the bottom of the slope, no more than a hundred feet below her, Maureen gave them the merest glance. Then she moved a few feet to the side into the cover of some alder. Once she had taken this precaution against frightening the bears, she went back to painting. It was then I realized how far Maureen had come.

Though the two things must seem totally unrelated, Maureen's new-found ability to coexist calmly with bears made me think I must be able to solve the considerably less complex problem of the chimney. The wind grounded me that day and the next, so I devoted the time to the assembly of an elaborate wind cap for the chimney that I hoped would baffle the downward flow. I had the leftover metal we'd used to cover the cabin. It was heavy and hard to cut, but it was all I had. I used pop rivets from my aircraft tool supply to hold it together. After three and a half hours, the wind cap was up.

We ate very late that night, and I found myself brooding on the recent events at Kurilskoy Lake. The situation was so far from what I wanted in my own relationship with bears, so contrary to the peace I wanted to believe was possible.

Many times that summer, Maureen's and my moods were on completely different tracks, and that night was one of them. Maureen was elated. Her painting had finally begun to feel good to her. Three new watercolours were drying on the walls, and she talked about the new self-assurance she was feeling in her solo hikes around the valley. We went to bed, poles apart, even while lying next to one another.

The wind subsided the next day and the fog rolled in right behind it. The fog clung to the valley for days, and there wasn't much I could do but think about Igor and Michio and the gas I had promised to bring them.

On August 9, the day dawned with a brilliance that meant the fog was thinning and the sun would soon burn through. In anticipation of blue skies, I strapped jerry cans to both sides of the Kolb and tied another two into the passenger seat. I told Maureen I expected to be back in a couple of hours, and as soon as I could see the sunny mountaintops through the mist, I taxied down the bay and climbed into the dazzling morning.

Most pilots agree that cool, still air is the best for flying, as the only turbulence is the wake of your own airplane. This was such a morning and, even with my heavy load, I felt completely comfortable cruising close to the rocks, skimming the ridges, shooting the canyon gaps.

As I neared Kurilskoy, I took aim on an ancient twisted birch on the edge of a bluff. Beneath the tree's outstretched branches, I slipped down the hill into the basin of Kurilskoy Lake. Flying above the lake, I saw that a thin layer of fog had yet to burn off at the south end where the cabin was. The mist was shallow, and the tops of the highest trees pierced above it. The cabin was visible and the look of it puzzled me. I thought it would be breakfast time for the crew, but there was no sign of activity. I looked for the canopy underneath which they prepared food, and it was gone. I wondered various things as I slowly descended toward the lake. Had they been forced to leave for lack of fuel? Could the canvas have blown away? Could they have started early on account of the lovely day?

The mist hugging the water made for a tricky landing. I couldn't tell where the mist ended and the water began, and had to lower through it slowly until I felt the water and knew I was down. By the time I had the Kolb moored to a willow, I was sure that the crew had broken camp for some reason. I walked up the slender dock and saw a piece of paper tacked to the cabin door. Knowing I would return with fuel eventually, Igor had left a note. Michio was dead. The bear had killed him.

Suddenly, I realized that I had been sitting motionless for some time. I had no recollection of sitting down and no sense of how much time had passed. The morning was so peaceful, as if the day itself was paying tribute to the person whose life had ended there. The whole caldera felt like a church.

Eventually, I got up and searched. Around the corner of the cabin, I found a pile of stones marking the place Michio's tent had stood. A jar full of wildflowers sat atop the cairn and the blooms were still fresh. Down the beach a ways, a female brown bear with two large cubs was fishing the mouth of the Khakystyn River, near the tower the cameraman had been using to film the problem bear on our visit two weeks earlier. Other bears strolled the beach west of the point.

Many years ago, I had trained myself to read the stories left in animal tracks, and I did so that day. It's hard to explain what I felt, but it amounted to a strong need to relive Michio's horror when he first realized what was happening to him. I needed to unsettle myself in the most basic way. The bear's tracks were highly visible in the lush summer vegetation, and I followed the trail away from the cabin into the thick willows. It was clear the bear had stopped there to eat some of its victim, then had buried the remains under a mound of moss and grass.

Later, I would be told how the camp awoke at 3:30 a.m. to Michio's screams. The bear had jumped onto his tent. Igor and Andrei rushed outside, but the tent was torn open and the bear was dragging Michio down the hill to the edge of the small lake where my plane had been the night I'd stayed at the camp. They grabbed pots and pans, a shovel, whatever would make noise. They advanced on the bear, screaming and banging. But the bear picked Michio up again in its mouth and disappeared into the tall grass and darkness. Igor had no gun and did not want anyone else to be hurt or killed, from what he had seen in the beam of his flashlight, Michio was already dead. He was forced to give up hope of rescuing his friend.

The story was all there, in the paw prints and the blood. I let the revulsion of it sink all the way into me, knowing I would never forget what I was seeing or what it was causing me to feel. It may sound odd, or even calculating, but I wanted this experience to shake my convictions to the core, so I would have to re-examine everything I thought I knew about bears. I felt alone and unsure, and what I wondered most was what Michio would say if he could talk to me right then. Would he tell me that he had made a fatal error, or would he say he'd been wrong to trust bears all along?

I had thought my share about how I might die. There was some appeal, frankly, in the idea of returning to the land, and being consumed by a predator was certainly a profound way of achieving that. I consoled myself with the notion that, after the initial horror at what was happening, Michio too might have accepted the end he met. His connection to nature seemed fathomless. This end might have been acceptable to him.

The trail away from the mound was also well-defined, and I followed it to where the bear had been killed and its body airlifted away. I was told later that Igor and Andrei had boarded the boat and motored across to the fisheries research station where Bill Leacock had a satellite phone. There they called Petropavlovsk for a helicopter and someone with the authority to kill the bear. They borrowed a rifle in the meantime and, returning to their camp, tracked the bear to where he had entered the willows. Then they waited at the cabin for the helicopter.

It had arrived at noon, with a Special Forces officer and a hunter. Igor boarded the helicopter and they flew to the thick bush at the edge of the lagoon. They spotted the bear, buzzed the brush until he flushed into the open, and shot him from the air.

After I'd gone to the research station to find out a few final things about Michio's death, I flew home. It was hard to go back, carrying such terrible news to Maureen, and imagining what effect it would have on her. Though she hadn't met Michio, she had listened enthusiastically to my retelling of our conversation. Now, that vibrant, creative, positive man was gone from the earth, killed by a bear.

We had planned to fly to the coast that day, but instead we spent most of it sitting on the veranda, thinking, talking, drinking vodka, sometimes exploding into argument about what we were doing there, and whether to go on. Our perception of what we hoped to accomplish, and our concept of bears themselves, had been blasted, cracked open like some kind of nut. It felt as though we had been torn out of ourselves and placed in the heads of our worst critics, the ones who thought we were dangerous lunatics, humorous fools.

The first principle of our research was that bears would not be dangerous to people without cause; that it was possible, given appropriate manners, given the following of a few fundamental rules, to live so that bears would never harm you. Now Maureen challenged me to consider the opposite, that bears simply had it in their nature to turn on humans. No matter how valid her words were in the face of Michio's death, it was still hard to hear my convictions, the fruit of my life's experience with bears, thrown open to challenge. The more valid the challenge, the more angry it made me.

Nothing could be resolved that painful, bitter day. The best I could do was stare at the lake, at the sculpted pine and alder hillocks, at the rising majesty of the smooth volcanoes, and of course, at the bears; to stare and hope that in some wordless way the marvellous place itself could repair what had been torn. That and the crude beneficence of alcohol got me through the day.

MAUREEN: When Charlie flew off to deliver gas to Igor and his Japanese film crew, I stayed behind and pursued my usual workday rituals. I went to the beach to look at the tracks along one stretch of sand, which I did once or twice a day, and then I went in search of a "bear bed with a view." I had begun finding these bedding places and painting what could be seen from them. The bear bed I found and worked from that day faced in the direction of Kurilskoy Lake. As I approached completion of my painting, I obeyed an instinct I will perhaps never understand, and painted the sky above the mountains blood red. When Charlie landed on his return home, I walked to him, carrying the new painting, dripping red.

My first reaction when told that Michio Hoshino had been killed by a bear was to register that I was not surprised. A series of emotions followed: graphic horror as I imagined what Charlie was telling me; anger that no one had prevented it; guilt that I had done nothing either. I had seen the danger and I hadn't acted. I felt like a wimp, and I am not one. However bad I felt about this, I recognized immediately that it was more severe and personal for Charlie, who had met Michio and liked him so much.

Inevitably, and I think reasonably, I questioned what we were doing at Kambalnoye, and whether we shouldn't pack up and go. Maybe it wasn't all a matter of bad food habits. Maybe bears turned against people for reasons of their own and always would. If that were true, we had no business where we were.

Since our arrival I had been following Charlie around like a kid. When it came to bears, I thought of him as an infallible god. It must have been irritating, the way I tailed him over hill and dale, stepping where he stepped, speaking when he spoke, using his tone and words. If he picked a flower, I considered if I should pick one too. Now, I was pulling away sharp and hard, speaking words he could hardly stand to hear: that he might be wrong, that his very mission in life might be misguided. As reasonable a man as he is, this angered him, though I knew similar thoughts were in his head. We had not come here to be martyrs. That wasn't our brand of heroism.

I still can't stand to look at the painting I created that day. Its blood-red sky still haunts me.

We rose early the next morning, and I followed Maureen to where she wanted to paint. She led me to a place along the creek above the lake where wildflower blooms dotted the mossy slopes. The creek explored its way down through boulders. Maureen climbed to a place where the bears had a bed and a nice view of the valley upstream. She set up there and began to paint, and I hoped the tough emotions were flowing out the tip of her paintbrush; a therapy I envied.

For myself, the only thing I could do was return to the past, to the experiences with bears that accounted for my being in Kamchatka that day. They were some of the best experiences of my life and, from them, I had sculpted out the system of ideas and beliefs that I was now clinging to with difficulty. I stared at the landscape, or perhaps through it, to where the Mouse Creek grizzly was always waiting. In wonderful detail, I relived our journey together in the rain forest on the day she dared to sit beside me and when I dared to touch her mouth and put my hand in her jaws.

I thought of the Spirit Bear—glowing in his jade world on Princess Royal Island—who had chosen to brighten his solitary life through friendship with us, who had confounded our filmmaking by getting too close, under the tripod, face in the lens.

I flushed my sore mind with these memories. They were not figments. They were not slight and inconsequential things that I had teased out into a theory that was now breaking off under its own unsupportable weight.

Back in the verdant canyon, in the moment at hand, a big male bear came poking its nose over the valley rim, as if we had hailed him with our thoughts. He sat down in a sea of globeflowers. Maureen had already packed her gear to go, but we stayed and watched for a while. The bear did not seem the least afraid, and that was a great balm for what ailed us.

When we got back to the cabin, I talked Maureen into a flight across the divide to the east coast. She had not yet seen the spectacle of bears hunting salmon in the surf and I was pretty sure we would see them at it today. From the air, I spotted bears near the mouth of the Gavrilova River. The way the river formed a long pool parallel to the ocean before it broke through the sand dunes made it a perfect place to land. I was able to come in low behind the dunes, staying out of sight of the sea, with the roar of the waves drowning out the sound of the motor.

Once on the ground, we peeked though the dunes and could see three bears fishing the river mouth. The blue-green waves towered over them before crashing onto the sand. A young female came out of the bush and walked along the bank towards us. She was obviously curious about the Kolb, the big bird that had just swooped over her back. We stayed close to the plane but out of sight. Twenty feet from the upstream wing, she stopped for a long look, then cut through the sand to join the others on the beach.

From behind a large driftwood stump, we had a grandstand view as the bears waited for the waves to strand some salmon. When the waves did roll some out onto the sand, the bears casually strode over to the flopping fish and ate. The fish were victims of slight mistiming. If the return journey to the river of their birth had got them there at high tide instead of low, when their freshwater target had been deeper, they probably would have made it to the spawning ground. Sometimes, apparently just for the fun of it, a bear would swim out into the surf to play in the waves, where harbour seals appeared in the vertical face of the breakers, as they too pursued salmon.

By the end of that day, both of us had made some progress. I don't mean our faith and confidence were fully restored, but a start had been made.

I have left something out of the story of Michio's death and I'm not sure why. I have already mentioned that Maureen and I flew to Kurilskoy soon after the film crew arrived there and that we went to the tower where the Petropavlovsk TV person was filming the problem bear. The bear was into the man's food, and we had wondered at the time if he was deliberately using his food to lure the bear so he could get a better shot.

After I flew in and discovered Michio was dead, I went to the research station and Katya told me the parts of the story I didn't yet know. One hair-raising fact was that, after getting into the TV man's lunch, the bear had traced the smell back to the helicopter and knocked out its window to look for more food inside. The cameraman recorded the bear doing all this, and it became the video the TV station played when it ran the story of Michio's death.

What I finally did make of Michio's death, besides mourning it, was to vow that I would learn from it. Much as I liked bears, and had faith in their good nature, I would never be lulled to a point where I was not alert to possible danger. When all my self-questioning was said and done, I still did not believe there was anything in a bear's nature that would make the animal turn on humans for no reason. There was always a reason. In the story of Michio's death, there were so many reasons it was almost pointless to number them.

I was more certain than ever that it was time for someone to go searching for peace with these animals. If no one did, the time would soon come when *all* relationships between humans and bears would be just a dismal memory.

What came finally was a rededication. I would give the next years of my life to solving the question of whether bears needed to be fearful of people. Meanwhile, I decided to stop trying to justify what I was doing. No longer would I chase myself around my own brain asking what it all meant. There would be plenty of time for that on the long winter nights in Alberta, when I would be dreaming of a way to return to Russia. Now, while I was still in Kamchatka, I had to get on with what I had come to do.

8

A Month of Hell

August 199 stands out as a month of hell. First, there was Michio's death, then the painful reassessment before we could commit to continuing our work. Hard as well was going through all that soul-searching and rededication only to have the project stumble on as before. We were still disturbing every bear we met, and I was finding it more demoralizing all the time.

I thought Maureen was coping better than I was. Probably because I'm not an artist, I often mistake effort for results. I saw her working, and I liked what she was creating. It always came as a surprise that she was unsatisfied with her work.

Less than a week after Michio's death, we watched as wispy mare's tail clouds rose up to form a high, thick layer of overcast. It was dark along the ground and ominously still. We had learned by now to recognize this pattern as the prelude to a storm, but the cyclone that hit that day exceeded all our previous definitions of what a storm could be. Driven by incredible wind, the rain jammed under the tarpaper and poured down through the nail holes. We erected the tent fly to direct the torrent away from the bed. I spent the first night securing the tie-downs on my plane and tightening the frame on the supply tent so there would be less strain on the canvas. It seemed possible that our cabin would be yanked off its moorings and roll windswept into the lake.

It was good and cold, and we looked at the stove with mixed feelings. The chimney extension that was supposed to solve the problem of the smoking stove had failed and I'd removed it. My second design, the cap over the stovepipe, had been working but was untested in high winds. During a lull in the cyclone, I struck a match and touched it to the kindling. The fire got off to a roaring start, and I was just beginning to look forward to its warmth when a wild gust hit the house, reversed the convection in the chimney, and filled the cabin with smoke.

We coughed, spluttered, and rubbed our eyes. I threw a dipper of water on the fire. I started to babble to Maureen about one more idea I had that I thought might work—but she was in no mood to hear about more inventions. As far as she was concerned, I'd had my chance and blown it. The only real option was to pile on more clothes and tough it out.

My pride was injured and, though I shut up about it, I didn't stop forging a plan in my head. I refused to be defeated by a chimney. But I also realized that this whole bear project, so replete with challenges and complexities, could yet be undone by that mere length of pipe. The weather was too tough here to do without a warming fire.

At that point, nothing much about the project felt like it was working, including our relationship. At two and a half years, our partnership was fairly new. We had come here with ideas of brilliant summer days among innocent bears and wildflowers. What we got was the worst weather I'd ever seen and bears as frightened and wary as those I'd chased with my father and brother all over Canada and Alaska in 1961. We had spent a lot of this summer cooped up together in one small room, a room that was often either cold or smoky. You could say with some accuracy that our relationship was undergoing a torture test.

During the second night of the storm, Maureen woke me and told me I should check my plane. We had gone to bed during a lull, but the storm's resumption had shaken her awake. She noticed that the wind was coming from a different direction, and it was good thinking on her part to realize this shift necessitated changes in how the plane was moored and protected. I pulled on my pants, coveralls, overcoat, hat, and headlamp, and left the cabin to face the elements.

The trail to the plane was slippery with mud. I crept along carefully, getting my face washed by each walloping gust. The plane had withstood the storm so far, but I added two more ground screws, one at each wing tip. Then a huge gust of wind from up the creek hit the plane from the tail. The velocity from that direction was punishing the control surfaces, attacking them from the direction opposite to what they're built for. Along the rudder, flaps, ailerons, and elevator I secured more control locks, so each hinged surface was as firmly restrained as possible.

Maureen was asleep when I returned, with the feather tick pulled over her head to deaden the roar. I found a towel, dried my face, and slid back into bed. For a long time, I listened to the storm and I found myself thinking about the Itelman people. I thought about them in their pit houses, in storms like this one. Somehow I felt certain they had done better with their smoke hole than I was doing with my stove and chimney and boxes and caps and baffles. On the day at Kurilskoy when I found out about Michio's death, I had gone to the Itelman pits on the point beyond Igor's cabin. I had stood there wondering whether days of such mourning had been commonplace for the villagers, or if the Itelman had devised a better way of living among the bears.

As I lay awake in the storm, it came to me that the Itelman people were my truest predecessors in this place, perhaps the only ones who knew what I was trying to find out. Perhaps they had evolved a true understanding of the mind of the bear. Perhaps they had learned respect out of their inability to conquer. If there was any way of finding out more, I had to pursue it. I had already asked Igor to look, while he was in Petropavlovsk, for any kind of written account of the Itelman past. I was hoping that he might have something when he came to spend time with us in September.

The next day, the storm was not any better. I did not dare climb on the slippery roof in all that wind, so I could not attempt anything new on the chimney. I worked out my plan on paper and gathered the materials I would need, but I kept my mouth shut.

When the storm finally did end, Maureen grabbed her rod and headed for the river to fish. I climbed to the roof and assembled a three-sided box around the top of the chimney, including the wind cap. The box was held up by two posts and was guy-wired to the ridge beam. For the record, this final desperate fix, while not perfect, worked well enough. It has blown off once and been rebuilt, but we have relied on it ever since.

During the storm, Maureen and I talked a lot about whether we should continue into a second year. It was by no means certain. We were pretty disheartened, both by the weather and the fearful bears. For people who like bears, it is no fun scaring them almost every time we encountered them, especially when our intention was the opposite.

On August 19 I turned fifty-five, and to mark the day of relatively good weather we took a long hike and saw twenty-five bears. We were hiking a great deal at this time, and though the majority of bear encounters that month were of the fear-and-flight variety, the odd bear reacted differently enough to give us some small measure of hope. The day the blond bear had sat and watched me fly in and land was still a major moment for us: the way he had calmly studied me, even as I taxied up to my ramp not far from where he was sitting. When I disembarked, he had not run away, but had gone back calmly to his meal of sedges.

Another time, early in the morning, we had been enjoying a cup of coffee in bed while the fire warmed the cabin, when a loud and plaintive crying came from outside. When we got to the porch, we could see a female bear swimming across the neck of the bay with a small cub (the source of the racket) forty feet behind her. The cub was crying mightily, and it took a minute to figure out that he was unhappy about more than the cold water. When we got the binoculars trained on them, we saw a second cub riding high and dry on the mother's back. The family continued like that to shore, with the wet cub howling and the dry cub visibly enjoying his advantage. Some parity was restored when the dry cub tried to hold onto his perch as the mother entered an alder thicket. In short order, the cub was dusted off by a branch.

After repairing nicks on the prop of my plane, changing oil, and going over all the flight control linkages, I was able to fly down the river for firewood. There were more bears than ever fishing the river, and more still had congregated at the coast where the berries were ripening on the tundra. On one trip I counted between eighty and a hundred bears.

But the bad weather resumed and put an end to my flying until the end of August. Maureen and I kept hiking in spite of the rain and the fog. Just as the bears were frantically feeding in response to the advance of the season, Maureen and I were desperately picking up the pace of our activities. Good people had invested good money in us. Maureen had a grant for her artistic endeavours—I was determined not to leave Russia without some of the answers I'd come to get. We had to show results, and neither of us was satisfied with what we had to present thus far.

All summer there had been an endless procession of bears past our camp. One week, the flow would be east to west over the divide. Next week, it would be west to east, as if they had all been to the same jamboree and were returning home. Kambalnoye was certainly a crossroads, and it was all spectacular to watch, but if the bears weren't spending enough time near us to come to terms with our presence, could I honestly say that we were any closer to our goals? The best I could say was that, although the bears and I were hardly bosom pals, neither had they decamped from the valley to avoid me. What I needed was a way to speed up the process.

An incident around this time made me realize that the whole issue of fearfulness was even more complex than I had previously thought. To keep from disturbing the bears, Maureen and I had learned to choose trails away from edge of the river. But there was one trouble spot that could not be easily avoided. It was a short stretch of river where dense alders pushed to the shoreline, forcing us to wade in order to get by. The river curved at this spot so we couldn't see ahead. It was an obvious place to call out a warning, but on that day I neglected to, with the result that I came face to face with a mother bear and three cubs.

The instant the bears had my scent, they leapt into the river to get away. I was talking, trying to calm their fear, but with all the commotion of four big bears galloping in two feet of water, I doubt they heard much of it. They fled without pause, right up to the ridge and over it. I continued on with the same anxious feeling in my gut that I always felt when contemplating how much happier the bears might be if I just got lost.

Such fear, I firmly believed, is a learned response. It had to mean a violent history in this place. Also, judging by the sharpness of the bear's anxiety, I was sure the cause was recent. Vitaly Nikolaenko, the veteran bear expert up at Kronotskiy Preserve, had told me that bears can pass down their fears to cubs for several generations as a way of keeping them from having to learn the fear first-hand in the face of actual danger. For a project like mine, this theory was not encouraging.

Later, when I came to the blind spot from the other direction, I had the breeze in my face, and confronted another mother bear with two spring cubs. The only difference from the earlier encounter, besides direction, was that the bears and I were on opposite sides of the stream and almost hidden from each other by alders.

Before I could duck into a hollow and hide, the female bear stood tall to sort out what I was. She saw enough to know I was not a bear, and I could tell she was getting ready to run. I really did not want to put another family of bears to flight, and I started telling the bear this, loud enough for her and her cubs to hear. Actually, I was begging. I put everything I had into it and, though I wouldn't have done this with a human audience, I went down on my knees to add abjectness to my appeal.

This display of mine, an audition for the nuthouse in human terms, seemed to work. Not only did the female not run away, she began to move in my direction. Her path took her behind a screen of alders, but by the odd flicker of a branch I was able to track her and her cubs' progress until they came into view again.

I was on a mossy terrace about fifteen feet above the river. When the bears were visible again, they were only about 120 feet away. The cubs were standing on either side of their mother, balancing themselves with a paw on her flank. I kept talking, and only looked at the mother from time to time. Something strange and powerful was happening. I felt that the emotion in my voice was a language that the bears and I were sharing.

Finally, the female bear was in the open, with her cubs peeking out behind. She was studying me carefully. I turned slowly, walked a few steps back, and sat, talking all the while. The cubs, feeling bolder, came to the front, craning their necks. The distance had now closed to about sixty feet, with only the river between us. About then, the adult bear sat down and her cubs started to tumble and play. Everyone was about as relaxed as they could be.

As I watched and participated in all this, I began to understand that the bear's "picture" of me was not complete. Through all of this scene, the angle between us had been such that my scent was bypassing her. I got up and walked into the bush, hoping that once I was out of sight the bear would come and sniff where I had been. As I watched from the bush, she jumped into the river and climbed out on my side. She strode over purposefully, with no hint of fear, until she was about two feet away from where I had been sitting. When my scent hit her, she stopped sharp. A shudder rippled through her body. In one bound, she leapt back into the river, throwing up a huge plume of water. She sped away, passing her cubs, who for a few seconds were at a loss to understand the change in their mother's behaviour. Then they ran too. Up and over the ridge they went, never slackening pace.

The closest thing I had seen to the physical effect of my scent on that bear was seeing another bear touch the electric fence around our cabin. But that bear had jumped back only a few feet, then had stopped to consider what had happened.

I have thought about this event a thousand times and still find it very hard to understand. The bear had been close enough to see if I had shaved that morning, and was unafraid. She heard my voice for a long period and was unafraid, perhaps even pleased by the sound. But my scent had stirred in her the deepest possible fear. As for what it meant, one could go to Nikolaenko's theory and imagine that the bear's mother had taught her extreme fear of human scent. If so, she had never seen or heard what went with that scent. It was possible too that, in her travels this spring, the bear had come across a poached bear, with human smell all over its dismembered remains.

But rather than try to draw a conclusion, I tried to resist one. I knew far too little about this bear to presume to understand what my little glimpse into her life meant. I preferred to have the experience live on in my mind as a mystery.

MAUREEN: For me, that August was about an ever greater sense of futility. I thought I was wasting my time. The bears were afraid of us and neither of us had any idea how long it might take to gain their trust—as in, how many years. I had no idea what we were going to tell our sponsors, or what I was going to tell my arts granter, about how we had used their money.

It is very strange to look back and see what exactly I was doing while all that frustration and despair ruled my mind. Twice a day, I was walking to a certain stretch of beach to examine the animal tracks there. Everywhere I went, I was listening, and understanding just how dead to sound my society back home had become. I was searching for bear beds so that I could look at what the bears looked at in their times of rest.

Tracks. Sound. The view from bear beds. The three points on which my art would focus for years to come. But I did not know it yet. Intellectually, I was still nowhere, while subconsciously I was making incredible progress.

Before August drew to a close, the fall season rushed in upon us. The bears were getting fat on the biggest salmon run of the season. They were growing the luxuriant coat that would warm them in their winter dens. Snow had begun to fall, heavily on the mountaintops and more lightly at our elevation.

In my echoing desire to do something to prepare for my winter, I began to think of an electric fence project for Kurilskoy's salmon research station. Because of all the salmon available, many bears use the area. Tensions arise because the bears get into people's gardens and garbage, and wander through the village. It might be possible to build a fence around the whole place.

Another possibility was an electric fence to keep the bears off the weir. The weir stretched across the river a short distance from where it drained from the lake. It's function was to force the fish to enter through a gap where they could be counted. The bears, being smart fishers, figured this was the place to be. The only problem was that they regularly broke the weir while fishing up against it. If I could deploy the fence to prevent this breakage, it would be a solid way of decreasing bear-human tension; a lasting contribution to the bears and to the people like Katya and Alexei who tolerate them.

Also about this time, on our hikes and in our cabin, Maureen and I began to hatch a scheme of raising a few poacher-orphaned brown bear cubs at the lake. In Kamchatka, cubs like these, if they survived at all after their mothers were killed, tended to wind up in the zoo at Yelizovo. They could only stay there while quite young, after which they might be shipped to a Taiwanese bear farm, where catheters implanted in their gallbladders would bleed off bile for sale as a medical remedy. These bears lived short, brutal lives in miserable conditions. Early execution was almost certainly more humane. But there could be a better solution.

The idea of bringing orphaned bears to Kambalnoye was very appealing. We believed we could wean them off their dependence on us over time and let them become wild. If we could do so in a way that did not erode their positive feelings towards people, we could test how and whether problems would still develop. It would be a good way to assess if fear is a necessary part of bear-human association.

A bear cub project would also be fast. The biggest problem with what we were currently doing was that we had no way of knowing how long it would take to gain the trust of the bears at Kambalnoye. We couldn't expect sponsors to go on with us year after year on the assumption of future results. The orphan bear plan would yield results quickly. We couldn't guarantee what those results would be, but we could guarantee the speed of them.

It was an exciting idea, and what's more, it was a plan for a second year. Formulating such a plan meant that we were both leaning towards returning. In fact, if we could get the cubs, it had the potential of being much more than just a second year. We could be in association with the cubs for a long time.

Of course, knowing the density and complexity of Russian bureaucracy, the adoption of wild bear cubs was bound to have miles of rules attached. At any rate, as soon as Igor came to us in September, we intended to ply him with questions and requests for help.

And that was how August of 1996 ended: with surprising optimism, and a couple of new and exciting plans rising out of the smoke and sadness and storms.

9

The Trail's End?

By September, it had begun to feel very much like the end of our year. All sorts of things in nature were drawing to a close. The last sockeye salmon run, the biggest and most important for the bears, was on the wane. Some of the bears had already left it to concentrate on pine nuts, which were full of fat and other things the bears needed in their preparation for winter.

When good flying weather resumed, around the first of the month, I went over to Kurilskoy to help myself to Katya and Alexei's ample and currently wasting garden. Katya had gone to PK to help her children get started in school, and Alexei was flying surveys up north. Bill Leacock and family had already gone back to the U.S.

I wasn't expecting to find Igor—because of all the bureaucratic problems he'd been having due to Michio's death—but he was there, overhauling his outboard motor and working on improvements to the Leacocks' dwelling for next year. He wasn't ready to come back with me to Kambalnoye, but he would be in a couple of days.

What Igor had by way of news was troubling. Sergei Alexeev, who had given me my permission to fly, was now in hot water over it. The FSB, the post-Soviet version of the KGB, had found out about me and were not pleased that a foreigner was gadding about their skies without supervision. When they first showed up at Sergei's door, they claimed that Maureen and I were already in prison. They kept that up for a while, then said they were joking. The real problem they wanted to talk about was my flying. They wanted me to stop.

All this worried me considerably and Igor not at all. He doubted they had the budget to hire a helicopter to fly to our camp and observe what we were doing, and otherwise how could they know if I was flying or not? His feeling was that they had known for a while and had been assuming, perhaps even hoping, that nature would take care of the problem. If I were to crash, that was by far the cheapest and easiest solution. When I stubbornly refused to kill myself, they decided they must take action. They were ordering Igor and me to show up at the Kurilskoy research station for a meeting with the chief flight inspector and a representative from the FSB on September 6.

Better news from Petropavlovsk was that Evgeny, the engineer who was building Sergei's Kolb, was half done. I was amazed. He was ahead of the schedule of any builder I had ever known, including me. I had worked continuous twelve-hour days to meet a work deadline, and Evgeny was bettering my pace even though he could not read English, the language the instructions were written in. Igor had watched him at it, and said that he took the manual home at night to translate the instructions he needed for the following day, using his English-Russian dictionary.

By the time I went to pick up Igor at Kurilskoy Lake on September 3, the weather had changed completely. Gorgeous warm days had come that felt very much like Indian summer back home. Igor was not ready when I arrived, so I made the first packing voyage alone. I was excited to see, in among the food and Igor's camera gear, two thick, heavy books printed in an ancient Cyrillic script. The Itelman information, I hoped.

Igor and I made the final trip together on the margins of darkness. Maureen had a wonderful supper waiting, and only when we were well into it did I urge Igor to explain to Maureen the FSB flying quagmire. I hadn't said a word, preferring Igor's way of explaining, which made it sound as consequential as a speeding ticket.

That night, we also talked about the orphan bear project. When we proposed it, Igor thought quietly for a minute, asked a couple of clarifying questions, then said he thought it might be possible. Sergei Alexeev was responsibile for orphaned cubs, and he might be receptive to our plan, especially if it brought some positive attention to the preserve. Igor guessed that some of the scientists would have concerns, such as mixing bear genes from north Kamchatka with the southern population, and about reintroducing bears into an area that already had lots of bears. Igor himself worried that the cubs might be killed by predator males. I suspected there would be many such problems ahead, but, if we got permission, I would be happy to apply all my bear experience to solving them.

The first big snow hit the volcano, turning the top half white. Most of the bears had moved to the coast, and we decided that in order to keep observing them we should do the same. We would fly down there and move into the cabin on the river for a while. Maureen and I had dropped in once since the time I had robbed the place of a handful of nails to finish the darkroom. With a little work we could make it livable.

But first we had to face the dreaded FSB. On the appointed day, Igor and I flew over to Kurilskoy. The research station, which had been all but empty on my previous trip, was now a hive of activity. The FSB could only afford the cost of the helicopter by sharing it with twenty vulcanologists doing fieldwork. Word had spread about what was happening, and everyone was curious to see the outcome of the meeting involving me and my plane.

As it turned out, the meeting consisted of Igor taking the chief flying inspector aside for a private chat. After that, I was served with a document for my signature. Igor told me to sign it and I did. For all I knew, it could have been my death warrant.

Not until we were back at Kambalnoye, having tea with Maureen, did Igor divulge the document's contents. I was grounded and was to remain so until they had written a new regulation that covered my kind of plane. If I needed to fly in the meantime, I must hire a Russian pilot and file a daily flight plan. As for my activity next summer, we would need to do the same thing.

To my ears, this was a nightmare, but Igor found it funny. In fact, he was laughing uproariously. I had signed a document that grounded me and then had flown off in my grounded plane, which symbolized the whole situation as far as he was concerned. After listening to the inspector's harangue, Igor had said that, of course, we would need to continue to fly for the rest of the season, and the inspector had agreed. If we came back next summer, Igor assumed it would be the same: a lecture followed by nothing.

So with that out of the way, we flew down to the coast and set up housekeeping in the other cabin.

The weather that week stayed wonderful. The vision of a prairie like the prairie back home—but covered in grizzlies—was even more intense for me now that the bear numbers were up and the weather was clear. While I studied how they used the coast, Igor harvested a bounty of white boletus mushrooms that were in full body on the tundra. He cut them into strips and set them to dry on old window screens. Through the grassy dunes and the driftwood stumps and the skeletons of whales and sea otters, Maureen and I stalked and photographed the bears.

MAUREEN: At the coast, the bears still ran away from us, but in the beautiful weather, it seemed to matter less. There was endless space. We were not crowding them. I was so sick of bad weather and the tense month that we had just experienced that living in the cabin at the coast in good weather felt like we had gone on holiday. We learned a lot too, such as the distance at which the bears could see us. The camera shots we were getting were better than we had managed to date, and that relieved some of my tension in regards to our eventual report to sponsors.

Among other signs of fall, at the coast and at Kambalnoye, were big flocks of geese that competed with the bears for the remaining tundra berries. They were getting ready to strike off for Japan or even more southerly points. The ptarmigan were also flocking, already wearing some of their camouflage whites. Hawks and falcons took natural advantage of the clustered bird life.

One day, as Igor and I were flying over the divide between the cabins, we spotted a herd of seven snow sheep just under the valley rim. I could see how the plane terrified them, and I gave them a wide berth lest they fall off the cliff in fear. Near the end of our stay at the coast, the mountain slopes turned bright red, the bear berry's vivid final flourish before the snow.

On those lovely evenings at the coast, Maureen, Igor, and I worked on the orphan cub proposal that we would present to Sergei Alexeev at the end of the season. Igor suggested we not mention the human coexistence part of the scheme. For the first time, he told us that he had been omitting this aspect of our project any time he made a presentation of our plans to the Russian authorities. He didn't believe his colleagues were ready for the idea of people and bears living together. As for what we were supposed to be here for, he had stated that our main purpose was to record bear behaviour on film and video. The $10,000 a year that we were being charged (two years of which was paid for with the Kolb) was to pay for this supposed filming. We had learned from Bill Leacock that he did not have to pay at all because of the scientific nature of his work, so our costs were really the high price of not being scientists. I was reluctant to continue the charade, but, as it goes with any deception, once you've started it's hard to stop.

Despite everything, Igor was optimistic. Sergei Alexeev was the one we had to persuade, and he knew more about our actual work and our ability than anyone, save Igor. Furthermore, during the winter, Igor planned to translate for us papers written by Dr. Valentin Pazhetnov, the only person in the world who was reintroducing brown bear cubs to the wild. He and his son had already been successful with twenty cubs in western Russia.

After about a week on the coast, we gathered up our effects and moved out. We did so with some regret, because it had been a marvellous time—bountiful bears, tasty mushrooms, and a stretch of fine weather better and longer than any we had experienced so far.

Any sadness we had about leaving was soon vanquished by changes back at Kambalnoye Lake. In our absence several bears had taken up residence in the bush near the cabin for the purpose of eating pine nuts, and they showed no concern when the three of us moved back in. It wasn't as if they were holding their ground against an enemy either; they really didn't seem to mind our presence. I had never seen bears eat nuts before, and now we could watch how it was done through our windows and from our porch. The close-up views of bears that we had been unable to get all season, we were now able to get without leaving the cabin. On still nights, we were serenaded by the crackling of dry cones between strong jaws.

MAUREEN: When we returned to the lake and our own cabin there, something had changed. It was as if the bears had sat down and had a meeting at which they decided to accept us. They came around our cabin to eat pine nuts and we were able to shoot big glorious close-ups right from our windows. One day when I went to the lake for water, a bear crossed the trail between me and the cabin. I talked to it. It stopped and looked, and then slowly walked by me. The bear seemed completely relaxed and later allowed me to take some great photos. This was a pivotal experience for me. I was overwhelmed by the changes that September had brought, and these changes were responsible for my decision to return.

The good weather stayed with us at Kambalnoye Lake. Battered by storms, the poor old wall tent looked like the veteran of a decade of bad weather rather than a single season. It had to go. The three of us set about building another cabin on top of the supply tent floor. We could never have imagined that a tent wouldn't be strong enough for storage. We gave the new structure the expansive title of "east wing," and joined it to the existing cabin with a covered walk. The result was an L-shaped edifice that buttressed the original cabin. The combined structure made the cabin stronger, and I was now confident it would survive the winter winds.

After a day of building, Igor and I would have a night of reading. The venerable-looking books he had brought from Petropavlovsk were indeed what he had been able to find on the topic of the Itelman people and another native group called the Koryaks who lived in north Kamchatka. The books were a two-volume set written in the eighteenth century by Stepan Krasheninnikov, titled *Exploration of Kamchatka, 1735–1741*. With the fire snapping in the stove, and pine cones scrunching in the bush, we sat beneath the light of our single bulb, and Igor provided a translation almost as fast as he could have read the book himself. We continued into the morning hours and only stopped when the solar-powered batteries weakened and the bulb began to fade.

I found Krasheninnikov's story fascinating. As a young science reporter, he had signed up with Vitus Bering's second expedition to Kamchatka in 1733. He left St. Petersburg that year and made it to Kamchatka's west coast four years later. He and his men were almost killed while crossing the Sea of Okhotsk in a decrepit, leaking boat. They were hit by a tidal wave caused by a violent earthquake just as they were landing at the mouth of the Bolshaia River (about one hundred miles northwest of our cabin). They lost everything, including two years' supply of food, but forged on.

When I got back to Canada, I went in search of an English translation of Krasheninnikov's work and found one, published by the Oregon Historical Society in 1972. The translation and introduction were by E. A. P. Crownhart-Vaughan, and the following paragraphs from that introduction are a good summary of what Krasheninnikov proceeded to do:

For three years, he traveled Kamchatka virtually alone. In that distant primitive land of mountains, avalanches, quagmires and volcanoes, besieged by hostile natives, mosquitoes and lack of food, Krasheninnikov observed, collected, noted. Seemingly nothing escaped his notice. He observed the appearance of the natives and noted in great detail even such seemingly trivial matters as how their hair was cut and how they sewed their garments together. He described their religion, myths, beliefs, customs, and even their language. He analyzed their manner of speaking and contrasted the tribes to one another. Not content with simply observing their food, he ate it. He candidly remarked it turned his stomach just to watch some of the dishes in preparation. For days on end he lived in the choking smoke of the underground "iurts" while he recorded every minute detail of Kamchadal festivities.

During these years he collected specimens of animal and plant life, amassed detailed data on the precise distances between stopping places along the various trails in Kamchatka, and often risked his life to journey to some inaccessible place to examine a hot spring or geyser or volcano. He experimented with raising rye and barley to see if Kamchatka might be used as an agricultural station for Siberia.

Even though Maureen was already asleep when we came to the bit about the "choking smoke," I woke her up and had Igor read her that part. Now I felt we had even more in common with those ancient people. Naturally, I was most interested in Krasheninnikov's observations of bears, and was disappointed when all Igor could find were two and a half pages, most of which was an account of how bears were hunted by the Koryaks from northern Kamchatka, and by other natives of Siberia. Of those pages, only one half page was devoted to how the native people of the south lived with the many, many bears that dominated the Kamchatka peninsula. Here, in translation, is that passage written by Stepan Krasheninnikov in the mid-eighteenth century:

> In Kamchatka, there are a great many bears and wolves. In the summer the bears graze in packs over the vast tundra in this country. The Kamchatka bear is neither large nor ferocious; it will never attack a man unless someone comes upon it while it is asleep. Even then a bear will rarely kill a man, being content with ripping the skin from the nape of the man's neck, slashing him across the eyes, and leaving him on the ground. When the bear is aroused to a fury, it will rip one's flesh to shreds, but will not eat it. In Kamchatka, one comes across a few men who have been treated in this manner. They are commonly referred to as "dranki" or "the frayed ones." One thing that should be made clear is that the Kamchatka bear will never harm a woman. In summer, when the women are out gathering berries, the bears follow them around like domestic animals. Occasionally the bears will eat the berries the women have picked, but that is the only harm they do.
>
> When schools of fish come into the river mouth, the bears come down from the mountains in regular herds to the sea and find a good place to take the fish. Since there is such a quantity of fish, the bears become particular in their choice, and only suck the brains from the head, leaving the rest of the fish on the bank of the river. But when the fish are scarce in rivers and there is no forage available in the tundra, the bears do not hesitate to eat anything they can find on the shore. Quite often they will even break into the Cossacks' huts along the shore to steal their food. They should be indulged, however, since they are

content to eat the fish they find in the huts, and do not harm the people. It is customary to leave an old woman in each cabin.

Once I got over my disappointment about how little material there was, I started to pay attention to what the paragraphs actually said. I had wanted to know how the Itelman people lived with the bears, and the Krasheninnikov book told me. I had heard this idea of women being excused from harm before. As I thought about it, I considered the pronounced difference in the roles played by women in these cultures as compared to men. The men, as hunters, were the ones who travelled farthest from the village, and were thus more likely to collide unexpectedly with bears at blind corners, or to surprise sleeping bears in the bush. The men, in other words, were more likely to trigger an attack.

Then there was the probability of a differing attitude between males and females. The men of Kamchatka were portrayed by Krasheninnikov as a pretty macho bunch and were likely gruff and aggressive compared to the women. If bears followed the women around the berry fields "like domestic animals," it implies that the bears did not fear them, and that the women perhaps did not fear the bears. Bears are intelligent, so it made sense for them to let the women do the picking and then rob them of the occasional basket. The women, by simply allowing it without threatening the bears, ensured their own safety.

That condition of relaxation was what I hoped to achieve and what I hoped would defuse the aggression that existed between modern people and modern bears. The fact that it had worked for the Itelman women two and a half centuries before was the best assurance I had found yet that I was on the right track. What I had to hope was that, as a man, I could be accepted into that circle of trust.

I pondered the words of this Russian scientist-adventurer over and over, and was often rewarded with new questions and insights. The fact that the bears were described as "not large" fascinated me. As I've mentioned elsewhere, the Kamchatkan bears of today are twice the size of the Rocky Mountain grizzly, and similar in size to the giants of Kodiak Island off the Alaskan mainland. I had been told before that there were bears elsewhere in Russia that were even bigger than the

Kamchatkan brown bears, but I had passed it off as myth. Now, I started to believe it.

I thought about the reference to the Cossacks' cabins being ransacked by bears. These people were colonizing Kamchatka at that time, and were drawn to the south shores in pursuit of sea otters. It sounded like they also capitalized on women having a different relationship with the bears than men. I wondered, were the cabins that were broken into the ones that had no old women available to protect them?

The Itelman built balagans, which were thatched roof huts on high stilts in which they could dry and store salmon during the summer, safe from dogs and bears. This system suggested a fairly sophisticated evolution towards making life easier and safer for themselves. In a way they were forced into being civilized by their lack of technology, but the introduction of firearms erased what they had known. It seemed fitting that now, in the same area, Maureen and I were trying to relearn their lost knowledge.

Perhaps the most important conclusion I drew, with the help of this piece of historical writing, was that maybe I shouldn't bother so much with the question of whether bears were naturally afraid of people. Maybe it didn't matter. What was more obviously true and important was that, in the absence of fear on both sides, life in close association between bears and humans was better for both.

One of the things that would continue to mystify me for some time was why Krasheninnikov had been so stingy in the space he devoted to bears in his huge, complex set of books about this country. Later, while doing literary research in Petropavlovsk, I asked that question of Irina Viter, head of the historical department of the Petropavlovsk museum. Irina had published several books on the local aboriginal people, and I had made an appointment with her to talk about both the Itelman and the Koryaks.

"Imagine travelling Russia as these people did," she suggested to me, "and consider that bears were numerous from St. Petersburg to the Bering Strait, a distance of 9,000 kilometres [5600 miles]. There were tens of thousands of bears and they would have been easy to take for granted." Krasheninnikov, being a writer trying to interest his readers, would have known that bears were too commonplace to excite them. She asked me to compare the mentions of bears in the books to the mentions of sable, the equivalent of the North American marten. Sable was Russia's most important fur-bearing animal at that time. Since the beginning of the seventeenth century, sable had been a form of currency in Russia. The "sable treasury" within the walls of the Kremlin held the royal reserve. Sable, as a result, got seventeen pages' worth of coverage in Krasheninnikov's work.

Another thing Irina Viter focused my attention on was the way bears were described in the Koryak sections, as opposed to the Itelman sections. Most of the mentions of bears had to do with the Koryak people, and virtually all these mentions had to do with hunting the bears, one of their staple foods. Just like hunters and outfitters today, the Koryak liked to tell tales about meeting the mighty bear head-on and emerging the victor. The Itelman, on the other hand, were fishermen and "pastoralists," which gave them a very different attitude towards the land and toward bears. They lived off salmon and wild berries. Even their boots were made of fish skin. Bears were not very important to their material culture and, hence, didn't even show up in their art. The Koryaks, who lived by hunting bears, included the animals in all their cultural trappings.

Inevitably our season of fine weather, wild blueberry pies, and wild mushrooms came to an end. On September 23, with the weather starting to go sour, I flew with Igor to Kurilskoy to check on the helicopter that was supposed to pick up Maureen and me at Kambalnoye in ten days. We discovered that there was some problem, but we couldn't find out what. Later that afternoon, I flew Igor to a creek near Ozernovskiy and dropped him off. Ozernovskiy was one of the places Igor had been told I was no longer to fly, so I didn't want to get too close. Igor assured me that he would look after the helicopter problem when he got back to PK, and all I could do was hope that he would succeed. He walked off in the direction of the village, and I got back in the air as quickly as I could. A storm was starting to roll in, and I just barely got home to Kambalnoye before it hit.

This, the final storm of our 1996 adventure, lasted a full nine days. Maureen grew steadily more upset because she was certain that Igor wasn't going to make it to Petropavlovsk, and we would be stuck here for the winter. We used the time to get everything packed. Towards the end of that storm, we were completely out of firewood and had to resort to burning green alder for warmth.

On October 2 the weather cleared, and we stared at the sky hoping for a helicopter to appear. It did not. I raced for the coast to get wood and on the way back was forced by fog to land. The little lake where I landed was not that far from home, but I was no less stuck for that. I could have hiked to the cabin, but that would have meant leaving the Kolb. So I got out my tent, pitched it by the lake, and prepared to stay the night. Just before dark, the fog rose a little, and I could see my way to fly. I struck camp, threw my gear in the plane, and headed home.

The next day was clear again, but still no helicopter. I flew to Kurilskoy to see if any message about it had arrived there. Nothing. By now, our situation was worrying me, as well. The snow was well down the volcano and would soon get to us. On several mornings there had been frost on the wings of my airplane. If we couldn't fly and weren't picked up, the result would be a long snowy winter of snaring snowshoe hares and ptarmigan, and burning green alder.

Finally, in the early afternoon of October 4, a small helicopter crossed the ridge into the basin and lowered to the ground. It was Igor and his friend Viktor, who taught helicopter flight at the flying school. They were ready to move us out. The first trip was to the research station with a load of things we were storing there for the winter. By the time that was done and our cabin was secured, it was getting pretty late. Igor and I left Kambalnoye Lake by plane and Viktor took Maureen in the helicopter. It felt strange to lift away, knowing I wouldn't be back for at least seven months.

When I landed in the flying school cow pasture, there was much amazement. Pretty well everyone had been sure I would never make it through the season in one piece.

The most important thing we did in Petropavlovsk in the days before returning home, was to meet with Sergei Alexeev about our orphan cub plan. Somewhat to our and Igor's amazement, Sergei liked the idea. We got as far as meeting with the owner of the local zoo, who agreed to cooperate when the time came.

There was progress as well on our other second year project: the electric

fence for the salmon research station. For that, we met with Katya and
Alexei at their institute in PK. The only real obstacle was their reluctance
to accept what they deemed charity. I argued that the fence was more of
a benefit for our study than an act of charity, and they relented. After these
two meetings, our plan for year two was in place, albeit without a crumb
of guaranteed funding.

The last days in Russia were quite pleasant for me, visiting and shopping,
meeting with Sergei, Alexei, and Katya, but I still managed to inject an
element of danger. I spent a lot of time at the flying school south of the city,
training the instructors how to fly a Kolb. These were the fellows who ran
the automobile windshield business in Nikolayevka, and they also had a
shop where they built small personal aircraft, often from their own designs.
They fabricated their flying machines out of parts scrounged from wrecked
military aircraft.

The pressure on me to train what seemed like half the population of
Nikolayevka in the use of my plane came from the fact that Eugeny was
almost done the second Kolb. They would all be flying it soon. And the
truth is, I am a lousy flying instructor, totally inexperienced—and nearly
crashed my precious Kolb as a grand finale to the season.

My first year as a Russian flyer ended on my last day in Kamchatka.
The Kolb was back on wheels, and we taxied it through the streets of
Nikolayevka to a big shed associated with the windshield business, where
it would spend the winter. When we closed the doors, I felt a wave of
elation. Against all odds, against the predictions of a great many people,
both my plane and I had survived.

From there I headed into the open market near our hotel in search of a
dry champagne. Whatever I had managed to learn of Russian and Kamchatkan ways, the language was not part of it, and I emerged from the
kiosks carrying a bottle of what I hoped was champagne, and not too sweet.
I marched into Maureen's and my room bent on a major celebration and
found my partner mired in a terrible depression.

While I had been risking my life and that of my trainees in the Kolb,
Maureen had been packing her season's creative output and feeling mightily unimpressed with it all. Everything she had done struck her now as a
big waste of time. She couldn't imagine facing the people who had given

her a grant for this work, and even more so her colleagues at the Alberta College of Art. She felt her career as an artist was over.

I had seen this insecurity in Maureen before and, so far, every time, the result had been the opposite of what she supposed. The more depressed she was about her art, the more successful it tended to be. Given that she was now more depressed than I'd ever seen her, I hoped it might mean that the work was the best she'd ever done.

I didn't say so. I accepted that we wouldn't be celebrating that night, though I expected we would sometime down the road. The following day, we returned, by way of Alaska, to our Canadian home.

For the record, our families, horses, and dogs were all fine when we got back to Alberta. Our sponsors were a lot more impressed with what we had done than we thought they would be, and the response to Maureen's season of work was wildly enthusiastic. When she had her fall exhibition, the paintings sold rapidly, which was both a pleasure and relief to us in that we were relying on their sale for a winter grubstake. We had arrived home close to broke.

For Christmas, Maureen's brother sent us air tickets to come to his place in Mexico for a big family celebration; not so much for our homecoming as for Maureen's mother's ninety-second birthday. When her family asked Maureen what her plans were for 1997, she said without hesitation that we were taking orphan bears to our cabin in Russia to raise. In the privacy of my mind, I had a chuckle. I was recalling her saying in the midst of the last storm at Kambalnoye Lake that I was to immediately commit her to an asylum if she ever suggested returning there.

Living under the volcano.

Kambalnoye Lake was a place to behold—in good weather. A rare photo with both of us in one frame.

At Kurilskoy Lake a big male looks down from eight feet. I was wiggling my fingers in the water, and he stood up to see if I had caught a fish.

Igor Revenko, our Russian fixer, who gave us the opportunity to live in his country and research bears there.

Rediscovering the delights of being free.

Our first meeting with the cubs, at the zoo. One look from Chico, at left, was enough to melt our hearts and solidify our determination to free them.

Male grizzlies catching char two miles downriver from the cabin. I estimated, on occasions when I saw a hundred or more from the air along the ten miles of river, that I was seeing fewer than half the bears each count.

Maureen warned me that the cubs would take advantage of the few inches above the door of their cabin to get out. I didn't believe her.

Young bears find fun in anything and everything. Their joy in life was infectious.

At this age bears have two speeds: full throttle ahead and complete stop.

Life was non-stop interesting. Biscuit and Chico were spellbound watching Maureen make oatmeal porridge for all of us.

Rosie was a slow eater.

Maureen decided to show them new territory across the bay.

Two small wires kept the bears from damaging the Kolb. Here I have completed the repair of my float.

I couldn't take this photo until I understood that there was a chance the damage wasn't permanent.

Once the cubs could hunt to fill their stomachs, next was to teach them the fine art of sport fishing.

I cut large driftwood logs
into stove-length sections
that fit upright in the
passenger seat, so I could fly
them in from the coast.
They carried with them
many interesting new smells
of the sea.

The cubs liked having us
with them along the lake's
shore, to deal with other
bears. It was a great place
to find scraps and
spawned-out salmon.

Chico, displaying her skill in dismantling a pine cone.

With Maureen back in Canada and the cubs in hibernation, this fox kept me company.

Denning time, 1997. Could the cubs, raised with us, do it on their own?

PART THREE

(1997)

10

Planned Parenthood

Planning year two meant figuring out how to be a bear parent—and tapping every resource, written and personal, that could help. At a bear conference in Canmore, Alberta, I made the acquaintance of Mike McIntosh, who at that time was saving about twenty-five black bears of all ages from injury and starvation in an area of Ontario highly populated with humans. He was managing to rehabilitate these wild bears, eventually restoring them to the wild. There was something familiar in the way he followed his own instincts, as opposed to the findings of any scientific body of thought. I asked him if he thought bears became hopelessly reliant on people after they'd been fed, and he had some pretty strong evidence to the contrary. He tagged his bears when he released them. To his knowledge, not one of over a hundred bears, all of whom had been fed by him, went on to become a pest.

Finding anyone with actual experience in rehabilitating brown bears was next to impossible in North America because it is against the law. The thinking is that you can not rehabilitate a brown bear cub without feeding it, and that you can't feed a brown bear without making it dangerous

to humans. The only person in the world who had been legally rehabilitating brown bears was Dr. Valentin Pazhetnov in western Russia. This
was the scientist whose papers Igor was translating for me.

At this stage, I did not know if the feeding-equals-danger theory was
true or false, but I knew that, at the very least, it was untested with brown
bears. One of the things I would be able to do in Russia, given a chance
with cubs, would be to test the theory to my satisfaction.

But what could we feed the bears? I relied on Lynn Rogers, principal biologist of the Wildlife Research Institute in Ely, Minnesota, to tell me. He is
unusually open to approaching the bear world in a way that could get him
into trouble with his scientific colleagues. In his estimation, all information
should be studied, whether or not they might challenge long-established
dogma. In a thirty-year study of black bears, one of the many important
things Lynn has nailed down is what food bears will choose if given a wide
choice. His surprising finding was that shelled sunflower seeds are the
favorite, even when the choices include beefsteak and salmon. He did not
test pine nuts because of their scarcity, but sunflower seeds are quite close to
them and relatively cheap. Given that advice, I found a source of sunflower
seeds in North Dakota and had 1,500 pounds sent to the port of Seattle.

Contacting my various acquaintances who work with bears, one of the
most interesting to talk to was Timothy Treadwell. Timothy wasn't so
much an authority on bear rehabilitation as a product of rehabilitation
himself. Several years ago, Timothy lived on the streets of Malibu,
California, a confirmed drug addict. He overdosed on heroin and very
nearly died. After surviving that, he decided he would save himself, and
chose a very strange way of doing so. Though a city boy in every way,
Timothy had a fantasy of surviving in the wild. He struck off for Alaska.

He wandered into the forests of Alaska with very little food and gear, and
no experience to draw upon. Perhaps the weirdest part was that he went looking for brown bears to live among, even though he was sure they were unpredictable predators. Somehow, out of his self-inflicted brush with death, he
needed to be saved through confrontation with a more natural threat.

One of his first encounters with a bear came on a path in an Alaska forest
at night. He met a big male brown bear. When Timothy tried to back away,
he tripped and fell. He lay there shaking, sure he was about to die. The bear

kept coming, smelled Timothy, and then stepped over him. It was late in the season, and Timothy remembers the bear's fat belly dragging across him.

From experiences like that one, Timothy developed a fascination with bears. Since then, he has spent ten summers living in bear country in a little pup tent, surviving on a diet of peanut butter sandwiches and Coke. The bears who live around him basically let him be. He walks the coastal beaches with them; he travels back with them into the deep forest. He considers them his friends.

Bear experts are always telling me that I will encourage innocents to do the sorts of things Timothy has done, so it's important to say that I am not responsible for what would appear to most people as reckless experiments on his part; when he made his life choice, Timothy had never heard of me, though I am pleased to know him now. His experiences, like many of my own, show a side of brown bear personality that many prefer to believe does not exist. None of us, not Timothy nor Maureen nor I, are about to start a commune in bear country, but our lives, our risks, and above all, our survival, go a long way towards proving something about the tolerance, trustworthiness, and patience of bears.

When I got in touch with Timothy that winter, he had heard about Michio's death. Michio is a legend in Alaska, where he did so much of his best bear photography, so his death was a blow to many in that state. Since Timothy lives alone among bears, in a pup tent with no protection whatsoever, we discussed all the details about what had gone wrong. I admit I gave Timothy some strong advice. I told him he should carry bear spray. He should also consider putting an electric fence around his camp. Also, Timothy tangles openly with bear hunters, accosting them in airports and the like. Given the high esteem in which hunting is held by Alaskans, I advised him to tone down that side of his operation too. Even though I wasn't convinced of his methods, I wanted to watch and learn from him. I promised to call again in a year.

Perhaps the strangest oracle I consulted about bear rearing that winter was James Capen Adams, otherwise known as Grizzly Adams, author of *The Adventures of James Capen Adams*, published in 1860 and reprinted in 1911. The latter was the edition we had in our library at home, which I had read as a boy. Despite some mixed feelings about Adams and his story, I knew there was a lot to learn from him about the raising of grizzlies. His experiences pointed out that even cubs orphaned at a year old would eventually become very loving and loyal to him, and did not become dangerous, even as adults. This information was important. I did not plan to discourage our orphans from being friendly towards us, ever. If they wanted to stay in the area of our cabin after they became independent, I felt this would be even more valuable to our study.

Adams was a professional hunter who had raised three California grizzlies. He raised them to be his friends and assistants. At the time of his adventures, he was supplying the 1850s gold rush miners with meat. One of his bears, Lady Washington, would pack heavy loads of deer and elk meat back to camp for him. Another saved his life during an altercation with a wounded grizzly.

That was the part of his story that always left me puzzled. Despite his obvious love for his amazing companions, Adams was not above shooting their kind whenever he came upon them in the California hills. The lowest estimate I have come across of the original number of grizzly bears in California is 10,000. They were completely wiped out of the state by 1908.

As spring approached, Maureen and I were in the same nervous position that we'd been in a year ago. We had to commit to everything by April in order to get our visas and ship our goods in time, but we were still well below the mark on funds. According to our modus operandi, we went full ahead, buying goods on credit and preparing to ship everything, including ourselves. We bought a collapsible boat and a ten-horsepower outboard motor. We bought enough electric fence to go around the Kurilskoy station. On and on the list of purchases mounted until the whole of it would just barely fit in a pickup truck. Then, on April 15, we got the exciting news from Igor that three orphaned cubs had been deposited in the zoo at Yelizovo.

I was in Seattle loading our shipping container when I got word that our funding breakthrough had finally come. A film producer in Vancouver wanted to do a documentary on our project and, on that day, had agreed to reimburse us a portion of the money we had paid for the Kolb we gave to

Kronotskiy Preserve the year before. Thanks to that last-minute windfall, we had enough support for year two in Kamchatka. We had pulled it off— or so we thought as we left Canada.

The extent of the pack ice in the Bering Strait and the unlimited wild snowscape of Siberia's east coastline got me quickly back into the mood for Kamchatkan wilderness on the flight from Anchorage to Petropavlovsk. We landed on May 16, and the first thing we noted was how full of snow Yelizovo and Petropavlovsk still were. Igor had to navigate around dirty piles of it as he drove us in. The country beyond the cities was still white, except for some luminous green strips in the valley floors.

Igor told us how the streets had been snow canyons just a month before. The old-timers were calling it the heaviest winter of snow they had ever seen. Later, when we caught up with Katya and Alexei at their office in PK, they told us to prepare ourselves for living in the snow for quite some time at Kambalnoye. The crew at Kurilskoy, a thousand feet lower, were still wading in three feet of it.

As soon as we were on the ground, our minds focused on the zoo and the three cubs. We were anxious to get on with the paperwork needed to free them into our hands. Accustomed to North American impatience by now, but feeling the need to educate against it whenever possible, Igor gave us a season-opening refresher speech on the realities of working in Russia. We were booked into a hotel for the next couple of nights, but he would help us find a cheaper apartment to rent. It seemed like he thought we could be here for a while.

The scary truth that unfolded was that Igor had encountered stiff resistance from the scientific committee of the Kronotskiy Preserve. They had not warmed to our cub reintroduction plan. Nothing could have shocked Maureen and me more, because we had steamed along all winter on the belief that we were already approved. We believed that Sergei Alexeev's okay, received before leaving last fall, was the final word.

Sergei, it turned out, was not even in Kamchatka. He had gone to Moscow to gain approval for the capture of a number of sea otters at Lopatka Point. He planned to sell them to zoos around the world to raise funds. Suddenly, our plans looked like a house of cards in a wind storm.

Had Sergei's endorsement been communicated to anyone but us? Did it mean anything? We even wondered if he had left in order to avoid us.

That night at the hotel was not pleasant. If we couldn't convince the science committee of the value of our cub project, we were finished here. All the months of planning and equipping ourselves, the thousands of dollars raised, would be wasted. That was not to mention the three cubs who were sitting in the zoo. Their future had seemed rosy in our minds. Now they were once again exposed to all the terrible possibilities. The only thing that consoled us was our track record. We had faced seemingly insurmountable odds the year before and had found a way to stumble through.

A few days after we arrived, it was time to go to the preserve office for a meeting with scientist Alexander Nikanorov, our chief critic. We entered the building well briefed and coached by Igor. Nikanorov was a biologist employed full-time by the preserve, a specialist in predators. He could read English, so Igor had given him *Spirit Bear* and the book Maureen had co-written called *Grizzly Kingdom*, in hopes that they would elevate us in his eyes. Igor believed that, if we convinced Nikanorov of our sincerity and competence the rest of the committee would follow.

Then we were in the man's presence, and I knew we were in trouble. A statuesque, craggy-faced, dark-complexioned man with a black beard, he seemed the quintessence of Russian science. His black eyes bored holes right through my confidence. Without delay, he let us have it. Our books had done no more than confirm his suspicion that we were "adventurers." If his point was that we were not scientists, fair enough, but I got the impression "adventurer" was a more pejorative term in his vocabulary than "non-scientist." He went on to say that our poorly conceived plan would only get us killed. Either Kambalnoye's bears would do the job, or the cubs themselves would turn on us. Injury was the best we could look forward to. The cubs were no more likely to survive in this scheme than we were, as they would likely be killed and eaten by adult male bears. Where was the sense in introducing bears in an area that already had ample? It would make more sense, he said, to introduce them where bears had been depleted by hunting. If the cubs survived into adulthood, they could then be harvested by hunters, yielding some commercial value.

The negativity, the insults and, finally, the cynicism of this tirade made me feel very much that I was being baited. I had to keep my head or we really would be doomed. I guessed that only one of his stated objections, that we weren't scientists, was the real one, and the rest were there for show and to demoralize us. The tradition of pure science is all-powerful in Russia, and, though poorly paid, scientists are greatly respected. Nikanorov was not about to see his territory eroded at the edges by pretenders.

Since then, I have come to understand that some of the problems underlying Nikanorov's position were never even stated in that meeting. Michio Hoshino's death the previous year had shaken people all over the world, and in Petropavlovsk particularly. The overseers of the sanctuaries of Kamchatka did not want a death like his repeated. They believed Maureen and I were the next possible candidates. Also, many of the scientists at Petropavlovsk blamed Igor for Michio's death. To some extent, the harshness with which we were received came from our link with Igor.

We tried to counter a few of Nikanorov's arguments, but it was almost pointless. We could hardly claim to be experienced bear raisers, nor could we claim to be scientists. It didn't help either that Nikanorov knew Dr. Pazhetnov, the only real expert on the re-establishment of brown bears. This relationship gave him a kind of expertise through association that he used against us. We were not in the same league as Dr. Pazhetnov. We should not have pretended that we were.

Under the circumstances, only one gambit seemed to have any potential. I asked Nikanorov what would happen to the cubs if we were not allowed to take them. Wasn't it true that they would wind up dead soon enough anyway, either killed when they were too big for the zoo or sold off for a slower, nastier death on a gall farm? Nikanorov was unmoved. If that was their fate, so be it.

We left the meeting thoroughly downcast.

Afterward, Igor took us to the zoo at Yelizovo. I had been there once before, so was prepared for its barnyard appearance. There were two buildings with a crude fence between them. Reindeer, rabbits, cats, dogs, and goats wandered around the place. Down a cluttered alley of outdoor cages, I could see ravens, hawks, eagles, foxes, and one Australian dingo.

In front of one cage stood a couple of Russian families. They were crowded so close we couldn't see past them and had to push in to discover the object of their interest: the three bear cubs. One of the fathers had just jacked open a can of condensed milk with his hunting knife and was dribbling the thick, sweet contents between the bars while the cubs struggled to get their pink tongues underneath. It was a lively competition that no one was winning. Most of the gooey milk wound up on their fur. At the same time one of the children was throwing popcorn into the cage. The condensed milk and popcorn made the cubs look like some bizarre form of candy.

Igor muttered about an article he had read in the local paper. It quoted Anatoly Shevlyagin, the zookeeper, as inviting people to come feed the bears as a way of keeping costs down at the zoo. The same article claimed the cubs had been brought in by men in military uniforms. There was no comment on how the cubs came to be orphans.

At length, the two families drifted off, and we were free to come closer and watch the cubs licking the last of their dinner off one another. Sticky, matted, and dirty as they were, the cubs were beautiful. One was dark and the other two blond. One of the blonds was almost white. As we watched them, the dark one particularly caught my attention. She had a lot of mischief in her eyes. Even in this filthy captivity, she looked to be having the time of her life.

The cubs stared at us until they were sure we had no food. Then they began to play. They took turns crawling up a section of tree trunk in the corner of their cage. At the top, each climber would leap off onto the others. Maureen moved in closer for a better look, and one of the blond cubs leapt at her, hitting the cage door with a spitting hiss. Maureen recoiled and fell. It was a sobering moment. Picking herself up, Maureen wondered aloud if we really had any business taking on these young bears, when they were already so conditioned to the wrong kind of treatment from humans.

Seeing the cubs in this place, treated as they were, I was beyond a rational answer. However logical misgivings might have been, I didn't have any. The indomitable cub spirit made even the dreaded science committee seem less formidable. While another father and son delivered up an offering of dubious nutritional value, I said to Maureen, "No matter what it takes, I've got to get these cubs out of here."

Anatoly Shevlyagin was in his office in the indoor part of the zoo. When we entered, he greeted us with genuine warmth. Though it was the last thing I wanted to do right then, he took us on a tour. We looked at his exotic prizes: foxes from the Sahara, monkeys, crocodiles, iguanas, mongooses, pheasants. I had seen most of it when Igor brought me here last fall—and I'm not a fan of zoos, especially not one so filthy and cramped. I tried to concentrate on Anatoly's fondness and concern for his animals. Or rather, the truth is that I tried and failed. My thoughts could not go anywhere but to the cubs. Their images seemed burned into my retinas. When I could politely turn the topic back to them, I did, and was delighted to hear that Anatoly was as eager as ever to release them to us. This was true generosity, because we had seen with our own eyes how the cubs drew customers. Yet he was willing to give them up.

Igor asked Anatoly how long it would be before the cubs outgrew their cage. He thought about a month. My feeling was that we would either sort this thing out in a week or not at all, but I kept it to myself.

Next day, Maureen insisted that we carry on as though we had approval: the bull-ahead strategy was our trademark. We outlined our needs to Igor and, as usual, he knew how to meet them. We wanted lumber to build a cub house and welded grids of iron bars for the windows. Igor led us to a small lumber mill and a joiner's shop tucked away on a back street, where the proprietors were only too happy to grant our requests. We also diagrammed a carrying case in which the cubs could travel and live until we could build the cub house. Again, no problem.

A lot got done that day. The ship with our container pulled into Avacha Bay, and I also went to Nikolayevka to make arrangements to work on my plane. Back in PK that evening, we moved from the hotel into an apartment. It was also the day when the science committee was supposed to convene to hear from Alexander Nikanorov about our project, but if the committee had met, we couldn't seem to find out the verdict.

For the next three days, we divided up our tasks in order to get the maximum done. Maureen and Igor took the customs detail and I went to Nikolayevka and put my Kolb through a regimen of maintenance and repair. Our previous experience of customs was that you could put in an entire day and come home having achieved nothing, so I felt I had drawn the better straw. At the village, my flying school friend Volodya Kudryavsev cracked open the building where my plane had sheltered over winter. The plane was dusty but undamaged. I spent many hours going over every inch of the airframe and wracked my brain to anticipate problems in the season ahead.

Basically, everything went as expected during these days. I got my repairs done with help from the flying school instructors. Maureen and Igor sat day after day in offices making headway that was at times invisible. One day they achieved *less* than nothing, due to a speeding ticket picked up while rushing between offices on a bogus bureaucratic errand. Meanwhile, our meeting to hear the science committee's verdict was scheduled, unscheduled, and rescheduled for May 26.

On the Friday before the Monday meeting, I finished with my plane. All the red tape about using a Russian pilot and filing daily flight plans had evaporated over winter. At the Kronotskiy office, I was asked to shade in on a map the places I wanted to fly. I made as expansive a claim as I could justify and was told in response to avoid a few places such as Ozernovskiy and Lopatka Cape. That was that. Then I joined Igor and Maureen at customs to participate in the continuing vigil. Finally, it was a half hour until closing, and we still did not have a deal. That was when Maureen reached the end of her rope. She started to push very hard on the customs person with whom she had developed an acquaintance, a woman of considerable wisdom in the ways of her department. Maureen pleaded with her to get the job done today, though closing time was literally minutes away. The woman summoned a particular man to help, stressing to him that it would be a huge imposition to make us wait until Monday. When he grabbed the key to the container and ordered a forklift, we knew we were in. The process that hadn't moved in a week was done in minutes.

That Sunday evening, the night before the meeting with the science committee, Maureen and I decided to give ourselves a break from cooking. We went out to a restaurant Igor had recommended, where the food was good but very rich. The next morning, I woke up with a severe pain in my stomach. I tried to soldier on as I got ready for the meeting, but the pain kept getting worse. Although I climbed into the car when Igor came to pick us up, I finally had to ask to be returned home. Igor and Maureen had to go without me.

I was still flat on my back in pain when they got back. The meeting had not gone well. A second scientist, Vladimir Mosolov, had been there alongside Alexander Nikanorov, and he was even more skeptical about our ability to achieve meaningful results with the cubs. Igor tried to be optimistic, claiming that the two scientists were not necessarily representative of the views of their committee, but it was no good. Maureen and I could recognize a brick wall when we hit one.

Later that afternoon, our friend Katya arranged for a doctor to pay me a house call. It didn't take her long to figure out that I was having a gallbladder attack. She gave me a prescription and said she would take me to the hospital for an ultrasound the next day.

That evening, loaded with painkillers, I sat down with Maureen and Igor for a long, candid conversation. We evaluated our chances of changing the scientific committee's view of our project. We put them at about nil. We considered every other option, and really there was only one. We asked Igor what he thought would happen if we simply took the cubs, assuming Anatoly the zookeeper would let us.

Igor thought this one over for a long time. Then he started to laugh. It would raise holy hell, he said, but the alternative was probably failure and a nasty end for the cubs. With that, all three of us agreed to give it a try. Petropavlovsk was about to witness a cub-napping.

The next day, the ultrasound found no gallstones, though my doctor was still sure I'd had a gallbladder attack, triggered by the fatty restaurant meal. Even without stones, it was possible. She told me to take a course of antibiotics and was also adamant that I have another thorough checkup when I got back to Canada.

That evening we went to see Anatoly Shevlyagin at the zoo. We laid out our plan to take the cubs to Kambalnoye Lake as soon as the weather would let us, and without the authorization of the Kronotskiy Preserve. Anatoly understood what that meant. The Kronotskiy officials might come back on him and make things hard for him at the zoo. He showed himself a true friend of animals by saying he would still release the cubs into our care.

The next day, May 28, may have been the most important day of our time in Kamchatka. I found it next to impossible to sleep the night before, as I listened to a snowstorm howl. The thought of flying into that snowy, wind-lashed world filled me with self-doubt. I would be landing and taking off on snow, and I had little experience of using the Kolb's float in that way. We had been warned of even more severe storms than last season, and I was not at all sure how I could secure the Kolb on snow. At the same time, I couldn't imagine going there without "the little plane that could." Oddly, Maureen fell silent on the subject of taking the cubs without permission. I suppose there was no more to say.

As Wednesday morning dawned, clouds and snow squalls were spilling over the mountains from the west. If the weather did clear, it would do so from the south, so we kept on making preparations. Out at Nikolayevka, I taxied the Kolb through the streets to the airstrip. I took it up for a test flight and did not care at all for the sound of the engine. It sounded like bad fuel, but I didn't know how to get any that was guaranteed to be better. Volodya had explained how PK businessmen were buying bargain car gas in Seattle and adding even cheaper diesel in mid-ocean. The waves did the blending. All I needed was fifteen U.S. gallons of good gas to get me to Kambalnoye. I had a supply of good fuel hidden there. Volodya said he would try.

I flew the Kolb over to Anatoly Kovolenkov's heliport next, where I exchanged the wheels for the Lotus float. Maureen and Igor were already there, having hired a truck and driver to bring our gear from town. We all got a rush when a weather report arrived saying the Kurilskoy research station was calm under broken cloud. The Mi-8 pilot who was flying Maureen and our gear said he was willing to go, provided we got him loaded and out in the next two hours. He described a route that started north and crossed the divide above the only road to the west coast. Despite the added distance, I decided I would follow his lead.

We asked the truck driver to take us to the zoo. Anatoly was waiting. He threw back the door of the cubs' cage, reached in, and expertly removed each bear by the scruff of her neck. We put them in the carrying box and slid it onto the flat bed of the truck. In a matter of minutes, we were back to the heliport with a box full of squalling bears.

We were well into our final preparations for takeoff when a telephone call came. It was Tatiana Gordienko, chief officer of the Committee for the Protection of Nature, announcing that she was on her way over to travel with the helicopter to Kambalnoye. She had been meaning to inspect our cabin all last season and would do so now.

When we got off the phone, Igor explained what he knew about Tatiana. She was a tough, smart woman, and if she wanted to go with us, Igor's advice was to not try to prevent it. She was not a member of the science committee that had turned us down, but we had no way of knowing if she supported their views.

I had to get busy and exchange the fuel in my Kolb for some Volodya had found, and Igor was coming with me as far as Kurilskoy to help Bill Leacock radio-collar some bears. It was once again time to rely on Maureen's skills of persuasion and diplomacy, as she would be the one meeting Tatiana at the helicopter. An hour after the pilot's deadline, we saw the Mi-8 rise from the heliport. That much at least was a good sign.

What I did not know was if Tatiana had already noted the presence of the cubs, and if Maureen and she were proceeding on that basis, or if Maureen had somehow got her aboard without her noticing.

Igor and I got into the air, heading north on the trail of the helicopter. As soon as I had gained a thousand feet, the rain turned to snow, though I was relieved to note that only a little ice accumulated on the plane through the transition zone. When I got to the pass that would take us over the divide to the west side of the peninsula, it was covered in many feet of snow and the cloud was low. I squeaked between the two mountains. Igor and I were so bundled up we could barely move, but we were still cold. Also, the condensation problem with the fuel had not been solved. Every time my rpms dropped below 4,000, the engine became rough and threatened to quit.

It was a good thing I had Igor to guide me. With low cloud everywhere, the volcanoes were not visible as landmarks. Trapped under cloud that turned the valleys into mazes, we were often boxed in and had to turn around to look for another valley trending south. Without Igor's knowledge, I almost certainly would have become lost. The alpine zone was a sea of white. Only in the bottoms of the lowest valleys had the contorted trunks and twisted branches of stone birch emerged from the winter snow.

My mind was in a strange state of turmoil. As the magic scenery poured by along the ground, various scenarios regarding the cubs and Tatiana Gordienko flew through my head. I would be flooded with the enjoyment of flying, seeing bear tracks wherever patches of sunlight illuminated the snow, only to be jolted by fear that Tatiana Gordienko might be carrying a firearm, as Russian protection officers were authorized to do. What if she killed the cubs?

We finally made it to Kurilskoy Lake. Despite the toughness of the winter, the lake had not frozen and it appeared as a Prussian blue island in the sea of white. I throttled back for my descent, and the wet fuel promptly killed my engine. I couldn't make it to the lake, but had enough altitude to glide in and land on the river, which was also open. We drifted for awhile until the heat of the engine had melted the ice in the throats of the carburetors. After about ten minutes, the engine started right away, and we flew on to the station.

The Mi-8 had already unloaded our gear at Kambalnoye and come for the things we had stored at the research station. It was now on its way back to the cabin. I was desperate to know what had happened with the cubs, so I said a quick hello and goodbye to everybody, including Igor, and got back into the air. As I climbed up the side of the Kambalnoye volcano and over the pass, I saw three dens with fresh bear tracks leading away from them. By a fourth den, a bear was lying in the snow, gazing over the valley. On the far side of the basin, the Mi-8 was flying away on its return voyage to PK. Tatiana Gordienko was certainly on the helicopter, but did she have the cubs in their travelling box with her?

MAUREEN: When Tatiana Gordienko arrived at the heliport, our pilot had the machine started and was anxious to go. This was a good thing because, if possible, I wanted to conceal the fact that the cubs were aboard. When Tatiana stepped out of the car, I could see she was a strong, determined woman. As I consider myself to be the same, this appearance sparked more respect in me than fear. I tapped my ear to indicate the noise of the helicopter and led her away. The cubs were fussing loudly about their latest upheaval, and I hoped to get her far enough away that their noise couldn't be distinguished from that of the Mi-8.

We introduced ourselves and I tried my first gambit, which was to suggest that we couldn't take her. The helicopter was already overloaded. In very good English, Tatiana told me I wasn't going anywhere without her. I didn't argue. I signalled the pilot that we were ready to go, knowing that he would immediately rev the turbine engines. The noise drowned out the cubs as Tatiana and I climbed on board. The cubs were far enough back in the cargo area that we couldn't hear them. Once we were underway, there was no possibility of trouble until the other end. Naturally, the cubs would be discovered then, but my preference was to deal with it there.

The flight took two hours. As Katya and Alexei had predicted, the valley was a sea of snow, with our cabin's clerestory roof poking out of it. I directed the pilot to land beside the cabin and the pilot, co-pilot, and engineer started dumping our belongings out the clam-shell doors at the back. I hurried Tatiana to the cabin and put her to work. Together we dug down to the doorways of the cabin and the studio/storage annex. We found hammers and a crowbar and peeled off the boards that had protected the doors and windows over winter. Tatiana, like myself, was no stranger to carpentry tools. I think we impressed one another in this regard. Soon enough we were inside the cabin and Tatiana was inspecting it. This part was over in a minute. She said she had never seen a better-built cabin.

Just then, as she was expressing her pleasure and I was basking in her praise, the helicopter flew off to Kurilskoy to fetch the second load of supplies. The sound of the helicopter faded, and the squalls of the bears rang out. Tatiana froze in mid-sentence and stared at me in disbelief.

"What is that?"

I told Tatiana that we had the three female cubs from the zoo. At first, trying to put a reasonable spin on things, she assumed there had been some change of heart from the science committee that she was not privy to. But I wasn't trying to fool her anymore. I told her that wasn't what had happened. We had taken the cubs without permission. We had done so out of concern for their welfare.

We walked out to the pile of off-loaded gear, and there in the middle of it was the carrying-box full of yelling cubs. Tatiana looked at the box, at the cubs inside. She looked across the lake and back to me. She was completely flabbergasted. She looked me in the eye and said, "You are completely crazy." Then, with a faint smile, the first I had seen, she added, "I like that kind of crazy." Even if it was a sentiment unlikely to be shared by her colleagues, she respected our determination to help these animals. Standing with the cubs, waiting for the helicopter to return, we had a frank discussion of what might happen next. She said she would do what she could to persuade the science committee to let us continue, but she didn't expect that to be easy. We weren't out of the woods, in other words. Kronotskiy Preserve still had jurisdiction over the cubs, and that would never change. In the end, I felt very sure that Tatiana understood what we wanted to do, if not why we felt so compelled and committed to do it.

Then the helicopter was back. After the men had it unloaded, they wanted to go. Tatiana and I shook hands; I thanked her for the chance she was giving us. And off she flew. It was only a few minutes later that Charlie arrived in the Kolb. He saw me. He saw the cubs. He saw that Tatiana was gone. When I told him what had happened, he didn't think we were necessarily any closer to an acceptance of our plan than before. I didn't agree and let him know it. Something very good had transpired here between Tatiana and me. I trusted her, and it was the first time I had trusted anyone in Russian officialdom. I felt certain our project had made an important friend and that our chances of keeping the cubs had greatly improved.

II

Chico, Biscuit, and Rosie

When I came in to land at Kambalnoye, after seeing the Mi-8 fly away, I swooped low enough over Maureen and our gear to see inside the cub box. My elation at seeing live cubs inside is my excuse for almost crashing the Kolb a moment later. The high overcast was creating a flat light and there were no shadows by which to decipher the contour of the ground. I chose to land on the lake, where I assumed the ice would be smooth. Touching down, I was suddenly catapulted back into the air by a five-foot drift. No thanks to me, the plane was not damaged.

There was so much snow in the Kambalnoye basin that, had our cabin been in a swale rather than on a hill, we never would have found it. The spot where I had parked my plane last year was under at least thirty feet of drift. In the distance I saw many bears, all on the move.

The three orphan cubs were playing wildly in their box, thumping its sides. I said hello through the grate, and they paused briefly to acknowledge me. Maureen had the shutters off the main door and one window, and water was boiling for tea. The cabin looked good inside. The snow had entombed it and protected it from harm. The one exception was a hole that voles had chewed through the inch-thick door. They had left a mountain of mouse dirt behind.

There was much to do before nightfall. Item one was to feed the bears. We had already christened them, without putting much thought into it, except that we wanted distinctive names for calling purposes. We called the dark one with the lively eyes Chico, and only remembered later (when she was already responding nicely to her name) that it should have been Chica. The largest blond became Biscuit. The smaller blond, and the smallest bear overall, we called Rosie.

Inside the travelling box, there wasn't room to give each bear her own bowl. We dropped in a big rubber bowl and sloshed it full from a bucket of porridge and milk. Pandemonium ensued. In a flash, Biscuit had Rosie pinned upside down in the milk and porridge, while Chico stood to the side slurping her fill. The noise was like a steam whistle with its throat tied open. These weren't barn cats, willing to sit politely at a common bowl.

After that performance, we worked non-stop to get our food and gear, and the sunflower seeds, under cover. It wouldn't do to let a curious bear get into it all on the first night of our new season.

We ended the day in high spirits, excited to be back, excited to have the cubs, and conscious of what a streak of good luck and good people it had taken to get the five of us here together.

The next morning dawned calm and clear, and there was no shortage of work. We had managed to cover the food and gear for the night, but now we had to get it into the storeroom and arrange it there. I patched the hole in the cabin door to stop the vole parade.

As soon as she had eaten, Maureen grabbed a shovel and started to dig a hole in the snow the dimensions of the cub cabin. She was digging into eight feet of wet, heavy snow, so it was no small undertaking. Maureen had shifted what seemed to be several tons before I could talk her into giving herself a break and tackling some lighter job.

Getting the cub house built was the obvious priority, as conditions in the travelling box were deteriorating fast. My chainsaw roared to life after its winter's rest, and I was soon happily building in the hot sunlight. (In that white world, the sun comes at you off every reflecting plane.) My goal was to have the cubs out of the box and into their new home that night. Whenever I glanced over, there were paws and noses sticking out of the iron grid as the bears peered out at their new mountain surroundings. I was waxing fanciful, imagining they could sense the freedom that awaited them there and were excited about it.

It was almost coal dark when I finally had the heavy tarpaper roof on, plus two barred windows and a door. We carried the travelling box to the cub house and contemplated the problem of transfer. We didn't want to lose them, especially in the dark. I decided I would imitate Anatoly's technique. Reach in, grab a cub by the scruff, lift her into the cabin, and quickly close the door. Even with gloves on, it was intimidating to reach into that dark space. I groped and finally made contact with a squirming cub in a far corner. I sorted out which end was which and got hold of the loose skin at the back of the neck, but could not hold her by the slippery fur. I shed the gloves and tried again. This time I could hold on. Squirming and howling, Rosie ascended into the open air. I dropped her into her new home. Chico, likewise, posed few problems. Biscuit, however, sensing she was alone and in trouble, dodged my hand again and again. She was screaming with pure fury, and had a lot of chances to bite, but chose not to. Finally, I had her in the cub house as well. All the grabbing and lifting had given me an estimate of their weight, about fifteen pounds apiece.

The new cabin was a big hit with the cubs. Biscuit expressed her pleasure the instant she was released by climbing a barred window and taking a wild leap from the top into the shavings we'd brought from the joiner's shop for bedding. We went to sleep that night to the sounds of the cubs still thumping around their cabin.

A little footnote to this episode is that we would notice much later that the cubs never bit each other on the paws, remarkable given that they grabbed and tugged at each other everywhere else. Maybe that was why they left my hands alone when I was fishing for them bare-handed in the box.

The next day, I decided to take advantage of the good weather and fly to the east coast for firewood. Maureen worked in the storage cabin, readying a place for what I brought back. She had decided to make a studio space for herself, also in the storage cabin, so she could have a work space that afforded privacy from the other human member of the camp—the sort of freedom from disturbance she was used to at home. The trick was to have room left after everything was stored.

Once I crossed the divide to the east the air was calm, even though the North Pacific was still heaving from the recent storm. A mist hung on the coastline, where breakers smashed the rocks at the base of some cliffs. I flew along the cliffs for a while hoping to see bears. While there was still snow on the ridge tops, the lower slopes were green with early grasses, a micro-climate the bears must have used for thousands of years to break their six-month fast. I found some females with yearling and two-year-old offspring, grazing slopes of such steepness they had to be near the point of falling off. That there weren't many bears suggested either other spring feeding spots existed, or that quite a few bears were still in the den.

The winter storms had done well by my wood supply. The area near the mouth of Gavrilova River that I had cleaned out the year before was replenished with drift logs and stray lumber. I landed on the quiet water near the river mouth, fired up the chainsaw, and cut a week's worth of wood. Though only a dozen miles from our camp here, the snow was gone and the warm, pleasant air was sweet with the scent of new growth.

It took the rest of the day to ferry the wood. Kolb as wheelbarrow. On one flight, I spotted Steller's sea eagles with two hatchlings in a nest atop a twisted stone birch. One of the adults flew up to meet me, and I throttled back to let it come close. The look in its eye was brave and fierce, as though it would tear into my wing if I let it catch me.

For a couple of days, our activity with the cubs was restricted to feeding them. We were starting them off on the porridge mixture Dr. Pazhetnov had used, according to one of the papers translated by Igor. Basically, it was oatmeal and raisin porridge. Maureen made a big bowl of it in the morning, enough for both meals of the day. Before she added oil and sugar, I would sneak in and grab a bowl for myself. (Maureen hates porridge and wouldn't go near it.) We served it to the cubs with milk. Right from the start we added sunflower seeds to the mixture, the idea being to increase the percentage as the cubs grew.

The immediate challenge was to get them to buy into a system of one feeding bowl per bear. As they had been fed in a common bowl at the zoo, they all jumped on the first bowl to hit the ground, starting an incredibly loud life-or-death battle for the right to eat. Rosie was the first to catch on to the principle of "one bear, one bowl." Very soon, she was going to her spot to wait for her bowl. Only when the bowl was in front of her did it become an object to be guarded. The smallest bear, she was also the most aggressive about food. But it wasn't too long before the feedings could be accomplished with some semblance of calm.

The matter of giving the cubs supplementary food was something we had agonized over. We did not want our feeding methods to make our bears dangerous later on. In my observations of animals, everything from chickadees to kangaroos, animals fed in some kind of feeder or bowl tend to be better mannered around people than animals fed by hand. That was our reasoning behind using three bowls. Maureen and I had an agreement not to feed them any other way.

Another of our feeding principles was something I had brought from my ranching background. I had found that I could condition cattle to associate the sound of a whistle with feeding time. I could call them with it. We reasoned that, if we could do the same with the bears, it would be a handy tool for locating them when they became separated from us. From day one, each meal was preceded by a loud toot on a whistle Maureen had found in her survival kit.

The next step was to let the bears out for their first taste of freedom. We had to screw our courage up for a few days before we did so.

We dedicated June 2—our fifth day in camp—as the day we would let the cubs out for their first run. It was a big day in their lives, and ours. We decided that, for the first go, we would let them out one at a time, so the siblings would serve as a lure back. Chico went first. For a moment or two, she looked the situation over. Her sisters were on the bars of one window, chuffing in vicarious excitement. Then Chico started to run. She ran in a circle around the cub house, and her sisters jumped from window to window, keeping track of her. Chico sped up but did not take on much more territory, apparently wanting to stay within a certain radius of her sisters. Besides running, she leapt off a few snowbanks and dug a hole in the layer of snow under their cabin. She was puffing by the time I put her back inside and gave the next cub her liberty. They each got fifteen minutes and seemed to be copying what the others had done before them.

The inaugural outing was a success. Next day, we let all the cubs out at once. We staged this experiment just before their usual feeding time. We threw open the door and called their names. The snow was compacted enough that we could walk on it without skis. Out a ways from the buildings, the bears started to run. As before, they ran in circles, but now Maureen and I, rather than the cabin, were at the centre. Occasionally they stopped to investigate some object of interest, but then were off again. The circles got bigger until they were including the nearest patch of pines in their circumnavigation. Some of the pines had melted out enough to appear as green islands in the white. We started to realize that we would be able to track the bears quite easily if they got carried away by their freedom. They were disappearing into hollows and behind bushes, then reappearing, always at full speed. They seemed to keep the cabin in view. Our biggest fear as we watched them tear around was that they would run into an adult bear in the bush, but there was no way of giving them their freedom without running some risk.

Finally, Chico, Rosie and Biscuit trapped themselves in a bay in the pines and got lost trying to navigate through it. Maureen thought it might be a good time to test the effectiveness of the whistle. She gave it a strong blast, and it worked like a charm. Within a minute, the bears were back, gulping down food at the compound.

It had been a banner day for all five of us. We relaxed a little thereafter in the role of grizzly parents. From that day on, we tried to stick to a regimen of two runs a day for the cubs, each lasting at least an hour. Only during severe storms would we leave them inside.

On June 6, a mother bear and a yearling cub came out of their den and spent their day snow-sliding. It was striking that bears coming off six months of living from their own flesh would have anything on their minds but food. Who would have expected them to play? But there they were, sailing down the long slopes. Any argument that it was transportation rather than play falls short of explaining why they climbed back to the top and had another go, and another. They played for hours, the mother with more gusto than her cub.

Our own cubs were full to the brim with wild enthusiasm for life, and Maureen and I found it completely infectious. With better weather, and with the cubs to watch and nurture, we were happier at Kambalnoye Lake that spring than we could have imagined possible. Our initial worry that the bad manners the cubs picked up in the zoo would create problems for us turned out to be unfounded.

Between walking and feeding our bears, we soaked up sun on our porch and made use of the spotting scope. A hole had opened in the ice by the lake's outlet, and there we saw the first ducks of the season. Closer to the cabin, the mountain ptarmigan, still in pure white winter plumage, were strutting their mating ritual. Red foxes took advantage of their distraction to hunt them. On another day we saw a river otter crossing the lake at a ropey gallop. It disappeared into the alders, not to be seen again.

We started to notice that, almost every morning, a male fox came by the cabin on the way to his den. One morning we followed him and found the den downriver, deep under a clump of alder. We saw the female fox, but no pups. Wherever the pups were, they must have been eating all the food the male brought home. Sometimes he had a ptarmigan, but lately we had seen him carrying some sort of rodent the size of a ground squirrel, an animal we had never seen alive. Maureen followed the fox's tracks backward and found that he had come over the divide at the end of the lake. Whatever the squirrel-like animals were, that's where they lived.

On another morning, the sun was at just the right angle to cast shadows off every contour and break in the pattern of snow. In this excellent light, I was scanning the slope across the lake when I focused on two grapefruit-sized snowballs rolling down. I followed their path up to the source, and there was a grizzly with its head poked out of the snow. I yelled for Maureen to come so we could watch the entire emergence. For a while, the bear stayed with just its head out, taking in the view of the sparkling mountains, the frozen lake, the cloudless sky. At length, the bear pushed itself the rest of the way out. Without looking back, it walked up to a naked outcrop. It lay there for almost an hour, soaking up the heat. When the bear got up again, it climbed to the top of the ridge and over. It was a great thing to see, a great chance to imagine ourselves in the mind of a bear at a moment that would only occur maybe thirty times in its long life. The last bear we saw come out of its den that spring emerged on June 17. If the bear had gone in at the normal time in mid-November, it had been under the snow for seven months.

I used the opportunity of that late spring in another way, and that was to go into the recently vacated bear dens to learn more about them. I found that some were quite shallow, while others were deep and roomy. One lazy bear's den was only a depression in among some pine roots, where he relied on a lot of snow drifting over him. The fact that the deep volcanic ash was easy to dig was one reason why this area was popular for denning. As well, good root systems of alder and pine kept the roof from caving in. When it got warm towards spring, a pool of water would form in some nests. When this happened, the bears dug a new room in the deep snow outside of the den, and that's where they stayed until early June. Another bear, who probably had several big cubs, had dug her den twelve feet into the mountain slope. The den went in and then upwards, then levelled out into a sizable cavity lined with grass. The way it was built, it could never be flooded, so it represented a superior design. Vents, like stovepipes made of ice, link the dens to fresh air. These vents aren't something the bear creates, but a natural phenomenon caused by their warm breath.

Naturally, the majority of our time in June was spent with our cubs, and happily so. Maureen liked to run with the cubs, and they loved it too. She would run and call in the high squeaky voice she used to communicate with them. Sometimes they would get carried away and grab hold of one of us, to give us a shake like they did with each other. We had to find a way to inform them we were more delicate. My way was to cuff them and say no. With Maureen, it was enough to say no in a non-squeaky voice when she saw they were about to grab her boot or wrap themselves around her legs.

The bears soon learned that we travelled slower that they did. Life was way too exciting to live at our snail's pace, so they forged ahead at full speed. They had two ways of keeping in contact with us. Either their tours would be big circles with us roughly at the centre, or they would rush back pell-mell to quickly visit. Often the three bears would converge into one large ball of rolling fur and flashing teeth, as they bit and shook one another's loose hides.

This tendency to remain in touch enabled us to keep pace and to exert a small amount of control. The exertion of these twice-a-day outings in the melting snow meant a serious workout, especially for me, not being particularly given to workouts. My level of fitness quickly improved.

The three sisters also liked to play around the cabin. If we were doing chores, we let them go at it for hours. There was a big snowdrift at the north end that they climbed and tumbled and slid on, and into which they liked to tunnel. I found that if I started a hole in the face of the drift with the shovel, they would spend hours expanding on it. It was as though they were practising digging a den. Everything was such a game with them that they could never dig long before one sister bit the one digging on the rear, touching off a wrestling match. It would be quite a while before any more digging was done. They would tunnel in and eventually dig upwards and break out the top. Then they chased each other through the tunnel. The uses to which the cubs put a snowdrift were about the same as human children would make. I had never seen an animal enjoy itself so much.

Even after we became comfortable that they weren't likely to take off, I kept an eye on the cubs whenever they were out. Because of the snow, I could not build an electric fence to protect the Kolb and had been parking it near the cabin as the next best thing. I had to guard a bit against the cubs in case they decided to have a big wild play on it. But all I really had to say was no. A change of tone was often enough to check them.

It was different when we were out on a walk. We got used to watching them head for trouble and our not being able to do anything about it. For example, they loved to run and play on the lake ice. It was still thickly frozen in most places, but dark patches indicated that candle ice had started to develop. Candle ice is a mysterious stage in the spring melt when vertical crystals form. The individual candles are maybe an inch in diameter, and they stand neatly stacked and sturdy until something disturbs them. What appears to be solid ice suddenly disappears in a shower of ice slivers. When the cubs were beyond our reach and playing boisterously on the ice, it was inevitable that one or more would hit a patch of candle ice and fall through. There would be a lot of snorting and struggling as the cold, wet cub fought around in the water, bringing down more of the ice candles until she found a solid sill to climb out on.

One thing we could do, and did do, to protect the cubs was lead them away from the river. The river opened up in sections, and the cubs with their energy and curiosity easily could have fallen into the fast water. If they had washed under a section of ice, they might have drowned. I sprouted plenty of grey hairs imagining such hazards, the various ways beyond predation that a mother bear's four, three, or two cubs could wind up being one or none by denning time.

We soon understood that, beyond differences of personality, our cubs were also differentiated by their roles. Chico was the leader and the others accepted her as such. On the first voyage together out of their pen, Chico struck out ahead. Rosie and Biscuit seldom went anywhere without Chico to lead them. We honoured this designation and tried to make use of it. If there was a danger we wanted to tell the bears about, we told Chico first.

Chico was also most interested in forging a relationship with Maureen and me. I never had the impression that she was seeking in us a replacement for her bear mother, but she did seem to want our companionship. She liked having us share her world.

Biscuit's role was a mothering one. She was always watching out for the other two bears. If one of her sisters was out of sight for a moment, Biscuit became alarmed. She would strike out in search of the missing one, chuffing excitedly. If she spotted a suspicious object, and she was usually the one who did so, she would begin a call that sounded like "chiia, chiia, chiia." Then all three would flee.

Rosie was in many ways the character of the trio. She was always off in a world of her own, checking into things that did not much interest her sisters. The others would be barging along and suddenly realize that Rosie was not with them. They would stop and wait, or go back for her. Maureen called Rosie the artist of the family.

Another interesting thing about Rosie was that she had the bear equivalent of a thumb-sucking fixation. Day or night, when it was time for the bears to rest, Rosie would go to Biscuit and take some of her fur into her mouth to suck. We don't think this is normal behaviour among bears, but rather something she gained comfort from, an orphan's lament. She would make the "churring" sound that bears make when suckling. At night we would often hear this sound coming from their cabin. Biscuit, with her mother persona, accepted this. Chico would not allow it.

From the start, the bears were more frightened of other bears than of anything else. The idea that another bear might be near was the one thing guaranteed to put them into flight. A danger during our walking excursions was that they would get far enough away from us, and disoriented enough, that they would not recognize us. If they thought we might be bears, their instinct was to get as far away as they could, as quickly as possible. We soon learned to identify this situation as it developed. We called out to them right then, and they were instantly calmed. It was very pleasing for us that they recognized our sound and were pacified by it.

The bears were also capable of scaring each other. If one disappeared into the bush and came back out at an unexpected place or angle, it often stampeded the other two. In this sense, Maureen and I had better communication with them than they had with each other. They had no linguistic way of reassuring one another of their identity.

Given the number of bears at Kambalnoye, and that our cabin seemed to be a crossroads, it was inevitable that the cubs would have contact with other bears. The first encounter was on June 7 as they were playing in the snowdrift by the cabin. An adult bear came by, and as soon as the cubs smelled him they bolted under the cabin and would not come out for about an hour. This was our first indication of their natural fear of other bears, so important to their survival. We knew it would be impossible to prevent the cubs eventually coming face to face with many different bears, and we could only hope that we could somehow prove wrong Alexander's prediction of their ending up in the stomach of a male bear.

During the previous winter, I had spent a lot of time thinking about bear food and how the bears, in the absence of a bear mother, were going to learn to identify natural foods. In my overheated imagination, I fancied myself as their hero and teacher. I imagined Maureen and myself pointing out good foods to the poor orphans and thereby playing a very personal role in their growth and fattening for winter.

How reality mocked us! The cubs seemed to know exactly what they needed to eat. Rather than blundering around waiting for us to show them things, they bolted ahead. If there was a bare patch on a sunny slope with shoots of green pushing up through dead mats, that's where the cubs would go. By the time we got there, they would have tested every available food.

False hellebore is a plant that grows in both Kamchatka and southern Alberta, and I was worried about the fact the plant is toxic until the fall frost. One day later in the summer, I noticed to my horror that Biscuit had just bitten off a stem of that plant, but she just as quickly spit it out. Something in the taste told her it wasn't for her.

What the cubs liked and didn't like did not necessarily correlate with our tastes. The previous fall, Maureen, Igor, and I had feasted plentifully on boletus mushrooms. At one point, I saw Rosie eat a big one, and I assumed that as the mushrooms became more plentiful they would be a big part of the bears' diet. Not so. When the mushrooms reached their peak later in the summer, none of the bears, including Rosie, ate them.

Another unshared taste was wild garlic. Igor had shown us how to identify it, and both Maureen and I were of the opinion that it was the best tasting wild herb we had ever sampled. We picked it by the armload and often built our meals around it. The cubs, to our surprise, didn't like wild garlic at all. Once we started to watch more closely, we saw that other wild bears didn't either.

Observing what the bears were eating often meant lying down with my face very close to their mouths as they foraged. The cubs would crawl right over top of me to get to the other side. One day in June, we were in this mode in a little grassy clearing when Chico crawled up into a crooked alder and looked down on me. She started making the chuffing noise that signals concern. She even started to make a popping noise, which is a notch up in the scale. Biscuit and Rosie, who were on the opposite side of me, began making the same noises and then proceeded to stalk me. Biscuit popped loudly and looked very tough. Chico came down out of the tree and then they all converged on me at once. I have to admit it was a bit scary. When they got to where I was, still lying on the ground, they went around me in a counter-clockwise direction, deliberately rubbing on me. Then, abruptly, they quit whatever it was they were doing and went back to feeding. It happened one other time, and again I had a strong sense of its being a game about looking tough. I thought that if they were still doing it when they weighed 800 pounds, it would be downright frightening.

We continued to feed the cubs at their cub house all summer, but we always fed them less than would have satisfied them, in order to to keep their interest in natural food strong. We figured out the amount by feeding them until they left food and then tapering it back.

On June 16, while we were out on our morning bear walk, we heard a helicopter. The sound came and went until finally the helicopter itself came over the north ridge and descended into the bowl on a trajectory for our cabin. It was by then breakfast time for all of us and we started back.

I walked like I had a lead weight on my back, because I assumed the visitors were the authorities about to have the last word on who could have cubs and what the proper channels were for obtaining them. It seemed likely that the insubordination of our approach to adoption was about to be punished, and I could barely stand the thought of losing the cubs.

Maureen stayed back with the bears as I went to meet the visitors. There were four of them and they were arrayed across a high drift near the cabin. Anatoly Kovolenkov, the pilot, was one. Igor was another. Tatiana Gordienko was the third. I didn't recognize the fourth, a man. What relieved my anxiety was that they were all smiling.

The unknown member of the party was a cameraman for Anatoly's television station in PK. It turned out that Tatiana had hatched a plan to smooth ruffled feathers back in the city. She thought that if Anatoly made a little television show about us and the cubs, in which we explained what we hoped to do, it might sway people into believing that our reasons for taking the cubs from the zoo were honourable.

The first shot was of Maureen arriving with her entourage of bears. I was very proud, as the bears behaved perfectly and trooped in as they normally did for their feeding. Then Tatiana hosted an interview with us in which we took pains to justify our program with the cubs. We were careful not to appear to be telling Russians about Russian bears. Rather, we concentrated on how sincerely privileged and humble we felt to have this opportunity. It was easy to say because it was true.

It wasn't long before Anatoly flew the group away again, and peace and silence returned. Maureen pointed out that she had been correct to trust Tatiana. Now that I had seen and talked to her myself, I was happy to agree. We had a friend at court who had gone to some lengths to champion our cause.

12

Upside Down and Lost

During the month of June, I took various flights with the Kolb: to the coast to get wood, and across to Kurilskoy Lake to visit the research station. On one trip, the air was so calm I was able to land among the steam plumes of a geyser basin high on the north flank of the Kambalnoye volcano. While there was still plenty of snow this high up, the hot springs were bordered by lush new plants. Several bears were feeding on the heat-assisted sedges. It was a remarkable place to be, and I could see much of the chain of volcanoes that stretched north for 160 miles. The Ozernaia River snaked off to the west. Beyond it, I could clearly see the Sea of Okhotsk.

That same day, on my return voyage from Kurilskoy, I came around the volcano to find that the Kambalnoye basin had filled with fog. I came in very high above the cloud and spotted something strange. On the far side of the lake from the cabin, there was a hole down through the fog. I flew over the small hole for quite some time and decided it must be caused by a down draft over the mountain. In one of those moments of strange and dangerous inspiration, I got the idea that I could fly down through it. I put on full flaps and made a tight spiral.

Entering the hole was like flying in an elevator, and I had to figure out fast how to get out of it without slamming into the lake. The place where the air of the downdraft bounced off the lake was like a big cushion and my sudden descent was slowed so that I was able to touch down softly. I taxied on a compass heading through the thick fog until I found the cabin—much to Maureen's surprise. She had given up on seeing me again until the fog had cleared. This was the first of many times that I flew "The Hole."

On my trips to the research station to visit and to pick up the loads of fresh vegetables that Katya brought us from Petropavlovsk, I noted that the snow was melting much faster than at Kambalnoye. I decided it was soon time to begin the electric fence project. In the winter, I had contacted Bill Leacock to discuss the idea of fencing out the weir and the research station village. He had volunteered to supply a share of the materials. At Kurilskoy, I had seen what he was able to ship over, and considering the total of his gear plus mine, I reckoned we could build the research station fence and have enough left over to do Igor's cabin down the lake.

On June 24 I loaded the Kolb with wire, insulators, and posts, and flew north over the flank of the volcano. As I started to descend into the Kurilskoy basin, I immediately felt happy. The people there loved their work and always seemed pleased to see me. The village was also about the only place in the world I had ever seen where bears and humans cohabited with a near absence of hostility and fear. Certain bears who had proven themselves trustworthy were even allowed to walk the village streets. Even the dogs understood that they were special cases and would not chase them.

Obviously, this situation had been altered by Michio Hoshino's death the summer before. Where the villagers might have argued at one time that they did not need a separation between themselves and the bears, they were now receptive to it. The facts were that the bears got into garbage and gardens, and into the fish curing shed (a bear tradition going back hundreds of years, according to the Krasheninnikov book). They also regularly damaged the salmon weir. If Bill and I could eliminate these frictions with an electric fence, it would be a gesture of thanks for the tolerance the villagers showed the bears, and for that matter, the tolerance they showed interlopers like us.

When I landed at the station that day, I found Alexei and Katya hard at work. Katya was putting the finishing touches on her enormous garden, and Alexei was putting the station in order prior to heading out on his salmon-counting aerial survey. At the moment, he was repairing a wind-driven generator and supervising the tearing down of an old building.

Alexei dropped what he was doing, and together we walked the margins of the compound several times, deciding on and marking a line for the fence. The station was a crossroads for travelling bears, and we planned the fence so as not to cut their most important trails. We also planned to leave a corridor so the bears could continue to fish both sides of the river and a small creek that skirted the village on its east side. We estimated that a thousand yards of fence would do the job.

We got a crew set up to start clearing bush and grass next morning. I finally left Kurilskoy to return to Kambalnoye at 10:30 that night, very close to dark. I had my usual reward of a silvery sockeye salmon, this one about six and a half pounds, to take home with me.

MAUREEN: When Charlie got home from Kurilskoy Lake that night, I met him outside and helped him tie down his plane. I had quite a story to tell him.

That evening I had taken the cubs for their second walk of the day when I suddenly realized that Chico wasn't with us. I stopped to listen and urged the other cubs to do likewise. When it was still, I could hear Chico howling, and though I couldn't yet see her, I went towards the sound. The intense crying came, it seemed, from inside the snow. As I got close, I saw there was a hole that the meltwater had carved straight down through ten feet of drift to the bed of Char Creek. There was poor Chico, clinging to a ledge with her front claws, with a torrent of water pouring over her, yelling desperately for help. Below her the swollen creek was flowing strongly. I reached in and grabbed her tightly by the scruff of her neck. I hauled her out. Beside me, Biscuit and Rosie were greatly excited, chuffing their approval of the rescue.

Of the three bears, I have always felt the closest relationship with Chico, and in some way it is mutual. I was shaken to the core by what Maureen told me about the cub's near disaster, especially after I had seen the hole and the creek surging fast underneath.

The morning after, I returned to Kurilskoy to continue the fence. Alexei's crew of university students and staff had cleared the fence line, and we lost no time putting down posts and stringing wire. We built swing gates at the major human crossings and made them easy to work so no one would be likely to leave them open. The post hammer we used was a gem of old-world workmanship made from scratch for this job by the village handyman, Sergei Bezrukov. He started with a six-inch diameter crosscut of the toughest green alder, reinforced it with steel bands, and inserted a handle in a way that prevented separation or twisting.

The only problem I encountered with my fencing crew that day and the next (it took us two full days) was getting them to position the lowest wire low enough. The perception is that the fence has to be high to keep bears from climbing or jumping over, but bears, in my experience, are inclined to do neither. They are much more likely to try to squeeze under. Ordinarily, I build a three-strand fence, but to give the people of the village more confidence in the fence, I added a fourth strand on top.

While I was at Kurilskoy, I found out from Bill Leacock that he was having various kinds of trouble with his project. He was using an Mi-2 to locate, dart and collar bears, and there were problems both with the helicopter and its inexperienced pilot. In the Mi-2, you had to fire the darts from the rear of the chopper, which was dangerous because there was no safety tie-in. All in all, he wasn't collaring many bears. Much as I liked Bill and respected the information he hoped to gather, I couldn't help cheering for the bears, as in any contest of that type.

Another major challenge for him was the scientist overseeing the project—Alexander Nikanorov. The only way Bill could keep Alexander from getting overly involved, and making endless interfering suggestions, was to claim that it would be overloading the small helicopter to have him aboard. To give Bill a break, I invited Alexander to come with me to Kambalnoye and have a bit of a flying tour. This was somewhat of a gamble because Alexander had never been an advocate of our having the cubs, nor had he seen them with us. But that was also why we decided to invite him—so that his imagination wouldn't run wild and create offensive scenarios that didn't exist.

June 28 was the day of the tour. As the air was peculiarly calm, I couldn't help but land on the flank of the volcano by the geysers on the way to pick Alexander up. As an added bonus, I had spotted a takeoff opportunity that is any mountain pilot's dream. After a pleasurable poke around the hot pools, I got back in the plane and taxied over a small crest so that I was at the top of a steep, snowy pitch ending in a cliff. My plan was to take off without using my motor and to glide all the way to the research station. Playing it safe, I did give myself a good boost with the propeller before closing the throttle to idle. The morning breeze gave me a lift at the cliff edge, and the five miles to the lake was an easy glide. I landed in pure silence.

Alexander Nikanorov showed no qualms about joining me in flight. Given our history, I was surprised that he would have that much confidence in me. On the forty-five minute journey to Kambalnoye, I showed him all the bear dens I had discovered between the station and the cabin, but I noted that birds interested the biologist more. One of the birds we spotted thrilled me as well. It was a pure white gyrfalcon, of which I had only seen one before.

Struggling with his English, and obviously excited by the vantage my plane was giving him, Alexander showered me with questions. He wanted to know everything I had seen of the region's wildlife on my travels; not many of his questions were about bears.

At our cabin, Maureen and I made a point of showing Alexander the copious notes we were taking of everything we saw at Kambalnoye, hoping to improve his rating of our ability as researchers. But the rudeness he had shown us in Petropavlovsk was absent. He was downright pleasant now, and even gave us a spring scale for weighing the cubs until they surpassed forty pounds. By attaching some netting to the hook, we got Chico swinging from the scale and weighed her at fourteen pounds. Alexander said she had been six pounds when he first weighed her at the zoo.

On the return journey, I took Alexander on a long route of his choosing. We were rewarded by sighting several minke whales at the mouth of the Kambalnoye River. It was a day well spent from a political point of view, and beyond schmoozing, I had found that I could like Alexander. I can never hold a grudge against a person so obviously enthusiastic about a landscape and its animals. I doubted he had forgiven us yet for taking the cubs the way we did, but I think he left our company a little more appreciative of our knowledge and the contribution we could make towards understanding the natural world we lived in.

The next morning, we took the cubs for their usual walk. We saw a wolverine digging in the snow at the foot of a slope, a pile of hair around him. The wolverine saw the cubs first and didn't bother to stop digging. When he saw me, he ran straight up the mountain. I went to his dig and investigated. What he was doing was digging out the hide of a brown bear that must have died the fall before. This was the first wolverine Maureen or I had seen in the area. There are many farther north in Kamchatka where there are caribou and other ungulates on which wolverines prey.

The fog cleared around midday, but the sky darkened in the afternoon. It was that dark, menacing, still condition that invariably heralds a major storm.

Two hours after we went to bed that night, an east wind started to build. I forced myself to get up and go outside. I wanted to see if the Kolb could in any way be made more secure. I had it tied down to a bare spot that was sheltered against every kind of wind but an east one. There was just no better place to put it. I torqued three more ground screws into the soft soil and hoped it would do some good. The ground here did not have the dwarf-willow root matrix that I preferred to screw down to. But the east wind was only moderate at this stage and the barometer was still reasonably high. I went back to bed.

At four in the morning, sheets of rain were lashing the cabin and the wind was definitely rising. I pulled on my rain gear and headlamp and stumbled into the open to see how things were holding. The mooring ropes had loosened, so I repositioned and tightened them. I checked the barometer and it was steady. Back to bed—but I did not sleep well.

At the first hint of dawn, I was up again. The wind had not changed, but I had a sense of worse things to come. I looked for something really heavy to add to the tie-downs on the plane. What I decided on were the two solar storage batteries. Each weighed seventy pounds and, tied onto the sponsons at the outboard end of the wings, they anchored the plane much more solidly. I returned to the cabin and fell deeply asleep.

The next thing I knew Maureen was yelling at me, something about my plane being upside down. I felt as if I had just closed my eyes, so I thought this might be part of some terrible dream. I jumped up, looked out into the morning half-light, and it was true. There was my marvellous airplane, lying on its back, at least thirty yards from where I'd moored it.

Maureen and I ran outside. If we got there in time, we might keep the plane from flipping again. Just then a tremendous gust of wind brought a wall of water the length of the lake and nearly flattened us.

Seeing the plane close up sickened me. There was a gaping hole in one wing. When the wind had picked up the plane and tossed it, the storage battery on that side had smashed right through. The plane must have cartwheeled, for the tail was badly mangled. An aileron was clipped as well. The only good thing I could think of just then was that the second storage battery, still attached to the other sponson, had managed not to hit the plane while flying around.

We worked fast. All the ground screws had pulled free, and we used them now to hold down the plane as it had landed, flat on its back. We reasoned that the wind would have a harder time getting under the plane with any force if it was left in that position.

Back in the cabin, I felt completely miserable. Maureen said that at least it was not a flying accident, but I was hard to console. I had never accepted that any kind of accident would happen with the plane, aerial or otherwise.

The barometer was now reading incredibly low, and I wanted to throw the thing at the wall. What kind of infernal device gives you no warning, but tells you there's a storm after your plane is wrecked? If anything, the storm was escalating, to a force we had not experienced before. The gusts kept peeling water from the lake and sending a never-ending sheet of it downriver to the sea, an awesome display of the power of nature.

I checked the cubs, and they were curled in a knot in the corner of the shed. Not a peep out of them about their missed morning walk. Smart bears, I thought. I then went back to the wreck to begin an itemization of the damage. Maureen brought her video camera to document the evil moment: wide shot of the wind ripping up the lake; medium shot of the twisted and smashed parts of the plane; intercut Charlie's long face. She had a hard time keeping her camera, tripod, and herself from blowing away.

As I did my inventory of damage, I felt the first flickers of hope. There just might be an outside chance I had the materials and tools to repair this mess. The tail boom had not actually bent under the force of the plane's tumble, and that was a great relief. The stabilizers were certainly smashed, but I had a supply of aluminum tubing that was possibly the right size to fix them. The tubing was for a camera mount for the documentary, but having a plane in the air was more important.

Another piece of damage was a wrecked propeller blade. It had stabbed into the ground, possibly preventing the plane from going for another roll. I had spare blades.

Most of the rest of the damage was on the wing, where the storage battery had crashed through. Luckily, the battery had gone between the ribs, slightly damaging only one. That would not be hard to fix, nor would the clipped aileron. There was a dent in the tubular wing spar that worried me, though. As for the torn fabric, I had plenty of Dacron cloth with which to replace it, having always expected a curious bear to someday rip a surface of the plane. The difficulty there would be heat-shrinking the fabric onto the wing, something you ordinarily do with a clothes iron. We didn't have one. There wouldn't have been enough wattage in the cells to heat it if we had.

When I looked at the plane from end to end, the only thing I was afraid I could not fix was the creased spar tube. This six-inch diameter tube supplied most of the structural strength to the wing. This part would be the hardest to fix, and there was no way of flying the plane unless I did.

I went back to the cabin and spent the next couple of hours matching the damage list to an inventory of tools and materials, everything down to the last rivet. Maureen helped greatly by coming up with ways of converting items around camp into needed parts. Her greatest coup was suggesting that the rudder of her Klepper kayak might become the needed patch on the damaged spar tube. The rudder was made of an ⅛-inch aluminum plate, which might well prove malleable enough to mould, and strong enough to reinforce the spar. We would replace the rudder with a piece of Lexan.

Though making good progress, I stayed a nervous wreck as long as the storm was blowing. The plane could be further damaged; there was no way to keep the wind from shaking it. As long as the wind could rattle the plane, the top wing surfaces could be injured in collision with the ground. It made for a long day of pacing and cursing. Finally, at 10:30 p.m., there was a let-up in the storm. I fell asleep, exhausted.

Next morning, there was hardly a breath of wind. My urge was to go to the plane and work on it non-stop, but we had other important things to do. Enough snow had melted that it was feasible to get the cubs out of their house, which was a definite priority. With a little trenching through the remaining snow, we could build an electric fence that would allow them to live out of doors as much as they liked. The other electric fence was needed again to protect our cabin from them. They had lately taken to rearranging the tarpaper on the outside of the studio/storage annex.

Even though they would be living outside, we intended to keep on with the cubs' twice-daily walks. The phenology of local plants progressed rapidly in the shortened season, and we wanted our bears to keep up to date on every new source of food. Flowers had begun to bloom on the tundra, and, when they did, we discovered the bears had a sweet tooth. The cream-coloured rhododendrons near the cabin didn't stand a chance. The cubs ate every one they found. It was the same with globeflowers. When they bloomed our bears ate them by the bushel.

After a long walk with our bear family that morning, we went to the plane and carefully jacked it up. To my relief, there was little damage to the top of the wings. One false rib had broken and a small area of fabric was stretched. By evening, I had the shattered tail removed and brought inside the cabin. The kitchen table was converted into my workbench. Maureen stopped producing art to help me. With no radio and no plane, we were completely incommunicado. If there was trouble, walking out would be our only hope.

The next several days were divided between fence building and airplane repair. We built the electric fence to a size of forty by sixty yards, enclosing two groves of twisted alders for the bears to climb. There was also room to run. On the evening of July 8 it was ready, and we turned the cubs loose into it. An instant hit. They raced around until it was dark, forgoing their usual sleep after dinner. That night, they slept in the bush.

Inevitably, the cubs got a few jolts from the fence before they accepted the limits of their freedom. It took time for them to understand that they were also protected by the fence. Two days later, we found the track of a big male bear that had come right up to the cub fence. When we took them out that morning, they were very spooked about the smell of the track and stayed close. They dug a hole in the ground near the north side of their enclosure and slept in it that night. Soon enough, the cubs understood that other bears would not cross the fence.

The cubs were such diverting company at this stage, it was hard to keep on with our other work. They could even lure me away from repairing my plane and Maureen from her art—things we were desperate to do. In the mornings, when we let them out of their pen, they ran down to the bay, a distance of fifty yards. From there, they went wherever their whim might take them, a randomness that allowed Maureen and me to discover places we never would have located on our own. Following the cubs often meant crawling on hands and knees through alder groves, or stumbling over the tops of tough pines. Beautiful grassy clearings and meandering mossy rills appeared out of nowhere.

This kind of exploration reminded me powerfully of childhood, memories complete with physical sensation that I never expected to have again. In just this random way, my brothers and I had explored our home ranch, visiting the familiar, discovering the new, respecting no obstacle.

Part of the cubs' exploration of the world was learning to swim. I am sure that cubs who follow their mother are forced to swim early in their lives when she heads across a narrow bay or crosses a river. We went around the lakes, so learning to swim was left to the cubs' initiative. For quite some time they stayed in the shallow end, but one morning I saw Biscuit lead the other two into deep water. Chico and Rosie turned back as soon as their feet would no longer touch. Biscuit made a loop back and then out again. This time Rosie followed. Chico seemed quite upset, as she was normally the leader, but deep water was not her forte. She ran beside the lake, look-ing back, hoping they would follow, but their new-found ability to travel through water was too much fun. Chico came back and reassessed her fear. Soon they were all in the drink and then began to play on a rock island fifty feet out. I'm sure they were challenging me to join them.

MAUREEN: I thought that it was important that the cubs learn to be good swimmers, and that they should not regard the lake as too big an obstacle to swim across. This is one reason I started to coax them into the water and to urge them to follow me in my kayak. Also, I just thought it a very cool idea to kayak along with three cubs swimming after me. They were already swimming across small lakes on hikes by then, but following the kayak was their debut in the big water.

Something else I did from my kayak, when I was just on my own, was experiment with calling to strange bears from a distance when floating in towards them, trying to get a photo. The trick was to keep them from running away. In order to make my voice project that far, it automati-cally went up an octave. What I noticed was how much the bears liked that sound, just as the cubs did. Their ears would go up; their interest would quicken. In some cases, bears would jump in the water and swim out to see what I was. It worked so well, I had to be cautious with it. That is, I had to be careful that I didn't attract bears closer than I felt was safe. During that year, I definitely learned to sustain a high-pitched voice when I wanted a bear to feel happy with me, or when I was really trying hard to communicate. Charlie calls it my "squeaky bear voice."

Early in July, I left the cabin with the cubs one morning and walked into a dense fog. Maureen had stayed back and was planning to join us later. Walkie-talkies were part of our equipment in 1997, so finding each other, even in a fog, was no great problem.

With their usual careless enthusiasm, the cubs dashed onto the snow by the lake, just as an adult bear materialized out of the fog on the far end of the drift. With nothing but the fog against which to measure him, the bear looked huge, and the cubs were horrified. They retreated at top speed and huddled behind me. While I stood wondering what to do, the big male bear flopped off the edge of the drift into the lake with an enormous splash, and started swimming across the bay. I turned around and saw the cubs leaving the country. They had given up on me as a protector and were depending on their legs instead. Almost instantly they were swallowed by the fog. At a fraction of their speed, I followed their tracks.

We had talked about what the cubs would do in a face-to-face encounter with an adult bear. Now we had our answer. As I walked on, wondering how far the cubs would run, Alexander Nikanorov's prediction about their fate was haunting me. He had been exaggerating the danger to make a point, but I knew from my own sources that adult male bears do on occasion kill and eat cubs, the progeny of other bears. It was also true that the cubs had a natural and profound fear of adults of their kind. As long as the cubs were running around in a panic in the fog, the chance existed, however remote, that they could encounter a bear that posed a danger for them.

Tracking, I came to a point where they suddenly veered in a different direction, another flight response. I alerted Maureen, who was just then leaving the cabin, to come and help. She agreed to make a large loop to the northeast. If the cubs continued in their current direction, such a loop would cut their trail. The speed at which the panic-stricken cubs could travel worried us. It was a big old world out there in the fog and there was no telling where they might wind up.

After another thirty minutes of searching, Maureen spotted the miscreants on top of a hill, a favourite place to which they had gravitated in the past. We cautiously approached, calling to them all the way. When we were finally together again, I had to stay on the hill for two hours before they could be persuaded to return to the cabin.

This was the first cub tracking adventure, but far from the last. Over the next three weeks, the rebuilding of the plane was often interrupted by the need to search for the wandering cubs. We also found we dare not skip one of their walks. One day when I was working on the plane and didn't want to stop, they went around the fence looking for low spots to slip under the lowest wire. This behaviour concerned me because I couldn't string a lower wire without shorting it out on the grass. What I finally did was string a fake bottom wire, one that wasn't electrified. The cubs had learned their lesson well enough not to challenge it.

Another day, Maureen was off with the cubs on her own and got separated because of dense bush. She was literally slowed to a crawl while they were travelling freely. When she got through the slow going, the cubs were gone. She tried the whistle, but it wouldn't bring them. By now, they'd figured out that the whistle had more to do with our being worried than with their getting fed.

At first, I didn't join the hunt. I was in the middle of a tricky repair and wanted to finish. Maureen kept looking, but by noon it was obvious they had gone somewhere far from the cabin. Over lunch, we planned a strategy. Maureen had walked miles by now, so we decided I should go on my own. I would hike a big loop that I hoped would cut their trail—if I could see it. There wasn't nearly as much snow as there had been, and tracking across blooming tundra was difficult. If I didn't hit their track and had otherwise run out of ideas, I would call Maureen to help me.

The circle I walked after lunch had a radius of about a half mile, with the cabin at its centre. I started at the lakeshore and kept to the snow as much as I could. The cubs preferred to travel on snow when it was available. I had just about completed the circle when I made out very faint tracks heading west down the river. This route would take the cubs farther from home, into terrain they did not know. They were travelling a southwest-facing slope on a sunny day, and their track was melting before my eyes. Soon, I couldn't see a thing. I made another big loop and picked up their marks again. They were still going away from the cabin and down the river.

Maureen decided to rejoin the search; it took her a full hour of fast walking to catch up to me. We were at least three miles out. At six that evening, we could no longer find any trace, and it was obvious that the cubs were lost. More than once, we returned to the last trace, but the large patches of brush and the absence of snow kept defeating us.

We split up again to cover more territory. I started on a big loop to the north, while Maureen slowly worked her way back towards the cabin. There was always the chance that the bears' inner compass would right itself and bend them home.

I found enough adjoining snow patches on my circuit to suggest that the cubs were inside the circle I had walked. To make sure I hadn't just missed their track, I went around a second time. Still nothing. It was a big area that took half an hour to circumnavigate. By now, I had a pretty good sense of the lay of the land. It looked like the cubs were headed into a big patch of pine, maybe fifty acres in size, probably in search of a place to bed down. I walked up onto a knoll on the back side of the pines and yelled out, "Hey, little bears!" several times.

About 300 yards away, three heads popped out of the bush, a joyous sight. Soon they were moving my way, navigating the dense pines with difficulty. When they made it out, Chico came to me. I bent down so we could touch noses, a form of greeting she liked. Usually only Chico did this, but today Biscuit and Rosie wanted to touch noses too. There was great delight in this reunion, and I radioed Maureen so she could share it. I started for home and, most of the way, the cubs walked close behind me. As we entered familiar territory, Chico passed ahead of me. She led the parade the rest of the way in.

After the trauma of being lost, the cubs were noticeably changed. They were a lot more attentive to where they were and what was going on around them. I'm not suggesting that there was never again a worrisome moment of separation. Just about any time there was a panic over an adult bear, a separation of some length occurred. I always tried to remember, in the cubs' favour, that bears their age did not normally have to concern themselves about orientation or even safety. Their mothers would have taken care of it. Our cubs needed to be more resourceful than most, and they became so at a very young age.

During the first two weeks after the plane smashed, we were surprised that no one from Kurilskoy came to see about our welfare. I assumed they would be worried, especially since I'd said I would come back soon to do the final hookup on the electric fence. After the savage storm, and then several very nice days with no sign of me, they had to be wondering what had happened. The helicopter Bill Leacock had been using was back in PK so that was not an option. I assumed they were waiting for Alexei to return from a survey, and that could take a good long while.

The work on the plane was slow, but we surprised ourselves with inventions. Maureen devised an ingenious way to heat-shrink the wing fabric. A friend had insisted we bring along a ridiculous little five-inch frying pan. It had hung on a nail all summer, and Maureen was staring at it one day when it transformed before her eyes into a "wing-fabric shrinker." I cut some metal disks to fill the inside of the pan and then a larger disk to cover it. These would add mass and enable the device to hold heat absorbed from the gas heater. Pressed against the fabric, the hot frying pan was like an iron.

On the tail stabilizer, we ran out of aluminum tubes before we were finished. We were able to sleeve together some shorter pieces to make up the difference.

The damaged wing spar was the final challenge: the item I was not certain I could fix. I started by removing the torn fabric until there were no frayed edges. This created clean-cut, two-foot diameter holes in the cloth, top and bottom, to be patched and painted later. From the aluminum-plate kayak rudder I cut an oval, which I carefully pounded for hours until I had the precise fit. It covered the damaged area with a two-inch overlap. Next, I drilled forty holes around the edge. I cleaned the edges one last time, filled the area with epoxy, set the patch, glued, and riveted it. When the job was finished, I thought it was beautiful.

This was the stage of repair on July 15, the day the village of Kurilskoy Lake paid us a visit. Alexei had returned with the survey helicopter, and the whole research station crew, including Igor, and several kids and dogs, piled in to come see what had happened to us. Finding us healthy and still laughing, our friends were in a celebratory mood, and we wound up having something of a party. Everyone met the cubs, who were much beloved by the children especially, and by Bill Leacock, who couldn't take his eyes off them. Our friends got to see Maureen's art, and there was great pleasure over that too. A nice bit of news was that they had started up the electric fence without me, and it was doing its job. The bears had already begun to make new trails to replace the few the fence had cut off.

Igor had also heard that the documentary film crew would be coming south, perhaps in a week. They were in PK, and he was heading there to help them through customs.

All in all, it was a great day. With the cubs giving us their incredible company, it would be a lie to say we were lonely during our first two weeks of grounding. But all the same, it was nice to see all that friendly humanity. The time between the storm and the visit was also sobering proof of how on our own we really were. Without our having a radio or their having a helicopter, all our friends could do was worry. If we had been in really tough shape, fifteen days would have been a long time.

13

Independent Filmmakers and Fisherbears

By the time the people of Kurilskoy Lake paid their visit, we had been in Russia two months. The season already felt jam-packed with activity, adventure, and mishap, but the real action of a Kambalnoye summer had not started. We had begun to notice a few salmon in the lake from the first sockeye run, which meant, if this summer mirrored the last, that Char Creek beyond our house would soon live up to its name. We were as excited as the bears at the notion that we would soon be dining on char, and that the bears would soon be lining the river banks, acting out the intense drama of their annual hunt.

Maureen and I were always thinking of things that our bears should be learning. We dithered most about anything we thought a mother bear would teach, as opposed to the cubs knowing it by instinct. For example, would the cubs have a strong instinct to fish? Another item was snow-sliding. The cubs had so far shown no sign of going to the big snow slides on the mountain for that purpose. Then one day, we led the bears onto the east side of the lake, where the steepest snow slopes were. About all we had to do was show them an almost vertical one-hundred-foot drift, and the coin dropped.

They scampered up the slope in great excitement. Watching from the bottom, we began to worry. This wasn't going to be a risk-free business.

The way the cubs went to the very top, rather than to the less risky middle, reminded me of my own foolhardy youth. Then down they came, completely out of control. They hadn't a hope of stopping where the snow stopped. They barrelled off the edge of the drift and continued to careen and tumble down the rocky scree. It was lucky there weren't any large boulders around. Veteran bears would turn onto their bellies and dig in their claws when they wanted to stop. Not so Rosie, Biscuit, and Chico. At least not today. They went back to the top for more runs and continued bouncing off rocks and plunging over cliffs. By the end of the outing, they had made some improvements, but were not yet masters of the glissade.

Another dangerous piece of learning had to do with climbing cliffs. Biscuit was the bravest of the three at this sport, and as a result, was the first to get herself into a precarious situation. Like many a novice climber, she discovered that ascending is easier than descending. She climbed into a spot from which she could neither climb farther nor seem to come down. Instead, she set up a strange distress call that drew her sisters to the rock ledge below. Rosie and Chico were long on verbal encouragement, but Biscuit stayed frozen on her perch.

I decided to get involved and climbed onto the ledge with Rosie and Chico. It wasn't the safest place to be. Maureen said it was quite a sight: me stretching towards Biscuit, with Chico and Rosie on either side standing on tiptoes and reaching. All three of us were talking at once. The performance started to work a change in Biscuit. Perhaps under the illusion that I could catch her if she fell, she began to inch her way down. When she got to where I could reach her with some leverage, I grabbed her by the scruff and lowered her to the ledge.

The early stages may not have been impressive, but the cubs all became adept climbers that summer. They eventually got so good that the cliffs became a major part of their survival strategy: they could climb to places other bears feared to follow.

By the third week after the plane wreck, Maureen and I were almost out of firewood. If a storm came, we were in for a cold time. I went on repairing the Kolb as fast as I could, but there was a limit to how fast I wanted to go. A plane is not something you want to fix badly.

By July 19 the work was nearly complete, but I did not reattach the wings. The weather was bad, with high winds, and the plane was safer in pieces than it would have been assembled. We were down to burning green alder, which I hated to do. First, it made a bad, smoky fire. Second, it was against regulations to destroy the slow-growing wood. But we had used up all the dead wood we could find and needed a source of warmth.

Ian Herring and his film crew were supposed to arrive at Kambalnoye the next day, but it was foggy—the fourth foggy day in a row. We used the time to build the collapsible boat we'd brought from Canada. We put it into the lake, hooked on the small outboard motor, and took a tour. We had been so preoccupied with the cubs and the repair of the Kolb that we were out of touch with our greater surroundings. As we poked into the various bays, we realized that a lot of salmon had already entered the lake and gone to their spawning grounds. Bears were fishing from shore. That meant the river must be alive with bears. Summer had snuck in under our noses.

During this tour, we heard a helicopter, but could see nothing. We imagined the pilot and film crew looking into the valley, seeing all the fog, and going back to Kurilskoy to wait. We brought our boat around and returned to the cabin just before dark, and were astonished to see a human figure in the mist. In all our time at Kambalnoye, no one had ever arrived on foot before.

Igor called out a greeting, and we were soon in the cabin visiting. As we'd thought, the helicopter had been Igor and the film crew, and they had gone back to Kurilskoy. Igor had asked the pilot to land him near the spot where he and I had landed the Kolb on our first trip together to Kambalnoye. He had climbed over the same pass. He was bringing us astounding—and irritating—news.

Because Ian Herring's budget would not stretch to include an additional helicopter charter, Igor had instructed the pilot and crew to unload everything at Kurilskoy before going back to PK. When I asked what good it did to have the film crew and equipment at Kurilskoy when the subjects were at Kambalnoye, Igor revealed his master plan: I was going to ferry everything—crew, two tons of camera equipment, and a month's worth of food—with my Kolb! How Igor, who had seen my plane in pieces on the ground only a week before, could have come up with such a plan, I did not know. My first response was to balk. If Ian Herring didn't have enough money to make his film, maybe he should use the money he did have to go home.

The next day dawned as foggy as the last four. Igor joined us on the morning walk with the cubs, and they demonstrated their new preference for swimming. Whenever a lake stood in our path, the bears would swim while we went around. They also swam the deep creeks that had hemmed them in not long ago. Chico, the leader on land, was still the least adept in water. In the watery element, Biscuit reigned.

The walk with Igor went very well. The cubs did not act up because of his presence, which augured well for the work we would be involved in soon with the film crew—if I could get them here.

That afternoon, with Igor's help, we put the wings back on the plane. We moved it to last year's summer tie-down, which was finally snow free. Maureen noticed the char were back in Char Creek, so she was able to catch us a plentiful supper.

The morning of July 22 dawned clear and calm, one of the really beautiful days that summer. The air cried out to be flown upon. I eased the Kolb into the lake and took off on my first test flight since the accident. It handled delightfully. In fact, it flew better than it ever had, because a few mistakes in the original construction had been corrected. To have repaired the plane out here with no support and with homemade parts was tremendously satisfying. I enjoyed that test flight as much as any flight I've ever taken in the Kolb, including the maiden flight of its storied life.

I landed after a time and beckoned Igor. He joined me in the cockpit, and we flew downriver to look at bears. In the first stretch of good fishing water, we saw seventeen. Beyond that, the river was still in fog, right out to the sea. Where we *could* see, the air was so clear that Igor and I were able to identify the fish the bears were catching. Not salmon as I had supposed, but char. This was the first time I understood that the char, like the salmon, migrated to the ocean.

Then we turned towards the pass to Kurilskoy. As luck would have it, that valley was also full of fog. I flew along the border of the cloud and found the eastern edge of the lake clear. I lowered to a few feet over the water and we squeaked under the cloud the six miles across to Igor's cabin.

Ian Herring was waiting for us, as was his cameraman, Mike Herd. We went into the cabin for tea. Ian was 37, a Vancouverite whom I had met in that city. His goal was to make films about how people relate to nature, and he had studied writing as a means to that end. I found him likeable, and was fairly certain we could work together.

Mike Herd was a different type. A Scotsman in his fifties, he had been in the film trade his whole life and was somewhat of a legend for the natural history shooting he had done in Africa. You could also tell that he considered himself a legend. Maureen, Ian and I had already agreed on a direction for this film, but Mike had other plans. He had a particular film in mind, and it wasn't the one I had agreed to.

We did not talk long because of the immense amount there was to do. By now, I had accepted the role of ferryman, and I knew it was going to take an almighty number of loads to get everything to Kambalnoye. I asked Igor to stay back and put together the loads. For the first of many times that day, I filled the passenger side of the cockpit and tied everything down. Then I filled my wood sack with equipment and tied it to the plane. Luckily, nothing in that mountain of gear was too heavy or too large for the Kolb to carry.

I got my fill of flying that day. By eight that night, I had ferried ten loads, and the fog was creeping back in from the coast. Ian and Mike had also made the journey. We finally called it a day and left Igor behind at Kurilskoy with three final loads.

Ian and Mike had seen enough bears during their trip across the pass to become thoroughly excited. Maureen had spent her day creating space for our guests in the studio/storage annex. We had built bunk beds there during bad weather a month before.

The fog stayed for two days. Watching our guests, I began to understand that their patience for bad weather was limited. I wasn't much more patient myself. When a southeast breeze started up around noon, I began thinking about the Hole, and wondering if it would be possible to fly out of it as well as in. If so, I could ferry in the last three loads and Igor.

I tried to explain the Hole to the others, but they couldn't fathom it. What they saw was a pilot in a very small plane taxiing off into a pea soup fog that quickly swallowed him. The apparent height of recklessness. I followed a compass heading and kept on it for most of a mile. The fog began to brighten and the brightness led me to the Hole. Sunlight. An open sky above.

What remained to be seen was if the Kolb had the physical power to fly up through the downdraft, which I could actually see: a waterfall of cloud spilling down the south side of the vortex. Cloud fragments skipped along the surface and were swept up again on the opposite side. There wasn't much room to circle up through.

I pointed the nose into the wind and took off. I found the spot where the downdraft air hit the lake and bounced. I climbed on that bounce as hard as my eighty horsepower could lift me. I circled to stay in the clear and eventually fought my way up above the fog.

Bringing a load back down the Hole was hair-raising, like being sucked down a drain. I extended my flaps, entered a spiral, and made for the upward bouncing air. It cushioned my fall as it had before. On the water, I followed the opposite compass heading back to the cabin. When I taxied out of the fog, the reaction was astonishment. Ian and Mike hadn't been able to see a thing the whole time I was gone, and yet I had managed to fly out and come back.

I brought Igor over last. Usually Igor was silent when we flew together, calm and confident. This time, as we dropped into the Hole, he said, "Be careful, Charlie. Don't kill me here."

While confined to camp by the fog, Maureen and I used the time with the crew to teach them a protocol for working around our cubs and other bears. When we finally did get sun on July 26 and the shooting began, the cubs carried on eating sedges and playing in mud puddles as if the film crew wasn't there. If they did become too interested in the people or the gear, I had taught everyone how to say no in the language the cubs understood. No grabbing at boots. No grabbing at anything.

Cub play features a lot of grabbing loose skin and shaking, and we had gone to some pains to convince the cubs that we were too fragile for that. At the same time, I had deliberately created a double standard where

Chico was concerned, for the sake of experiment. The game Chico and I played most was that she approached me with her head down, and I grabbed her by the fur between her ears. She pushed against me and swung at my legs with her forepaws. She didn't swing wildly. There was no attempt to hurt or any risk of being hurt. We must have played this game a thousand times. I keep her away by gripping hard and keeping my arms straight. Eventually she puts a paw on one of my hands and flexes her claws into the back of it until I let go. It's as if she must remind me of her true strength.

At the same time, Chico was able to understand that she wasn't to touch Maureen. Chico's idea of a joke, on which this prohibition was based, was to sidle up to Maureen and bring her teeth within inches of the tempting rolled-down flap of her hip wader. She waited for Maureen to say no and threaten to whack her. The look on Chico's face was pure devilment.

As for the film crew, I told Chico in no uncertain terms that she wasn't to touch them, and she never did. The cubs' manners around the strangers were impeccable, from start to finish.

A fact that I have to confess about this documentary film is that I was never very interested in it. I have severe reservations about nature films or even nature photography. Because I love animals and landscape, I like to watch the pretty pictures as much as the next guy, but I'm very unclear on the purpose. Often, I think the images are pacifiers. The message of their beauty is that everything is okay out there, that healthy wilderness and wild animals abound, so let's all relax. For that reason, I want any documentary I'm involved in to have a prominent and useful message or purpose. My fear was that Ian Herring's production would be just another pretty natural history film, and if so, I didn't want any part of it. It would be a waste of our time.

Maureen did not agree. She had worked in documentary film quite a lot herself, and she was a strong believer in the power of motion pictures to send a message to the world. If we were going to change attitudes about grizzly bears, a film could be a huge help. The result of this difference in our opinions was that Maureen worked harder to get the production to happen than I did.

The great irony was that, when Ian and Mike actually got to Kambalnoye, Mike took an instant dislike to Maureen and, for the first part of the shoot, virtually refused to point the camera at her. He treated her like a camp cook from whom he wanted quick service. Mike wasn't crazy about having me in the shots either. He simply did not like including people in a wildlife film. Given that our only interest in the film was to show the world a positive model of bear-human interaction, this approach was somewhat of a disaster.

In all of this, Ian was piggy-in-the-middle. He was interested in the film that Maureen and I wanted to make. At the same time, he was reluctant to pull rank on his experienced cameraman. In the end, enough footage was shot to make the film, but just barely. It was an often uncomfortable struggle, and not our favourite part of the magic first summer with our cubs.

Another irony was that Mike became greatly interested in me, though probably more intrigued by my flying than by my being a student of bears. He and I fashioned Ian's telescopic soundboom pole into a camera mount for the plane and took off shooting aerials. Such was Mike's enthusiasm for this activity that Ian had to put a stop to it, lest they run out of film stock.

In the evenings we devised an overall plan. When the crew had what they wanted from Kambalnoye, it was decided they should go back to Kurilskoy for a few weeks. The bears were gathering at the creek mouths there for the biggest fishing action of the summer, which was the sort of thing Ian wanted. When I first looked at Ian's script, I had to shake my head, because it was entirely built around the premise that south Kamchatka was full of places like Alaska's McNeil Falls, where great numbers of bears mass on a single chute to fish. McNeil Falls is the way it is because it is the only really good fishing opportunity for bears in many a mile. South Kamchatka is full of good fishing spots, and the bears, sensibly, spread themselves out so as not to create tension and unnecessary competition. The creek mouths and berry flats at Kurilskoy were the closest thing Ian was going to find to what he had come to Kamchatka expecting to see.

The rest of the plan was that Maureen and I would commute to Kurilskoy a couple of times to take part in the filming there, to show how we could wander among bears without feeling in danger. In September, the crew would return to our cabin and film the cubs at a more mature and independent stage. Ian had a satellite phone, so we were able to arrange with Alexei at Kurilskoy to have his survey helicopter come and pick them up.

The day before Ian, Mike, and Igor left, Maureen and I decided to try an experiment for the camera, an experiment in fishing. Although our bears had learned to gather dead fish as they washed up on the lakeshore, it didn't appear that they were going to learn to fish for live salmon or char on their own this season. Maureen and I were convinced they needed this valuable high-protein food to grow and fatten for winter, so we decided to enter the picture as set-up people and teachers.

We were not sure it was possible for the cubs to learn to fish so early in their lives. It takes a lot of skill and dexterity for an adult bear to catch a live fish, and I had never seen a first-year cub even attempt it. Normally, cubs the age of ours would sit back and wait for their mother to bring fish. They will go on doing so until they are weaned, around the age of two and a half. Bears are often three and a half by the time they leave their mothers. We knew, in other words, that we would be asking a lot of our cubs, who had only emerged from the den for the first time a few months ago.

Igor, Maureen, and I went in search of a particular kind of small stream with a firm, rocky bottom. The idea was that we would catch some fish and put them into the stream at a place where the cubs could experiment with catching them. Between two small lakes, we found what we were looking for. We caught a dozen foot-long char and conveyed them to the fishing hole in the big tub we used for washing clothes.

The instinct to fish was not instantaneous. First, we placed some dead fish underwater to teach the cubs to put their faces in the water, find the fish, and get hold of them. After eating a couple of these, the cubs began to transfer the idea across to the live fish swimming in the dammed-off area.

Rosie turned out to be the fastest learner. She quickly became good at putting her face in the water, right up to her ears, and looking under the overhanging creek bank. It was she who caught the first live fish, though Chico took it away from her. She caught another, and Biscuit stole that one. Finally, she got one for herself. In time, the cubs had eaten all the fish they could hold, and Ian and Mike had the whole thing in the can.

■   ■   ■

The helicopter came for the film crew on August 2. To celebrate our renewed privacy and independence, we took the cubs for a long walk. The cubs went straight to the fishing hole, anxious to take up where they had left off the day before. We recharged the hole with fish a few more times, until we were pretty sure all three had the hang of it. They were far from expert in the fishing department, but were still two years ahead of their non-orphaned counterparts.

Through all of this, it was impossible for Maureen and me not to feel like parents. We were as proud of our beautiful orphans as we could have been. We were thrilled every time they learned something new. As for whether the cubs thought of us as some hairless version of their mother, I doubt it. We were too slow, clumsy, and dull to have that lofty a role with them. Watching us have difficulty with obstacles that were nothing to them, I think they even felt sorry for us. At the same time, I know they enjoyed our company.

Our feelings were a mixture of affection, joy, and worry. We were ever watchful for danger and were willing to fight to the last breath in defense of our cubs. But it was also increasingly less necessary to worry. The adult female bears of the lake had little or no interest in the cubs, beyond a certain astonishment or amusement whenever our bear-human parade went by. Then they would often stand up for a better view, as would their cubs.

The biggest danger had always been that the cubs would get lost. As our explorations together widened, this worry declined. The bears knew the terrain well, especially Chico. They had become expert at recognizing those places that interested them. An example was a stretch of steep river-bank where Biscuit dug out a vole and the other two bears spent an enjoy-able hour of digging for more. Two weeks later, I came at that spot from the opposite direction. Well before we were there, the cubs suddenly went barrelling off. When we caught up, they were back at the cutbank, digging.

While Maureen and I were promoting the cubs' independence by teach-ing them to fish and snow-slide and climb cliffs, we had to recognize that we might be hampering them in other ways. We had to be willing to extend their freedom as they became ready to handle it. On August 12, we took a major plunge forward and opened the two gates of the electric pen. The cubs were at liberty to go.

It was touching to see how they left the pen and started to run off, but stopped and looked back to see if we were coming. When we made no move, they continued down to the bay and played in the shallows. Then they came loping back into their yard, as if to make sure that this was a deliberate change of plan and not a mistake.

As if they finally understood that their boundaries had changed, they left the second time through the north gate. We went up onto the roof to watch. The bears swam and played in a little waterfall that spilled into Char Creek. Then Chico stood up on her hind legs and had a final look back at the cabin. Convinced we were not coming, she struck off towards a big swampy area that the cubs all liked.

After the bears were gone half an hour, Maureen and I followed. We snuck up onto a knoll where we could see them and not be seen. They were happily grazing on the horsetail and yellow orchid in the wet moss. It felt tremendously important, like seeing your child strike off from home for university. Finally, still within an hour of leaving the cabin, the cubs came galloping home. They stayed in their enclosure with the gates open for the rest of the afternoon. For a few more days, Maureen and I closed the gates at night. The cubs were probably ready for twenty-four-hour-a-day freedom, but we were not quite there ourselves.

During the next few days, the cubs made several tries at harvesting washed up salmon along the lakeshore. Each time, they were frightened away by a big, scary-looking bear who was after the same provender. The crowberries were ripening on the tundra, so the cubs weren't going hungry, plus we were still feeding them sunflower seeds at home, but it did make us wonder how the cubs were going to get the growth and fat they needed for winter survival if they couldn't feed on the fish that all the other bears were getting.

We decided to make sure that they got plenty of fish by fishing for them. We had watched how bears would almost grow and fatten before our eyes during the fish season, and we didn't want our cubs to suffer from the lack of that advantage due to the absence of a mother. Growth would help them survive by enabling them to travel over the thick, low mat of pines. Extra fat would see them to the far end of winter in their den. Each day we took the motorboat out to collect dead salmon and catch live char. When the cubs returned to the cabin from wherever they wandered, a huge meal of protein awaited them. They grew as quickly as any bear cubs thereafter.

With the added size came added confidence. Maureen was out with the cubs on the lakeshore one day when a big female without cubs strolled into the bay along the path from the pass. The cubs spooked up the mountain-side onto a cliff, a place we had noticed they preferred to go during the day to sleep. As the big bear passed beneath them, they acted secure, even a bit cocky. When the bear approached Maureen, the cubs started a chorus of chuffing to warn her of the danger. Maureen was moved by this generous show of concern on their part.

August 25 goes down in the history of our project as the day the cubs achieved full independence. That night we did not close the pen gates after they returned for their evening feed. When the gate was still open at nine o'clock, we could tell that the cubs understood that something was amaz-ingly different. Even though it was growing dark, they left the enclosure. We both thought they would eventually come home to sleep, just for the security of it, but they did not.

At midnight, we realized we were both awake. We imagined where the cubs might be and what they might be doing. We imagined dangers. Where would they sleep? Were they safe? Neither of us got a wink of sleep that night.

When light began to return to the mountaintops, I got up and made coffee. I went out and filled the cubs' bowls with sunflower seeds, just as I would have done on any morning. Then I crawled back into bed and we had our coffee there, still worried, but quiet. At a quarter to eight, we heard the sound of galloping feet. The cubs rushed into their pen and set upon their food. They all looked fine, none the worse for their night's carouse. The dew showed their incoming track clearly, so Maureen and I walked it until we found their bed. The trail went straight as an arrow north into the heart of a patch of alders. There, in a pleasant depression, they had slept. We felt a little foolish on our walk back. Returning to the parents-of-teenagers metaphor one more time, it was as if we had spied on our offspring, expecting misbehaviour, and had found none.

As if to emphasize their new freedom, the bears slept out for several nights in a row. After that, their point made, they slept sometimes in the bush and sometimes at home. Gradually, their enclosure and their cabin seemed to become places of nostalgic value for them. If they were feeling insecure, they would come home to be reassured by the familiar sights, and hopefully by Maureen and me, the familiar people. Once in a while, they would even enter their cub house, a place they had looked down upon after they were freed from it. It consoled us to realize that the cub house, the cub yard, and we ourselves still formed the bears' concept of home.

While Ian and Mike were filming at Kurilskoy, Maureen and I paid two visits to Igor's cabin to appear in that portion of the film. On both occasions, we were troubled by the possibility of getting cut off from the cubs by bad weather. One of the sequences had us hanging out on shore watching bears fish the salmon run. In the actual film, some of what we appear to be watching happened when we were thirty miles away, but there are a couple of moments that happened as they appear to have. One involved a male bear, a real giant, whom Maureen and I had been watching since we first arrived in south Kamchatka. A photograph that Michio Hoshino took in 1996 of the same bear has since shown up in calendars. It wasn't just the bear's impressive size that drew us; it was his disposition. He was a very relaxed animal, comfortable in the vicinity of well-intentioned humans.

In the film, the bear is fishing the shallows and patrolling a stretch of shoreline. With a big salmon in his mouth, he heads for the trees to eat. He passes Maureen and me so close that both of us could have reached out and touched his fur. It is a scene that people often comment on, a moment that dramatically conveys how close to the bears we were accustomed to being.

What I like about the scene is the way it shows a male bear in a position of trust and ease with humans. Despite the fact that a lot of human-bear problems have to do with people blundering in between mother bears and cubs, there is a stereotype that male bears are automatically aggressive and dangerous. The scene in the film counters that idea, as does the book that my friend Timothy Treadwell published that same year. Quite a bit of space in Timothy's book is devoted to the good nature of the male brown bears around whom he lives during the summers in Alaska.

Another interesting sequence in the film involved a young female bear who put on a big display of standing on her hind legs, bending willows and letting them snap up again. She goes at it wildly and is quite definitely performing for my benefit. In my experience, a performer like this one will often have been a single cub. Whereas our cubs looked to one another for play, single cubs have to learn to entertain themselves—or their mothers. They develop solitary games and are often interested in humans as audience.

When September got underway, the film crew was supposed to return to Kambalnoye Lake, but did not on account of bad weather. It was September 5 before the weather broke and I was able to fly over and see what Ian Herring's plans were. I happened to get there just as the helicopter was loading gear to bring them to us. Ian decided he might as well fly back with me. Just as we were about to take off, another helicopter entered the Kurilskoy valley. We waited to see who it might be.

When the chopper was on the ground, Tatiana Gordienko climbed out of the cockpit with two men in suits and ties, an unheard of costume in this location. Tatiana asked me where Igor was and I told her he had just left in a helicopter for Kambalnoye Lake. What she said next really floored me. She and the two suits had come south, she said, because Igor was in big trouble with the authorities. He had been operating a tourist business for years without a licence, which meant he had been evading tax on his operations. What startled me wasn't so much that Igor had no licence, but that it mattered so much. As Igor had explained things to me, people all over Russia did what they could to avoid taxes that sometimes soared to sixty per cent of their incomes. Deals were made with the tax assessors. My impression was that whatever Igor had been up to probably hadn't been much different than what a lot of Russian entrepreneurs were doing.

But the demeanour of these visitors was extremely serious. The city-dressed men were a prosecutor and his interpreter. Igor had transgressed, and they were present to collect evidence to support their charges. They took Ian and me aside and grilled us on our arrangements with Igor. What role did he play? How much were we paying him?

After they were done with us, they took off for Kambalnoye. Ian and I followed in the Kolb. By the time we got there, the atmosphere at the cabin was strangely celebratory, given what was going on. Taking a quick read of the mood of her guests, Maureen had decided it was time to haul out a precious bottle of Scotch that we had been reserving for some hallmark occasion. The prosecutor asked Igor some questions, then consented to join us in a drink. I studied Igor for a reaction to his predicament, but it wasn't easy to tell what he was thinking. He wasn't smiling, but he didn't seem badly thrown either. The Scotch was less than a total success because the Russians had never had it before and grimaced at the taste. Nonetheless, they were a fairly cheerful group when they took off.

For the remainder of that evening, and the rest of the bottle of Scotch, we tried to figure out with Igor how much trouble he was really in, and what impact it was likely to have on our project. Igor tried to pass it off lightly, but none of us, I suspect including him, believed it.

The next day, the weather remained good and we went back to filming. One of the last things on Ian's shot list was a sequence of me flying to the coast to cut and haul firewood. On September 9, Mike Herd and I set out to fulfill that mission. We had flown downriver about five miles when I saw something I could scarcely believe was real. A huge, tracked vehicle, a real monster, was moving up the river, rolling over and crushing everything, alders and pines, that came in its path. It was crossing rivers and driving through the hearts of lakes. Behind it, an ugly scar of broken wood and torn tundra stretched as far as I could see.

The roof of the machine's cab was rolled back, showing five men, each with a rifle. The main vehicle was hauling a trailer about half the size of itself. The rear part of the all-terrain vehicle and the whole of the trailer were covered by tarpaulins stretched over metal hoops, so I couldn't see what load they were carrying. As we watched, the tracks swivelled and the machine started up Quiet Creek, the next watershed south of Kambalnoye. They thrashed their way up the side of this pristine river, leaving it pristine no longer. Fifty years, was what I was thinking: the length of time, at the absolute minimum, it would take nature to heal this damage. Given their rifles, the tarps likely covered the bodies of poached snow sheep and bears. Kamchatkan snow sheep are similar to the Dall sheep of northern Canada and Alaska, and are coveted by hunters for their long curling horns.

In the cockpit of the Kolb, I was cursing them at the top of my lungs. I can barely describe my rage at seeing this mess and knowing that poachers were killing bears and sheep so close to where Maureen and I were trying to raise the cubs. The sight made our work seem pointless. Mike was staring at me as though I'd gone berserk, which was close enough to the truth. My calming down was unlikely so I snapped off the intercom so he wouldn't have to listen.

I continued on to the coast, but my interest in what we were to do there was nil. I cut and loaded some wood, but had scant patience for Mike's instructions on how to stand and what to do over again exactly as before. I kept staring at the cabin that Maureen, Igor, and I had stayed in last year. Smoke was wisping out the chimney, meaning the ATV revellers had slept there. I couldn't stop thinking about them and the sheer, careless obviousness of what they were doing. By coming so close to where we lived, they were showing a complete lack of concern about being caught. Of course, we would see. Of course, we would know and report it to the authorities. Why didn't they care?

Finally Mike gave up on me. We got back into the plane and flew for Kambalnoye. I was at 1,500 feet when we reached the junction of Kambalnoye River and Quiet Creek. I could see the ATV now a long way up the Quiet Creek valley, trailing its mark of destruction. In my life, I have seen my share of offensive things. This was one of the worst.

Within a few moments, we were back at Kambalnoye and Igor was asking me to calm down so I could tell him what I'd seen. At the end of my description, Igor and I had an exchange that still seems remarkable. By my description, he knew what vehicle it was. A 500-horsepower Vityaz all-terrain vehicle, the ATV he had hoped to hire back in 1996 to bring our building materials to Kambalnoye over the snow, the only vehicle of its kind in Kamchatka. He agreed with me that the group was probably poaching bears and snow sheep.

When I kept expressing amazement, Igor got angry. He said, "Charlie, you are so full of naïveté, it's a wonder you've survived this long."

When I asked him what made my anger so naive, he told me that the poachers were probably guests of Valery Golovin, the director of the South Kamchatka Sanctuary. He was probably out with friends on a fall hunt. Shocked all over again, I let fly another outburst. I asked Igor why he was angry with me, when Maureen and I had been specifically led to Kambalnoye as a place to rear cubs on his assurances that it was safe. If anybody should be mad, it was us.

Igor said he wasn't angry with me, just disgusted at the situation. The irony of the prosecutor's visit was on both our minds. Here they were investigating the work of people (Igor, Maureen, and me) who actually cared about the land and its animals, when the real barbarians were freely rooting up tundra by the mile and blasting away bears and sheep.

The first thing we did was phone the Environment Committee in Petropavlovsk on Ian Herring's satellite phone. We also alerted the head office of the Kronotskiy Preserve. It was perhaps a foolish, or at least time-wasting, thing to do. We couldn't find anyone able to do anything. As I tried to wake up from my naïveté, I had to consider the possibility that they knew Golovin was involved and didn't want to help. The overall director of the Kamchatka preserves, Sergei Alexeev, was again conveniently out of the office. Giving up on the phone and the authorities, we came up with a more direct plan. Igor had his video camera. He and I decided to take the risk of flying in on the poachers and getting their performance on tape. Igor also carried to carry a rifle since Michio's death, and he took that with him too.

Igor and I took off and climbed north. At 6,000 feet, I turned and flew towards Quiet Creek. Even at that exceptional height, we could easily see the scar left by the Vityaz. It went around the curve of the valley in a generally southern direction then veered sharp west up a steep, pine-covered ridge. At the top of that pitch, the ATV was parked on a narrow bench. I throttled back so the engine was almost silent and told Igor to get ready.

I pulled the flaps all the way down and pointed the Kolb almost straight at the ground. We descended in a silent, spiralling glide. Igor's trust in me as a pilot has always amazed me, and this was the ultimate test. He seemed relaxed, hanging against the shoulder straps, looking out intently, as the world rotated in front of our eyes. Two men with rifles had gone to a rock promontory that overlooked the mountain's long slope to the sea. This side of the mountain was opposite the one the ATV had climbed. A bear was sunning himself just out of rifle range.

The other three poachers were standing beside their tracked vehicle. The dark smudge of exhaust meant the oversized diesel engine was running and they would not hear my approach. After thousands of feet of spiral descent, I levelled the plane out suddenly, passing first over the two with rifles and then over the group of three. It worked perfectly. No one saw us until we drifted over their heads. I could see the surprised looks on their faces. In seconds we had slid into the valley and were turning behind the ridge.

I was grinning ear to ear, ready to whoop out loud at my cleverness. I looked at Igor and he wasn't smiling. He was fiddling with his camera in a way that told me his news. Over the intercom, he confirmed it. He had missed the shot and wanted to go back for another try. The risk was much greater, and I wasn't sure to what extent he realized it. There was no way I could surprise them a second time. They would see us coming, and they were armed to the eyeballs. The only way they could keep us from documenting what they were doing was to shoot us down.

We would be pushing our luck beyond all sense. I pointed the Kolb for home. But somehow, before I got there, the plane turned almost of its own accord, and we were again heading for the mountain above Quiet Creek. The only nod in the direction of safety was that I stayed farther away. I came at them from behind the ridge this time, suddenly dropping over the top. When I saw that more of them now had guns in their hands, it felt like the most reckless thing I had done yet in Russia. They didn't shoot, as far as I could tell, and this time Igor's camera was rolling.

After the second pass, Igor asked me to set him down somewhere nearby. At first I said I wouldn't, but I gave in. I had spotted a green place on the top of a ridge. I flew around it closely and confirmed that moisture from a little spring had made the tundra lush. I came in fast below the green and swooped uphill at a steep angle, holding off until the last second so that I landed like a hawk does on a power pole. A nice piece of flying, I have to say.

Igor told me that on the first close-range pass, he had seen Golovin's sour face clearly enough to recognize him. Now Igor wanted me to leave him here with his camera for the rest of the day so he could watch what the poachers would get up to next. We agreed that I would pick him up at 7:30 that evening at a small lake in the valley. I lifted the tail of the Kolb and pivoted it 180 degrees so the nose pointed down slope. I took off and left him there, gun and all. I didn't know what he had in mind. Maybe he wanted to confront them. If it were me in that situation, I wouldn't want to be armed.

When I came back that evening, landing on the appointed lake at the appointed time, Igor was waiting. The ATV crew had turned around and gone back down the mountain after I'd left. He had shot more video of them crossing the valley to the other side, then climbing another mountain there. The ATV was still on that mountain, just below the ceiling of cloud, a place where I'd often seen snow sheep. We made one more pass at a safe distance so they would understand that we were still watching. The clouds settled down over them before we got close. Thus ended our feeble attempt at harassment. We went home.

There were things about that day that Igor and I did not know. It is amazing that we ever found them out, given the lack of other witnesses. Through the following winter, because of our actions, the activity of the poachers and their ATV were part of a substantial law case in Petropavlovsk, a widespread legal action taking in various other putative wrongdoings in South Kamchatka. Part of the investigation was the seizure of a videotape that the poachers themselves had taken. With our tape, and this thoughtfulness on the poachers' part, the prosecution had a pretty easy time of it: two audiovisual accounts of the same crime.

The following paragraph from a Petropavlovsk newspaper account of the trial contains a description of what happened that day, on the other side of our brief air war. The translation into English is a bit rough but also poetic in its way. I've inserted a couple of corrections and clarifications in brackets:

The Vityaz all-terrain vehicle climbed the *sopkas* [mountains], making its way through the prostrate cedar [dwarf pine]. It was easy work for a such a monster vehicle in comparison with that of ordinary CTT [caterpillar tractors], which is like a mongrel in front of a mastiff. The thunder of the engine and the caterpillars [tracks] drowned the crunch of broken branches. Resin plastered the windshield like drops of blood so that the driver could not see where to move. Then a man sitting on top had to take away the sticky coat with the help of some sharp iron thing. Afterward, he [Valery Golovin] would say, "I can't imagine how all this happened. I blacked out." Suddenly a small float plane appeared out of low clouds and, having come near, began to circle persistently. "We shall shoot when it makes the third circle," said those on the Vityaz. But fog on the tops of the *sopkas* was ready to conceal the vehicle [that] bristled with rifles for the tiresome observer. "Too bad the ATV is moving into the clouds," said the floatplane pilot.

The report was gleaned from courtroom testimony based on both Igor's videotape and that of the poachers. There is little doubt of its authenticity. When I read this, it made the little hairs on the back of my neck rise up. It is one thing to think you might be fired upon by rifles, another to know for a fact that the bad guys had that intention.

But the fact was that Igor's and my persistence in aggravating the ATV poachers had not deterred them at all. They had stayed another two days. Director Valery Golovin's eventual excuse in court was that he had "blacked out." Given the time that elapsed, it has to be one of the longer blackouts in the history of psychiatry.

14

The Cubs in the Care of Others

Ian Herring's film shoot ended on September 12, and Ian, Mike, and Igor left by helicopter. Igor's final message was that he would do his best to divert the prosecutor's attention away from himself and onto Director Golovin.

The day after the crew left, so did Chico, Biscuit, and Rosie. They had been growing steadily more independent since we opened the gates and had lately taken to missing the odd meal. This time was different. By midday of September 14, they had been gone for over 36 hours. Maureen and I were fussing and worrying that something terrible had befallen them. It was a confusing business. Obviously, their independence was exactly what we wanted. The worrying went on nonetheless.

After lunch that day, we struck out walking. The previous year we had walked hundreds of miles in this country and enjoyed it. Now, without the bears for company, hiking was a lonely and strange pursuit. Mostly by fluke, using binoculars we spotted the cubs high on the far end of a ridge about three miles from the cabin. We decided to sneak up for a closer look but made a pact that we would not interrupt if all was well.

From the closer vantage of the knoll, we could see that the cubs were eating green pine nuts and playing in a dense patch of pine bush. Sometimes they were on top of the bush, sometimes underneath. They seemed to be having a whale of a time and we were amazed at how big they looked. With difficulty, we left without calling out to them. We retreated to the cabin and sat there full of mixed emotions. We were thrilled at the bears' independence. We also felt betrayed. After all we'd been through, how could they be so happy without us?

The next day, I went for a long fly over the area of ATV damage; I estimated it was seventy-five miles long. Besides taking in that depressing sight, I also paid attention to what various bears were doing. Though the pine nuts were not ripe, a lot of bears were eating them, as our own three were. The snow on the volcano was already bountiful.

Since it was a nice day, I made the rash decision to fly to the top of the volcano to get some photographs. In rapid succession, two potentially disastrous things occurred. First, I was flying on new fuel that Igor had brought from Kurilskoy, and when I throttled back at 8,000 feet the engine died. Five seconds later, in the eerie silence, I heard a loud bump beneath me. One of the bladders from inside my float was hanging out and swinging in the breeze. Expansion caused by being so high had blown out two of the float's back compartments. I glided down two thousand feet. At that altitude, the plane engine caught first try, and I managed a thrill-free landing on the herniated float.

The following day, Maureen and I put Humpty Dumpty back together again. With a heavy-duty hand stitcher from her sewing kit, we sewed new partitions in the float. Then the cubs came bounding home, full of themselves and delighted to see us. They spent the day sleeping and hanging around while we worked.

The cubs were still home next morning and followed us out on our planned excursion beyond the place we called Itelman Point, after the nearby remains of an Itelman village. Maureen wanted to paint there. When she was set up and working on the hillside, the bears took turns looking over her shoulder like seasoned connoisseurs. It was funny to watch, especially when Chico got her paws and nose too close and Maureen had to tell her to stay out of it.

The cubs were becoming more confident all the time. As a result, they were getting more spent fish to eat along the lakeshore. When a big male came along where they were fishing that day, the bears ran up the cliff, but only far enough and long enough to let him pass. Then they were quickly down again and back to fishing—quite a change from the not-so-distant days when they would have fled into the tundra and hidden all day.

On September 18, a helicopter came into our valley and landed by the cabin. The prosecutor was back, this time accompanied by Tatiana, Katya (our friend from the research station), and a fierce-looking forestry official. The purpose seemed to be to discuss the ATV incident, and I was more than willing to help. Among other things, I drew the path of destruction on the helicopter pilot's map so they could go look at it. But the prosecutor was also back to old themes. He interrogated Maureen about Igor, how much we had paid him and so on, to see if our stories tallied. Given the much greater evil of the ATV damage and the poaching, I was perturbed. Even worse was the forestry official. She was harsh and bullying and spent far too much time measuring every little cut we had made through the alder for our electric fence. She also measured the ground dimensions of each building.

Maureen and I did manage a little private time with Tatiana, who told us that not only did it look like Director Golovin was at fault for the ATV caper, but that the incident would be used as evidence towards having Golovin's boss, Sergei Alexeev, removed from his job. But Igor was being caught up in the sweep as well. The way Tatiana was carefully giving me all the credit for videotaping the poachers, not mentioning Igor at all, was a clear sign of what was going on with our friend. What Tatiana did not say was that another thrust in the case against Sergei was that he had given us permission to build our cabin here, and had supported our cub program.

I flew to Kurilskoy the day after Tatiana and the prosecutor's visit. My intention was to help Katya take samples of zoo plankton in three high volcanic lakes. She had wanted to study these lakes for years and now saw a way to do it, if I would help her with my Kolb. That idea was put on hold, though, when I discovered that Igor and three visiting Moscow photographers had found several dead bears in the vicinity of Igor's cabin, and still more along the lakeshore. Igor had become aware of the problem when Bill Leacock reported that the signal from one of his radio-collared bears wasn't moving. He and Igor tracked the signal and found the collared bear dead. All the dead bears had been killed and mutilated in the same way: shot in the head from close range with a slug from a shotgun and their gallbladders removed. There was also evidence that whoever was doing this was also illegally harvesting salmon caviar.

This sinister development, on top of the recent events near Kambalnoye, took the heart right out of me. Here, just twenty miles over the mountain from where Maureen and I were having the time of our lives watching fine young bears grow up to be wild, poachers had been killing as many bears as crossed their path. In an area devoted to the study of salmon and bears, it was open season on both. I felt surrounded by threat.

Maureen and I were both scheduled to leave in a couple of weeks. My original plan had been to stick around until I was absolutely sure our bears had denned, but there had been a screw-up with my visa and it was about to run out. Because a visa cannot be applied for or renewed from within Russia, I was going to have to return to Canada and then come back to Russia. Maureen's visa was also running out, and her plan was to put on an exhibition of her art in Petropavlovsk, then fly home for the winter.

My biggest concern was having someone feed and keep an eye on the cubs while I was away. All along I had assumed Igor would do this, but he was so on the outs with Russia's environmental bureaucracy at the moment, it was impossible. Then, to my complete surprise, Bill Leacock volunteered. Most of his radio collars were being monitored by satellite. That circumstance, combined with his whole family's fascination with the cubs, meant he was willing to move his wife, Tip, and daughters, Grace and Nina, across to Kambalnoye for the period of my absence. It was an enormous favour, which they did as if it were nothing.

For the remainder of September, Maureen worked furiously to ready her work for exhibition, and we both indulged in a final frenzy of worry and joy over the cubs. The cubs were gone much of the time, and seemed to be favouring the heights of the nearest mountain to the east. As the mountain had no name, we began to call it Biscuit Mountain. For three days, we didn't see the bears at all, and then I spotted them on top of Biscuit Mountain.

That evening they came to see us. They barely touched their sunflower seeds, so I like to think it really was our company they'd come for.

The next day the bears were still around, and we went for a walk. It was a beautiful day and the cubs led us to some marvellous spots. One was a valley full of the lushest moss I'd ever seen, fed by water seeps on all sides. Our bears looked great in their heavy winter coats, all bushy and clean. In this different hairstyle, their colours remained roughly the same as when they were cubs: Chico, dark; Biscuit and Rosie, two shades of blond. All three were over a hundred pounds.

The recent poaching at Kurilskoy and downriver from our camp made this time a highly emotional one for Maureen and me. We were most haunted by the idea that our bears would go right up to a poacher because of the trust of humans we had taught them. Our lot was to agonize, it seemed. That day was hardest on Maureen, who would fly out soon after the Leacocks flew in, any time now, and would not return until spring. For her, this was potentially goodbye to the bears we had poured our hearts into all summer long.

The Leacocks, along with Alexander Nikanorov, came on the last day of September, so it was a very full house that night. Eight people slept in the cabin and annex. For the past few days I had been cutting and stacking wood down at the coast, and the helicopter pilot and I went there and brought back three big loads to see us through the season.

By morning, the pilot was getting antsy. He was low on fuel and still needed to pick up Igor and the three Moscow photographers at Kurilskoy. He couldn't afford to be turned back by weather. When the frost finally melted off the wings of the Kolb, around 9:30, I flew over to check the weather at Kurilskoy. When I got back with the all-clear, Maureen's gear and her artworks were already stowed. The pilot, Maureen, and Alexander left immediately.

The Leacocks and I spent that day at Kambalnoye splitting and stacking firewood in the annex. The cubs did not come home that night and the whole family was pretty disappointed. I spent a fair amount of time scanning the bears' favourite areas with the spotting scope, and at two the following afternoon I made them out on the cliff above the lake on

Biscuit Mountain. They were sleeping. When they began to stir, Bill and I went over to visit them. As I hoped they would, the cubs followed us home. Grace and Nina were thrilled to see the bears, and the bears were equally fascinated by them. The bears were so full of fish they barely looked at their sunflower seeds, which in other circumstances might have encouraged them to leave again. But they were far too interested in the children.

Just before dark, I looked out and all three bears were lying with their noses a few inches from the wire of the electric fence. The two girls were stretched out on the other side, also with their faces near the wire. There couldn't have been a foot between the noses of the girls and the noses of the bears.

The following day was another beauty, but I was getting anxious to go. Storms start up so quickly here, and the October ones can last ten days. What I needed to do before leaving was make sure these people, adults and children, understood how to behave around the bears. Though it may sound weird, I also needed to educate Biscuit, Chico, and Rosie how to behave towards the new people.

I had put a lot of thought into how the bears should be treated so things would be safe and would remain so. It was all about manners, and my conviction that bears treated with kindness will respond in kind. It was one thing for Maureen and me to expose ourselves to the risk of its not being true, but quite another to expose others, especially children.

My greatest concern was Chico. Although Chico clearly understood she was not to play physical games with Maureen, I had to be absolutely certain before I left that she also understood the Leacocks were not be touched. My worry centred on six-year-old Nina, with whom Chico was clearly intrigued. Chico was being careful, but as soon as I saw her tagging along behind Nina, bear body language for a request to play, I intervened. I showed Bill and Tip how they could stop any behaviour they didn't like by simply saying a firm no. Bill quickly caught on how to talk to the cubs, and set the necessary limits on any games that might have developed. Bill and Tip soon knew that they could control the bears around their children and themselves, which was a huge relief to me. That day, we walked along the lakeshore and the Leacocks saw how well the bears had learned to fish. We also sat for a couple of hours and watched them eat pine nuts. By the end of the day, I was confident all was well. The cubs were acting politely towards the Leacocks and vice versa. These were not people who would adversely change the cubs' feelings toward humans.

On the morning of October 4, it was obvious that a weather change was in the works. I wanted to go immediately, but I had a few more things to tell Bill, who was already off somewhere with the cubs. From the roof, I spotted him and the cubs by the swamp, and I hiked up there as fast I could. I said my goodbyes to the cubs and gave Chico a scratch. Then the cubs jumped into the lake, swam across, and disappeared into the pine bush. Bill and I discussed the last few points, and I boarded the Kolb.

It was a good thing I hadn't waited longer. A big storm brewed up that kept edging me farther and farther east. By the time I was within fifty miles of Petropavlovsk, I had been forced right out onto the east coast, the only place I could see to fly. That meant I was headed straight for the wrong side of the nuclear submarine base, the dreaded "Secret City." If spotted, I would get us into even more trouble than we already were in. I skimmed low along the west side of the bay, then ducked into a little valley that I hoped might take me behind a ridge and down to the village to Nikolayevka. Luckily, I was right.

When I skidded in for a landing on the grass by the flying club, I felt a great relief. My plan for the rest of the season was to fly into and out of Kambalnoye by helicopter, which meant that the landing was also my last of the 1997 season. I had survived again, and it was time to put the Kolb away for another winter.

It just so happened that my friends at the club were test-flying their latest home-built plane, a slick fibreglass two-seater powered by a Subaru car engine. They didn't want to stop until they had finished the test, a sentiment I fully understood. When darkness forced them down, one of the flyers took me to his apartment so he could make a phone call. He was going to take me into the city, but needed to know the location of the apartment Katya had arranged for us. While he was phoning, I looked into the living room, where his wife was watching TV. She was watching Maureen, who was talking through an interpreter about her show and inviting the people of Petropavlovsk to come down to the Science Library for the opening next day. Eventually we caught up with each other at the apartment and were able to swap our stories.

Maureen's art show was a great success, thanks in part to the positive boost given it by the local media. The people of the city flocked to the Science Library to see it. By now, she and I had become either famous or infamous locally: the people who had stolen the bear cubs from the zoo; the woman who painted wild bears from life; the man who flew a tiny home-made plane all over the wild south country. It's not exaggeration to say that almost everybody in PK knew about us by the end of our second season.

MAUREEN: My art exhibition in Petropavlosk was titled *Views from the Bear's Nest (The Bear Who Looked for Beauty)*. I had discovered early on that bears dig out indentations in the tundra for sleep. Biologists call these sites "day beds." How boring a title for such a phenomenon—and limiting, as the nest-like sites are used both day and night.

What astonished me was how these sites always overlooked stunningly beautiful vistas. Some were high, above Kambalnoye Lake, and some were low, on rocky outcroppings at the lakeshore. I decided to sit in a collection of these nesting sites (my name for them) and to paint the views from the bear's eye level, interpreting the scenes as they would do. Some twenty views of the landscape emerged, all painted from different nesting sites.

The people who visited the exhibition accepted the idea that bears could appreciate a beautiful view. Why not? But Maureen, they said, do they see all the very bright colours you see? My response was that bears enjoy life on such a high level that surely they must see what they like very vividly.

Also included in the exhibition were drawings of Chico, Biscuit, and Rosie as young cubs, often sitting in their own nesting sites. What I left out were the times they tried to taste my paint or criticize my work!

We saw old friends at the show and made some new ones. Anatoly Shevlyagin, Alexander Nikanorov, Tatiana, Katya and Alexei, the Revenkos, and all my friends from the flying school attended. It could have been wishful thinking, but the indications seemed to be that the rift created by our taking the cubs without approval had begun to mend. By October 10, the exhibition finished and my Kolb was stowed away for the winter. We climbed on a jet and flew home.

15

A Hike into
the Heart of Darkness

Thirteen days later I was back in Petropavlovsk. The snow was much farther down the mountains, and I was anxious to get to Bill and his family, but bad weather prevented it. Bill managed to call me on his satellite phone, so at least I knew that everything was all right. The most nerve-racking episode had been when Rosie became separated from the other two bears and went missing for three days. Finally she showed up on the cliff above the lake, and Bill had been able to coax Chico and Biscuit to follow him there. The cubs were happily reunited.

The helicopter pilot finally consented to take me out on October 28, in less-than-super flying conditions. Reputed to be one of the best pilots in Kamchatka, he did a good job of feeling his way through the foggy valleys. As we got farther south, the weather improved, and the trip became more relaxing.

My uncertainty about the time of arrival meant that the Leacocks were not ready to roll when we got there. The pilot was impatient lest the weather close in on him. As it turned out, the cubs had not been seen for the last twenty-four hours and the kids were highly upset at the idea of having to leave without saying goodbye. It was difficult all around because everyone had stories to tell and only minutes to do it in. The pilot said that he was taking off at 4:15, with or without the Leacocks. We literally stuffed the gear into the helicopter and the family in on top. Then they were gone, back to Kurilskoy Lake.

The helicopter was disappearing over the north ridge when I remembered what I had not told Bill. He and I had agreed to share a helicopter out of South Kamchatka on November 23, a deal that could save us both a lot of money. But back in PK, Anatoly Kovolenkov had offered to pick us up at an extremely reduced rate on one of his supply trips. Having forgotten to tell Bill meant that two helicopters would be coming. Now I had no way of letting Bill know.

What prevented me from thinking about this further right then was the arrival of the three bears. They came running into the yard, looking very large and important. After they'd had a few seeds, I went out and watched them eat pine nuts for a couple of hours. The last time I'd seen them at it they had been pretty clumsy. Now, they were experts.

A bear's method of eating pine nuts is worth describing. First, it finds a place in the bush that has lots of cones in easy reach. The bear sits back, or slumps, under the bush. The bear hooks the claws of one front paw over a branch to create a surface to work on over top of its belly. Just behind the last knuckle on the top of its paw is a little depression. The bear holds the cone in that depression with the claws on its opposite paw. When the bear has the cone firmly in place, it bites one side. Inside the mouth, the bear separates the nuts from the scales and lets the scales fall out. Then the bear rotates the cone on its paw-table and takes another bite. Three or four bites completes a cone.

The few nuts that fall out of a bear's mouth with the scales land on its belly and catch in the fur. After tossing out the core of a finished cone, the bear very quickly picks the nuts off its belly with its tongue. Their tongues are so precise they never pick up a scale instead of a nut. In a good spot, the bears can harvest about ten cones. When they've exhausted one place, they move and find another, but if they have a particularly comfortable depression, they will go, fill their mouths with cones, bring them back to the good spot, and work on them one at a time.

There is one set of ideal conditions where bears can eat pine cones on the move: when the cone is so dry and ripe that the nuts separate out easily. A bear will put the whole cone in its mouth and roll it around. The nuts seem to fall out and under its tongue. When the bear is done, it spits the stripped cone out. Bears do this while walking.

The morning after I arrived, I found Chico lying by the fence as though waiting for me to feed her. The other two cubs were still sleeping in the bush. I walked out to the gate but she didn't move. She stayed where she was, looking at the cabin door. She wasn't interested in what I was doing. It was strange behaviour, and I spent considerable time figuring it out. Then I remembered Tip telling me that Grace and Nina had a ritual of chatting nose to nose with the cubs at the fence each morning. It was obvious Chico was waiting for the girls to get up and come for a talk. It took her an hour to accept that they were gone.

The sensitivity of the bears, their capacity for caring, was something we had seen a lot of that summer. It never failed to touch us or cheer us up. In September, Maureen and I had a pronounced disagreement about what it might mean for us to be implicated in the case against Sergei Alexeev; that is, whether we were apt to be prosecuted ourselves. The argument got heated, and Maureen left the scene for a favourite sitting rock back on Char Creek. The cubs came loping along the trail and, seeing Maureen, veered over to say hello. Instantly, they picked up on the melancholy of her mood. They stopped playing and lay down in front of the rock, looking up at her. When Maureen was calm again, the four of them went off to look for salmon along the beach.

The bears were attentive and protective of each other as well. We never saw them separated for more than a moment without showing concern about it. Biscuit was particularly inclined to send up the alarm the instant she could not see or smell her siblings. As they got older, their high-pitched chirping distress call turned into a mature chuffing. They made the sound while they ran back and forth looking for the sibling who was currently misplaced.

One of the first things I noticed that first full day back was how far down the mountain the snow line had come. It looked like the next good storm would bring winter to the level of the cabin and the lake. With that in mind, I spent the day organizing the camp for winter. I tightened the fence and patched a rip in the tarpaper roof. While I worked, I dithered about the two-helicopter situation. I finally came to the unhappy conclusion that hiking twenty-five miles across the mountains to Kurilskoy Lake and telling Bill Leacock in person was the only way to prevent it.

In the evening, I put together a pack for the hike. It didn't include a tent because my travelling tent was inside the Kolb. In lieu of a tent, I packed a sheet of clear plastic. I put my sleeping bag and some light fleece underwear in a waterproof bag inside the pack. I didn't include much food because I wanted the pack small. I was going to be travelling in some dense bush, and a wide pack would be murder.

The next morning, I got myself up two hours before the light. The cubs must have been sleeping in the yard, because they were up and waiting by the time I had my breakfast. I fed them, and, while they went to the creek for a drink, I set out another meal of sunflower seeds for them to have later. Then I shouldered my pack and got on the move. My idea was to get a jump on the day by hiking the part I knew best before dawn. There was no wind, no clouds, and the stars were still bright. The bears caught up and walked with me until they figured out that I wasn't going anywhere that interested them.

An hour and a half of walking brought me to the top of the north ridge. I dropped over the far side and crossed the small valley that forms the base of the volcano on that side. I followed a deeply worn bear trail that I knew led to Kurilskoy Pass. I was making good time despite the need to twist and contort, and even crawl, through the dense groves of alder. I met a couple of bears on the trail coming from the opposite direction, and they let me have the right of way. Once I was over the pass, I entered a pretty alpine basin. It was great to be in the sunny, warm zone, where the walking was dry and unimpeded. I passed a family of four very black brown bears on a small creek there.

The alpine interlude ended where the meadow dropped off into forested canyons. I knew from flying this route that there was no avoiding the alders until the forest changed to willows near the lake. It was going to be hard travelling. The first difficult obstacle was the Khakystyn River, which eventually drains into Kurilskoy Lake near Igor's cabin. There were no good crossings on this river for miles, and I chose the one that the bear trail led to as probably the best of a bad lot of options. The water was high, the current strong, and the footing along the bottom rocky and slippery. If I lost my balance, I could easily be swept down through a churning chute full of boulders.

To improve my odds, I cut a straight staff of green alder with my jack-knife. Wading in, I prodded ahead, finding places between stones where the staff could wedge. I leaned on the staff while I felt with one foot then the other for underwater holds. The swift water was soon at my waist, freezing cold of course. I was nervous all the way but made it without inci-dent. I couldn't waste the daylight required to build a fire and dry off, so I continued on soaking wet. But, before I left the river, I stored my staff carefully where I could find it on my return.

The struggle through bush-filled canyons continued. Gruelling and exhausting is about all you can say about it. It was soon obvious that I would not make it to Kurilskoy in daylight, not even to Igor's cabin, let alone the four miles beyond that to the research station.

When the true darkness came, I was crossing a big berry field. My esti-mate was that I had about a mile and a quarter to go. An inlet, swampy and narrow but also deep, meant that I couldn't go straight but had to loop around the end of it, through heavy willows. I had gone most of the way, groping in the dark, when I heard the roar of a very angry bear. To get around the tip of the lagoon, I had to go towards that sound. I shuddered at every scream until I was very near the source. I have rarely heard that particular sound, and I couldn't think what would make a bear voice such rage.

Finally, by the bit of light, I made out a big male. He was caught in a cable snare and was fighting for his life. He ripped and tore at everything in sight. If he pulled loose with me there, I would have no hope of convincing him I had nothing to do with his torture.

The situation made me sick. I knew instantly what was going on. Bear poachers had set this snare and now they were leaving this great bear to rage and fight the night away because his fury would swell the gallbladder, which was all they wanted out of him. The bear would make short work of me if I got anywhere near the snare, so there was nothing I could do to help him. If I'd had a gun, I would have ended his night of misery right there.

Finally I passed between the raging bear and the lagoon. As I rounded its tip, I came out on the shore of the main lake. I was starting to move towards Igor's cabin when I saw the glimmer of a fire through the bush at the mouth of Khakystyn River. Totally exhausted now, cold and wet and in bad need of rest, I hung there for a time, until something close to pure hatred drew me to the light. I worked my way in until I could see the campfire. Near an old tent, two poachers sat on stumps staring at the flame. A few feet away, a shotgun leaned against a tree. It was a single-shot twelve-gauge and, looking at it with binoculars, I saw that a wire wrapped around the grip held it together. It was the crude weapon they would use to end the life of the bear when he had suffered his value high enough to suit them.

I studied those men for a long time. It was almost certain they were the ones who had killed all the other bears Igor had found here in the berry bushes and along the lake. They were grubby-looking men, rough and bearded, their ragged clothes and gaunt faces blackened from weeks in the bush. The tops of their hip waders had been cut off and discarded. I tried to tell myself they were just two more people desperate for a way to feed themselves and maybe their families in the endless economic confusion of post-Soviet Russia, poor and ignorant people being paid next to nothing for the supposedly valuable organs of these bears. That is, I tried to feel that way, but all that was truly in my heart was a murderous loathing.

I stared at their gun and measured my distance to it. I imagined various scenarios. I could probably get to it before they did. But I passed on that in favour of another idea. I thought I would wait for them to retire to their tent. I would find a good stout alder branch with a cudgel end. I would quietly approach the tent and blast a stream of pepper spray into it. As they came out coughing and spluttering, I would brain them. My intention was to kill them.

It is not easy to admit this impulse to my friends and family, and to the people out in the world whom I hope to influence in the direction of a more benign treatment of bears. I consider myself not exactly a pacifist, but certainly peace-loving. A world without violence appeals to me. But the events of the previous two months, the betrayal of his mission by the South Kamchatka Sanctuary's director, the bears already killed by these men, the bear out in the bush fighting desperately for his life while these two brooded indifferently by their fire—above all, the threat that these two and their kind might kill Chico, Biscuit, and Rosie—all of it had pushed me beyond the borders of my normal morality.

The slender margin that kept me from at least trying to kill these men was my own utter and complete exhaustion. Lying cold and wet in the bush, I stiffened up so badly I could hardly move. To ensure my own survival, I had to get away. I edged back out of their range of hearing, then stumbled my way in the dark to Igor's cabin. Inside, I fell on a bunk and was quickly unconscious. My final thought that night was that I would attempt the remaining four miles to the research station and Bill Leacock the next day, if I felt up to it.

At four in the morning, I got up and checked the weather. There was still the occasional roar from the bear. I may have accepted his fate, but he hadn't yet. It was misting over and turning nasty. By 8 a.m., it started to pour rain. The decision had to be made fast. If it started to snow, I might never be able to get back to Kambalnoye. If the cubs' instincts did not guide them to den, I would not be there to intervene and help them. In the final analysis, it was simply more important that I get back to the cubs than that I talk to Bill. There seemed no reasonable way to do both.

One of Bill's telemetry posts was up on the hill towards the end of Igor's point, above the big Itelman village. I left a short note folded in a piece of plastic bag and tacked it exactly where he would set his transceiver. The note directed Bill to another more detailed note in the attic of Igor's cabin. If he got to that one, he would know to call off the second helicopter. It was the best I could do.

Then I set out in the rain. Though I had a raincoat, I knew I could be in for plenty of trouble because of how tired I was. But if I took long enough to rest up, I could miss my chance of getting home. I got to the swift river about noon. I found my alder staff and waded in. The fact that the water was rising and that I was still overtired meant I was not as sure-footed in the river as the day before. I slipped about midway and went in up to my neck. By twisting into an eddy behind a big boulder, I managed to catch myself before I washed into the raging water and rocks. Climbing out of the river, I was damn cold and very tired, an ideal victim for hypothermia. On the ascent towards the bench below the pass, the symptoms of that quiet killer gathered: uncontrollable shivering, then drowsiness. At about 1:30 p.m., I was at the edge of open country, the alpine zone. It was still raining hard and it came to me that I must not enter that open space today. What I had in my favour was the dry sleeping bag and the dry underwear in the water-proof pack, plus the sheet of plastic. I changed clothes and crawled into the bag, doing so under the plastic as much as I could. The condensation soon turned everything damp.

It might sound goofy, but what saved me that day was having recently read Don Starkell's *Paddle to the Arctic*. This intense, intrepid Winnipegger had confronted and survived no end of life-threatening situations. I convinced myself this pickle of mine was minor by comparison. After I'd thought that thought for some time, I became downright cheerful and even a bit warm. Nonetheless, it was a long afternoon, and I still had all the night to cope with.

The day got colder and the rain turned to heavy snow. By midnight, there was at least eight inches of snow on the tarp, which was good as far as insulation went. The dropping temperature caused the condensation from my breath to freeze, ending the rain of drips off the plastic. When I finally got up to go at 8:15 a.m., it was winter outside my plastic-lined icicle. This was a critical time because I was getting cold again. I knew I would have to move fast and hope to be warmed by that burst of activity. I squeezed a cup of water from the foot of my sleeping bag before cram-ming it into the stuff-sack. The dry socks I had gone to bed in were wet, and it was a struggle to work them into my frozen boots. I left behind the clear plastic tarp and the sopping wet running shoes I'd worn in the river. I would try to return by air to rescue them in the spring.

Breaking trail through a foot of snow over the pass warmed me up considerably. I made it through to the cabin by three in the afternoon. The storm was slackening by then. It was November 1.

The first thing I checked when I got home were the food bowls. The sunflower seeds hadn't been touched, which made me happy, because it was one more indication that the cubs were fat enough to den. In the cabin, I built a fire and got a stew bubbling on the stove. I set out my wet things to dry and soaked up enough of the heat to warm myself. A couple of shots of vodka aided in that process.

I reconsidered the last thirty hours, the forty miles I had travelled, and it seemed like the toughest of all my journeys. There was no denying either that it was partly due to my age. At first, this thought made me feel puny before the immense obstacles that were still ahead of us on this project. How could I ever achieve what I had set out to do, in this tough wilderness, in this foreign land, in this aging body?

It turned into one of those solitary nights when your whole life comes under review. I revisited various episodes of my life's journey, especially the wonderful, vivid scenes with the cubs this summer, and gradually, while I warmed by the fire, I warmed back up to my own life as well. In the end, I came as close as I ever have to thinking that I had lived fruitfully enough, had done enough. It felt like two lifetimes, really.

Though I would soon be back to worrying about the cubs and trying to accomplish more with our project, it was a satisfying reprieve on a day and night that could have been disastrous.

16

Denning Up

There was a ritual when the cubs left the yard in the morning. They would disappear into a dip, then reappear on a knoll. Chico would stop there, while the others continued. She would rise onto her hind legs and look back to see if I was coming. On November 2, a sunny day that swiftly melted the last storm's snow, I obliged my friend by following.

Walking with the cubs, I was astounded all over again by their size. Each was probably over 150 pounds now, quite something considering they were fifteen pounds when Maureen and I brought them here at the end of May. When they arrived at a good pine cone location and started to eat, I decided to have a try myself. I found cones that were out of the sun, good and soggy, and I took a bite out of the side of one. I sorted the scales from the nuts in my mouth and spat out the scales, just as I had seen them do. The relatively small size of my mouth, compared to the cubs', slowed me down. I was at least two times longer eating each cone, and after five I was stuffed. The bears could eat five cones' worth of nuts in seven minutes, and they kept it up for hours.

Rosie had found herself a luxurious spot on the tundra, and for the sake of another experiment, and to be friendly, I started tossing her cones. I became accurate enough to land them right on her belly. She was like a harem queen being fed grapes by a favourite slave, and obviously loved the whole arrangement. I continued for about twenty minutes, until I had exhausted the cones in easy reach around me. I decided to stop and let her do her own bush crawling. When I sat down in the bush to have a rest, Rosie came after me. She walked up and cuffed me one, as if to say, "You start a good thing and then you slack off." I decided not to make a practice of cone fetching after that.

This was a good lesson about feeding a bear. There is something very different about providing food from your hand as opposed to putting it in a bowl for them. As good friends as we all were, a disaster could still occur if we or anyone else started hand-feeding these bears food that was not available to them any other way. In such a situation, it would not work to simply stop. They would demand more and become obnoxious, even dangerous.

On that day, as on many days, I thought about how the bears had improved my experience of being human. By allowing me into their world, by tolerating my limitations and the baggage of humanness, they helped me expand that humanness. Through their acceptance of me, and by following their lead, I had become more than just an observer of the land. I had become part of it. There is a great freedom in the way animals live, and my senses had changed a little in that direction, thanks to our bears. The subtleties that I had become able to sense were more the norm for an animal than for a human—a modern human at least.

Much of what people have lost has been due to an insistence on things being safe. We work away at the odds, putting them ever more in our favour until we're up millions to one. Still, we can't get over the weird illogical certainty that we will be "the one," the unlucky one, and so we go back to stacking the odds even more. With equal absurdity, we like casinos. Biscuit, Rosie, and Chico taught me to assess and accept the real odds. This was how I learned to trust them, rather than to fear them.

The bears did not come to the cabin at all the following day, so I went out looking for them. They were on a hill to the north, lying in the sun in a deep drowse. They were definitely slowing down these days. They walked more than they ran. They slept a lot. I made a decision to cut off their supplementary food on November 12, if they hadn't cut themselves off already. I didn't want the food I was providing to be a factor working against their instinct to den.

Chico and I played our pushing game for a while, and then we all set out on a leisurely walk. Something that happened with Biscuit on this trip showed me another aspect of the bears' relationship with me, which was forgiveness. We were walking a trail across a steep slope about eight feet above the lake. I glanced back and saw Rosie up on a rock, looking beautiful. I lifted my camera and, while trying to get a better angle, stepped right onto Biscuit's paw. It must have really hurt because she grunted and threw herself back. As my weight was still on her paw when she did this, it was like having the rug pulled out from under me. I went down, and both Biscuit and I slid down the slope into the lake. I was right side up at least and was able to keep the camera dry, even as I went into the icy water chest deep. I thought that Biscuit would be mad at me, so I apologized sincerely first thing. I could tell by her eyes that she appreciated the moment was a mistake. She showed no sign of trusting me less, right then or any time afterwards.

The bears stuck around that day until the scent of another bear made them run for their favourite haunt on Biscuit Mountain. I watched with the spotting scope and saw them at various times appearing and disappearing in the snow squalls. At one point, I saw that they had been joined by their friends and tormenters, the ravens. A nest of ravens hatched and raised on Biscuit Mountain had developed a relationship with the cubs based on a mutual sense of owning the place. The ravens' ideal situation was when the cubs were in a natural updraft. Then they would hover just above the bears, pestering them. If a cub swatted at them or jumped, all the ravens had to do was open their wings and let the updraft lift them out of harm's way. If the bears were sleeping, the ravens would land and sneak up, pecking the cubs on a hind paw or their hind end.

What was fascinating was the reasonable good humour on both sides. Like my games with Chico, it was basically a kind of inter-species play. Interestingly, Chico was the ravens' favourite target.

Over the next few days, the bears spent most of their time on Biscuit

Mountain or in the basin on the other side. I took to calling it Chico Basin. It was snowing now almost every day, and the bears were more inclined to visit when it was clear. When they were away, I walked to where I could look into Chico Basin and catch glimpses of them through the storms. Something about how they played in that bleak place warmed me to the core and told me they had everything under control. I only had myself to worry about.

I recall one pleasant day when they came down to visit and spent most of a day lying in the snow, snoozing. I sat with them, scratching Chico's ears. When at length they wandered off into the bush, I followed. Though they were taking cones off the pines, I noticed they were spitting them out whole. I picked up a couple and found they were frozen solid. The nuts were locked inside too securely to bother with. A really hungry bear could have broken into them, but our cubs weren't that hard up. They were fat and moving slowly, and still had quite a few salmon to harvest along the shore.

On November 7, I saw a bear digging its den, the first one I'd noticed. I had been following the dark trail the bear made by knocking snow off the pines. When I saw the bear was digging, I went up the north ridge where I could watch without disturbing it. That day, the cubs didn't bother with their second meal of seeds. They spent the whole day sleeping.

Next day, with the overnight snow whirling into vortices, I hiked into Chico Basin again and saw the cubs high on a slope of alders. Through the dark shadows and the slivers of sunlight, I watched them climb to the top and disappear over the ridge. I returned to the basin several times in the next few days, but the cubs did not come back. I watched a new bear enter there, harried by a Steller's sea eagle as the bird descended the basin in a big S-curve, then climbed back up to bed down by the pines. Within a day, the bear began to dig. I saw two more bears digging dens the same afternoon. I began to understand that I had probably seen the last of our cubs for this year.

The lake had frozen now, reaching that dangerous stage where it looks strong but isn't. A few fish remained, char spawning in the lakeshore places the salmon had spawned in earlier. I counted fifty Steller's sea eagles and saw a number of white-tailed eagles and two golden ones. The golden eagles were hunting ptarmigan while the others fished. When I saw two young bears taking turns digging the den they were about to share, I wondered about Chico, Biscuit, and Rosie. What kind of place had they chosen? Who had done the most work? How much room had they given themselves?

With the belief that the cubs had denned came a profound loneliness. The days were short and windy. The snow continued to fall, at times heavily, and to drift. It was not yet cold, which was a good thing, considering I was almost out of firewood. To conserve the remainder, I spent more time outside, taking long hikes.

Winter worked some uncomfortable changes in my cabin life. The powerful wind that brought the snow drove it through the walls. Snow entered through pinholes I could neither see nor find to close. After one terrible night of wind, I woke under an inch-thick blanket of it. The bed and the whole inside of the cabin were coated. When I went to light a fire that day, I discovered the wind baffle contraption had blown off the chimney and so had several sections of pipe. I had to piece together a new facsimile before I could use the stove.

I had set up the tripod and spotting scope in the middle of the cabin and could often observe bears denning out more than one window. One time, I watched as a young male bear worked all day perfecting his den. Just as he was putting on the finishing touches, a female with cubs came by and scared him off. She commenced digging in a snow bank nearby. I assumed she was about to den, but the next morning she and her cubs took off, heading down to the water to fish. At the lake, they were mobbed by sea eagles. The bears were fat and not too hungry, and there was lots of salmon left for the birds.

Next, the mother bear took a notion to venture out onto the ice about forty yards. I had the scope on her and was thinking she was taking a chance. Sure enough, she fell through. Once broken, the fractured ice would not hold her when she tried to climb back out. All she could do was break a channel towards shore, and it took considerable effort. Just as our bears would have done, her cubs came out about halfway, looking very concerned. When she got close to them, she smashed the ice they were on, and the whole family was in the water. The cubs swam behind their mother among the swirling cakes of ice and finally made it to shore. I assume it taught everyone a lesson, including me. On the rest of my hikes, I only went on the ice where I knew the water was shallow.

My daily fire-conserving hike was usually a circumnavigation of the lake. Not long after the cubs left, I found a huge male bear track heading right towards the big patch of bush where I thought the cubs' den might be. Even though the snow was deep and hard to travel through, I followed. When I could finally tell the bear was headed over the mountain in the direction of the east coast, I retreated.

Farther along, I found a sea eagle that was unable to fly. Four primary feathers on one wing were broken and, as long as the air was calm, the bird was marooned. Even on foot, the bird was managing to catch char. I came within a few feet and the bird stared at me with that hard look that eagles have. A breeze came up and, as soon as the bird sensed it had enough head-on air, it leapt and was on its way. Foxes were catching fish where the springs kept the lake water open. It was a funny sight: a fox carrying a three-pound fish in its mouth.

Some bears who came into the basin continued on through, but a great many stayed to den. It was definitely a place to which bears gravitated for that purpose. I would see a dirty patch among the leafless alders and there would be a bear just about melting into the ground. It would complete digging in just a few hours, then devote a few more to interior decoration. After scratching up grass and leaves, it would back into the hole, pulling the debris for its bed after it.

There were big hare around the cabin as well, not unlike the big white-tailed jackrabbits back home. I watched them closely and saw they were eating pine nuts too. The weather was brutal: powerful winds as swift as ninety miles per hour, and heavy snow that turned to rain and back to snow. My roof leaked and I wondered if the cubs had dug in far enough to be dry. The barometer was up and down like a yo-yo. The strongest earthquake of the year hit on November 18, preceded by the ominous rumble that I had by now heard quite often. On my hike that day, I saw a rare wolverine track and two young bears lying beside the mouth of their den.

■   ■   ■

The helicopter was supposed to come on November 23, but there was no hope. All week, the days were blizzardy and impossible for flying. Visibility was no more than thirty feet. I hadn't seen a decent flying day for some time.

Finally, I broke down and went out to cut alder for firewood. The first time, the forestry gods caused my chainsaw to break. I still had a small bowsaw that I used after that. Made shy by the scolding I'd received from the forestry official, I went far from the cabin and dug out the base of an alder. I cut a single stem low to the ground, then cut it into stove lengths. I used my trusty green canvas sack to travel it. The next day I went to a different grove and cut another. I vowed to bring an oil-burning stove if we were allowed to return in the spring.

Each morning, I looked at the sky and knew that no helicopter was coming. As November drew to a close, the thermometer slid lower. On November 29, I had to chop an inch of ice out of my water bucket before I could drink. I thought I had seen the last of denning bears, but that morning I saw another one digging away on the south side of the lake. It was the fourteenth and last bear I watched den up in the fall of 1997.

Without my bears to play with, I made a friend among the foxes. A beautiful fluffy red, this fox had a real love of play. He would run ahead of me about thirty feet and hide behind a puff of snow, a rock, or in a depression. He wasn't exactly hidden most of the time. He was like a child, thinking that if he couldn't see me, I couldn't see him. I would get down low and pretend to sneak up. He would let me come within five feet, then would bound off in search of the next hiding spot. We had seen the same fox playing this game with Rosie earlier in the fall.

Throughout this stormy time, I observed that the sky, if it cleared at all, would clear in the evening, when it did no good. What I needed was a clear sky first thing in the morning, and the cycle of weather seemed locked in the opposite pattern.

My position wasn't critical, as I had two weeks of food remaining. I could make biscuits and pasta, and if I was truly desperate for meat, there were some cans of horrible stuff from China remaining. You always come down to your worst food in the end.

November's last day dawned with some clear sky in the southwest. Visibility was good and there was no wind. I got busy first thing in the morning and packed and hauled everything down to the helicopter pad, a flat spot about a hundred yards from the cabin. I had put much of the gear into big aluminum boxes. I tied a rope to the handles and slid them across on the hard snow. I nailed the metal coverings on the windows too, except for one. This was my concession to the possibility that the helicopter might not come—and it did not.

In the late afternoon, I threw the process into reverse and dragged everything back to the cabin again. The boxes were good and heavy, and so were the solar batteries. Just before dark, I cut another alder and made a fire. I wasn't very optimistic about the helicopter coming tomorrow as the sky, in the fading light, suggested another storm.

That night I did an inventory of my food: a few cans of vegetables; a couple of cans of meat (did I mention they were horrible?); lots of pasta but not much in the way of a basis for sauce; some flour for bread (but I didn't want to use the wood needed to bake it); a little sugar; some powdered milk; some tea and coffee. Definitely getting down to the basics.

My journal for the morning of December 1 reads: "What a wild night!" Wet snow drove in on a northeast wind that shook the cabin hard. At 2:30 a.m., I was woken by sudden silence. I got up and went outside. The temperature had risen to two degrees above freezing. I could even see a couple of stars. The wet wind-driven snow was plastered thick on every upwind surface. I dug the barometer out of its aluminum box and it showed a drop of twenty-four points. My conclusion was that I was in the eye of the cyclone, an observation proven true a couple of hours later when a fresh storm raged in from the opposite direction.

This extraordinary blizzard continued into the light. From the time I checked the thermometer in the night until next morning, the temperature had dropped twelve degrees, to minus ten degrees Celsius. Inside the cabin, there was ice on the water pail again. When I went to light the fire in my stove, the room promptly filled with smoke. Corroded by the alder creosote, the stove pipe had snapped off in the wind where it extended above the roofline. The creosote was rotting everything, including the tin

May 1998 still looked like winter, and a combination of strong winds and deep snow contoured the landscape. Even the bushes conformed to its whims.

Chico, Biscuit, and Rosie rolled in the scent of my tracks after not seeing me for seven months.

The predator male.

A swing by the cabin to say hello.

Char Creek in late June as it melts a channel through the last snow.

Chico followed me deep into this snow tunnel, which was carved by the creek.

Maureen in her proper spot. With this lineup, Rosie could keep unobstructed vigil behind and carry out her duties as rear guard.

One day like this, on the north ridge, made up for five stormbound days stuck in the cabin.

The green time in July, before life gets serious. The abundance of lush vegetation slows the depletion of a bear's fat left over from the previous fall, but the bear does not build new fat reserves. So bears require ample supplies of pine nuts, berries, and salmon in the fall.

Rosie's freedom in paradise.

The cubs needed to be fast
and skilful to catch salmon
in the lake.

Taking full advantage of
the summer.

Chico and I have a special
affection for each other.

Chico deftly secures a hard, strong female sockeye, fresh from the sea on its way to the lake.

A few weeks later, Chico caught a male sockeye—big reward for a small bear.

Hanging out with Queen Biscuit.

Chico and I continually explored what it meant to trust each other.

Chico loved to lock fingers and claws.

I asked Chico if I could examine her find—a bear skull—for signs of a poacher's bullet.

Chico will not let me have it—at least not without first teasing me.

On the fourth try, she relented.

Brandy was a mother to behold. Remarkably, when she needed a break, she would occasionally entrust Gin and Tonic to me as her babysitter.

Maureen with Tatiana Gordienko, during our trip to St. Petersburg. Tatiana worked unceasingly to keep our cub program alive.

Biscuit in late September 2000, at nearly four years. She will turn seven in the fall of 2003.

stove. I had to be careful putting in wood lest I knock out the stove's side.

I stared at the stove and pipes and contemplated life without fire. I had no more materials with which to make repairs. Such was the howling blizzard that I made no attempt to go outside and look at the damage. I climbed into the rafters inside and looked for holes in today's upwind wall. I stuffed toilet paper into a few with the edge of a kitchen knife.

By noon, it had not let up. I donned my gear and pushed outside. In a couple of frustrating hours, I affected a very imperfect fix on the chimney and was rewarded with a smoky fire just short of what it would take to asphyxiate me. When I went to cut more alder and fetch water, the drifts were to my waist and the air so full of snow, it was hard to breathe.

By 6 p.m., I was somewhat comfortable in the cabin and contemplating the fact that my scheduled flight back to Canada had been in the air for one hour. If no one in PK notified Maureen about the storm, she would be meeting my connecting flight to Calgary in a few hours. She would have no idea why I wasn't on it.

In fact, no one did tell her. She did meet the plane that I was not on, and she did worry. Finally, she got through by phone to Katya, who briefed her on the storm.

As if the weather knew it was now December, it got much colder. After another cabin-shaking night of wind, I woke on December 2 to find snow all over everything and the water bucket frozen almost to the bottom. With a screwdriver, I chipped a hole down to the remaining liquid. I heated it and poured it back to melt more, to produce enough for coffee. I swept the snow into a heap by the door, but when I tried to get it outside, it blew back in, and more. The stove melted a little circle around itself.

The day outside was bleakness itself when I suited up and went for wood and water. I decided to haul the second solar battery down to the helipad, an exercise in wishful thinking. My friend the fox came to play, running ahead, pressing his body to the snow, nose between his paws. I knew how lonely I was by how happy I was to see him.

My first sensory impression the following day was the sound of snow pellets hitting the chimney. I rolled over and went back to sleep. When I woke next, sun was streaming in the window and the room was silent. No wind. I jumped up and yanked open the door on a perfect day. Without eating or having coffee, I started packing and dragging gear through the fluffy snow. I did not stop until everything was by the pad and the windows and door of the cabin were covered. It was noon.

By 1:15 that afternoon my dream of rescue had begun to dim. A huge wall of cloud was building over the sea and looked to be coming my way. Then I heard the helicopter. As it lowered, I was pleased with myself for having everything ready. My preparedness would allow us the margin of escape.

When the Mi-8 lowered to the pad in a swirl of snow, the wind was already up and the sun behind the edge of cloud. I studied the rim of blue to the north, our destination. The door of the helicopter opened and who should emerge but the bloody prosecutor, followed by his interpreter. The two idiots were again in suits and ties, albeit with winter boots. There was a third man in a suit whom I did not know, and Tatiana. They confirmed that Bill had received my note. The three men, like something straight out of Kafka's *The Castle*, marched for the cabin, nodding to me merrily on their way by. I did not know what to make of this madness, so I ignored it. I threw my stuff aboard, assisted by the engineer. The pilot was Viktor, and it was on the fact that he was such a good pilot that all my slender hopes resided. He kept the engines running. It began to snow, wet, sticky flakes.

Viktor was agitated, as he should have been. To be in this type of closing weather and not moving was enough to drive us both mad. He yelled at Tatiana to fetch the other three. She ran up the trail. I ran beside her asking what the hell was happening. She said that the prosecutor and the others were looking for proof that the cubs had damaged the tundra. At the cabin, the truly daft tableau was of men in suits chopping at the frozen ground. One of them saw me and made a hacking motion. He wanted me to fetch an axe. By now, the blizzard was raging. I grabbed him by his arm and hauled him down the path towards the helicopter. He allowed it, but when I let him go he walked back towards the cabin. I had to get away. I was close to doing something foolish.

Tatiana and I went back to the helicopter, which was now covering up nicely with ice. All I could think of was that seven of us would be stuck down here with no food and no wood, reliving some scene from the Franklin expedition. Finally, the smiling bastards groped their way out of the vortex of snow. Viktor advanced the turbines to full throttle before they were aboard and lifted off with the last one still on the step, clinging to the door frame.

The ground disappeared instantly. The windscreen was covered with ice. After all my flying here, I felt I was about to die in the air in someone else's craft, because of someone else's foolishness. I stood in the open cockpit door and studied the instruments. I could see by the compass that we were headed for Kurilskoy, but the altimeter read 1,800. The pass between the valleys was at 2,200 feet, the mountains to either side being much higher. Viktor was climbing, but far too slowly in my view. We had to be very close to the pass. I was so sure of the danger, expecting a wall of stone to appear through the cloud at any second, that I tapped Viktor's shoulder. He looked at me questioningly. I pointed up. He did climb, but in no way steeply enough to allay my fears. I went back to the cargo area, not wanting to be between the load and the bulkhead when we met the mountain.

The sickening crunch did not come. We flew on. One circular window near the back was open and I looked down through it. Just then, we broke through the leading edge of the storm and far below was Kurilskoy Lake. We were at least 8,000 feet above it. Only then did I understand my mistake. The altimeter on my Kolb read in feet, while the altimeter on the Mi-8 read in meters. When we landed I told Viktor the source of my agitation, and we had a good laugh.

We stopped at several hunters' cabins along the way to PK, and I was amazed by the amount of ice we were packing. Each time, we chipped off enough to get us airborne again. At no time was Viktor able to see forward. The one thing the hectic trip accomplished was that I thought little about the actual fact of leaving. My mind was kept off the cubs, who were hopefully fast asleep in their winter home of earth and snow, some-where beyond the ridge of Chico Basin.

A final footnote to the year was that, after Christmas, Maureen and I went out to Vancouver to help Ian Herring rescue his film. The fact that Mike Herd had been so reluctant to point a camera at us had indeed become a handicap in post-production. Ian shot cutaways of us that were cheated into the final film. He made two visits to Alberta that winter to tape voice-overs. The film was first broadcast by PBS under the title *Walking With Giants*, and in accordance with Maureen's beliefs, and in spite of mine, it did do a tremendous amount of good for our project. Instead of our having to seek people's attention and explain what we were trying to do, people who already knew were coming to us.

PART FOUR

(1998)

17

Russian Roulette

After our first summer with the cubs, the story we were able to tell generated excitement for our project. Fundraising for the third year was not the last-moment, nail-biting business it had been for the first and second years. People wanted to know the next chapter in the cub saga and were willing to contribute to help us discover it.

The questions asked during our promotion and fundraising often amused us. "Will the cubs recognize you?" was a favourite. To the cubs, we were at least on the level of older siblings or close friends. How could they fail to know us? Some even asked if we would know the cubs. You have to be patient with a question like that—like asking if you'd recognize your dog after a six-month separation, or your child.

People who have not had a lot to do with animals tend to see them as all alike. When I was a rancher, I could recognize every one of my cows, and there were 180 of them. In Kamchatka, Maureen and I could recognize every bear who called Kambalnoye Lake its home.

In the midst of this fundraising, I remembered that the Russian doctor had insisted I go for a complete physical when back in Canada. First, my doctor, Bill Hanlon, checked out the possibilities pertaining to the painful episode in Petropavlovsk. He concurred that it was gallbladder related: a temporary spasm brought on by a fatty meal. Then he discovered a much greater problem. Below my kidneys, I had an aneurysm two inches in diameter. I needed an operation and the insertion of a man-made part to repair the area. Until the patch was on, the aneurysm could burst, an event that would likely kill me in five seconds.

The good news was that Dr. Bill had found the aneurysm before it blew, and that medical science had a solution. In this way I was lucky and should have been damn grateful. But it was hard to feel lucky and grateful when I considered the ramifications for our project. Maureen and I were on pins and needles all winter about the cubs, a condition of suspense that could only be relieved by a reunion in the spring. Now I was being told that, due to a backlog in the Alberta health system, I would have to wait six months before the surgery could be done.

This bad news/good news visit to Dr. Bill happened on March 20, 1998. In the week or two that followed, I thought about it pretty much all the time. The idea of sitting around Alberta all summer, not even knowing if the cubs had survived the winter, was intolerable. Maureen was so determined to see how our bears had fared through the winter she was threatening to go without me. In my desperation, it was inevitable that I would strike upon the idea of returning to Kamchatka, aneurysm and all.

When I told Dr. Bill, he looked at me like I be been kidding. When I assured him I wasn't, he said he would ask a specialist for a second opinion on how foolhardy it might be. It helped to have a doctor who was no stranger to the concept of risk by choice. Dr. Bill was at that time planning to climb Mount McKinley.

The answer that came back from the specialist was that I had about a ten per cent chance of dying that summer, if I stayed in Alberta. If I went to Russia, the chance of my demise rose to fifteen per cent. To me, it wasn't a big enough difference to warrant scrapping our summer plans.

I have to admit I wasn't telling my advisers the whole story. Dr. Bill was assuming I wouldn't fly my Kolb over there, that I wouldn't be that crazy, and I did not challenge his assumption. But I did intend to fly. I spent a lot of time figuring out how to do so without radically infringing on the primary rule regarding my condition: "Do not lift." I imagined applying considerable Zen to problems like getting fuel barrels to rise and making my plane swap ends on the ground.

Maureen, who knew a lot more about Kamchatka, and about me, made one thing abundantly clear. If I did go to Kamchatka with my aneurysm—stop—and if I did insist on flying my Kolb—stop—she would not fly with me—full stop!

In the end, I decided to take my chances. The odds of not making it were about one in six, which seemed appropriate. In Russian roulette, given one bullet in a six-shot revolver, the odds of survival are the same.

Quite a few times that winter, I was asked how I was documenting our story and whether or not I intended to write a book. Because I had already written *Spirit Bear*, the concept of a book on the Russia project was hardly beyond the pale. As I considered the matter, I decided there would have to be a couple of improvements. Instead of scribbling in longhand, I wanted to join the twentieth century before it was over by acquiring a computer and learning to type.

Maureen, also, was not a computer person, so when I bought a laptop computer in mid-April, it represented a beginning for both of us. A crash course commenced as the date of departure rose swiftly on the horizon. As the computer savvy reader will guess, I was not exactly a super-user by the time I had to leave. There was a ton left to learn and the technological ante was about to rise.

I boarded a plane for Seattle on May 4. Maureen would follow me to Russia in three weeks. The shipping of our cargo container from Seattle was a well-oiled system by now, and I boarded my flight to PK the next day. The irony of the flight was that it was full of American hunters, also bound for Kamchatka, also dreaming of bears. But the bears they were seeing were at the centre of crosshairs permanently mounted in their imaginations. I eavesdropped on their seemingly endless, obnoxious anecdotes about previous hunts, and wished hard that I hadn't packed my notebook in the cargo bay. I was also thinking of Timothy Treadwell and what he might do in this situation. Given his track record, he would probably trade seats to be closer, so as to be able to tear into them with provocative questions and furious argument. My version was to grab the air sickness bag out of the seatback and scribble the following mini-essay up and down both sides of it: "Have been reading in *Time* magazine about a new wonder drug called Viagra, a potency pill for men. It occurs to me, while sitting here on a plane full of hunters, that the pill, if it can do what it says it can, might save the lives of a lot of bears. All these men are on the same quest: to kill a grizzly bear. All consider it the profoundest proof of their manly potency. So bring on the Viagra. Feed a bottle to every man. Get their self-esteem UP, so they won't have to kill bears in pathetic search of it anymore."

MAUREEN: Charlie was barely out of the country when good friends of ours, Barb Gosling and her husband Derek Small, got in touch with me to see what I thought about having a website for our bear project. Barb is a native Calgarian and her brother James is the inventor of the Java programming language, and is also vice-president of Sun Microsystems. The deal was that James (through his company) was willing to fund and manage our website. Part of that funding would be a satellite telephone and a digital camera. Our side of things would be to post a diary entry a couple of times a week from Kamchatka for instant publication on the site. The digital camera would allow us to post photographs as well. It sounded great and naively (in the sense that I had little idea what I was committing us to technologically) I said thanks and yes. It really was a wonderful offer.

Within a day or two, I had bought the camera and the satellite phone, and Barb was teaching me everything I needed to know to send e-mail messages and photos through the sky via satellite. It was three weeks of total immersion before I was on the plane to Kamchatka with my armload of new toys.

When I got to Petropavlovsk, I went to our friend Jennya's apartment. Jennya is a psychology teacher and her husband, Viktor, is a businessman. We had an arrangement to stay with them whenever we were in PK. Jennya saved the bit of rent we paid for the day when she would return to university for a psychology degree.

Soon after I arrived, I went out on Jennya's balcony and set up the satellite phone and computer, and began sending my first report with a photo of the PK waterfront back to James. The wind was blowing hard but I got a signal. It felt pretty shaky, but I soldiered on. Grisha, Jennya's son, was yelling at me urgently from inside, I wasn't sure about what. When I finally shut down and went in, I was told that I had transmitted the message during the worst earthquake to hit PK in months. I had been so uptight that I hadn't noticed.

When I landed at Petropavlovsk, Tatiana Gordienko was waiting. She quickly told me the outcome of the winter lawsuit stemming out of the all-terrain vehicle disaster last fall. For starters, Igor Revenko could no longer be our Russian agent. The main targets of the trial had been Valery Golovin and Sergei Alexeev, but Igor had been tarred by the same brush. Golovin had lost his job and been fined 56 billion rubles (US$9.3 million), which was so ridiculous an amount it was like being fined nothing. Basically, Golovin got off scot-free, having pleaded the equivalent of insanity.

Sergei Alexeev had also lost his position.

Igor had been nailed for various infractions, but his biggest error was probably being too close to Sergei Alexeev. Igor had already told me by e-mail that his business had been shut down and that he could no longer be our agent. He had also told me he was planning to emigrate to Canada—which he and his family eventually did, winding up in Vancouver.

What the lawsuit meant for Maureen and me and the future of our project was not yet clear. A new regime for the Kronotskiy Preserve was in the works, and, while officials in Moscow mulled over a permanent replacement for Sergei Alexeev, Vladimir Mosolov was appointed temporary director. Vladimir was a member of the science committee that had met last year over our cub rehabilitation proposal, and he had been vehemently against it. Make no mistake, Tatiana told me, there were still major objections to our project in the minds of these people. I would be meeting with Vladimir Mosolov in a few days, and Tatiana's advice to me was to "be clever."

In the months of preparation for year three at Kambalnoye, the one thing that I had not considered was that our project could be scrubbed before we got there. We had another shipment of 1,500 pounds of sunflower seeds steaming across the Pacific. In fact, Maureen and I had been hoping to expand our program with more orphaned cubs if any were available. Despite all the dire warnings and predictions, I tried not to believe that the end was any nearer now. I missed Igor's knack for downplaying disastrous trends and forecasting unlikely success.

Tatiana delivered me to Jennya and Viktor's apartment. Their boys, Misha and Grisha, greeted me at ground level and carried my heavy bags up to the third floor. I hadn't told anybody here about my condition, but it was as if they had intuited it. If this was being an invalid, I could get to like it. Upstairs, I was greeted like an old family friend by Jennya and her daughter, Dasha. Viktor was away on business in Moscow.

Another friend in PK, Olga Yefimova, had translated a few newspaper articles about the ATV trial. I read them with amazement and fury. When I had given my testimony to the prosecutor, I had asked that he leave Maureen's and my name out of things, while using the facts we were able to supply. I was truly concerned that our lives might be threatened if certain people knew we were actively working to bring down their poaching activities. But here was the news, with our names plastered all over it, and no end of questionable and downright false accusations levelled at us.

In making a case against Sergei Alexeev, the prosecution had singled out his promotion of the projects of foreign citizens. Our buildings and our electric fences were set forth as illegal, and who had given us permission to break the rules but Sergei? Our taking the cubs was certainly illegal, and Igor and Sergei had helped us take the bears' "fate into our own hands."

"In the opinion of the experts," one piece read, "the cubs' reintroduction didn't exclude close contact between man and bear that could be dangerous to both of them." The cubs had apparently denned successfully, the write-up continued, but "nobody knows for sure what can happen if in the spring, having awakened, the cubs will go to look for the people who had been feeding them and bringing them up." Michio's death was thrown in as if the cubs' potential danger was somehow proven by it. We were accused of damaging the local forest as well. The total value of the destruction caused by us (mostly damage the cubs had done to the tundra inside their pen) was calculated at 89,300 rubles. This amounted to about

US$14,800, which was nothing to sneeze at. With Tatiana's help, we would eventually negotiate it down to US$300 and pay that amount.

The fact that I was the one who alerted the authorities about the ATV disaster was called "the major paradox of the story," as if I was a hardened enemy of the environment who, by reporting the Vityaz debacle, had done an uncharacteristic environmental good deed. In another part of the story, Maureen and I were referred to as probable "fanatics."

To keep from blowing up at all this, I had to remember that the report was partly media hype and partly the authorities trying to nail one of their number using us as the hammer. It probably did not represent the true feelings of those who would be weighing our right to continue. I certainly hoped not anyway.

Two days later, as scheduled, Tatiana picked me up and delivered me to Vladimir Mosolov's office. "Be clever," she had told me, and what that meant in the actual meeting was biting my tongue as I listened to charges that were either untrue or unproven. There was much talk, for instance, about what a dangerous track we had embarked upon, how our project would almost certainly lead to injury to ourselves or to some innocent passerby. They had not yet decided whether we should be allowed to continue and were sending Vitaly Nikolaenko (the Kronotskiy Preserve expert we'd met in 1994) south to Kambalnoye with me to assess the situation. Vitaly, with his interpreter, would spend three weeks with the cubs and me, and would decide if the project should stop or go.

It was a lot to swallow. To date, we had been our own guides and stewards while on the ground at Kambalnoye. We had never really had to put up with anyone else's opinion. Now, I would have to share everything— my dwelling, my experience, my cubs—with a near stranger. I did not object, of course, as that would have been project suicide. In my head, I tried to lessen the objections as well. It was ironic that they would send a man who was no more a scientist than I was to decide our fate, but they had. I kept telling myself that Vitaly was a very experienced bear expert. If I listened, I could probably learn. From the time I left the meeting until we loaded up the helicopter and headed south, I chanted these positive slogans and tried hard to believe them.

What was amazing in a way was how all of this went on with no one

knowing for a fact that the cubs had survived. I had a lot of confidence in
them, but, nonetheless, the suspense kept spiralling upward. I could not
wait to get there and would have waded any river of bureaucracy towards
that goal of reunion.

On May 11, Vitaly Nikolaenko, his interpreter, Stas (the same interpreter
he'd used in '94), and I boarded a helicopter bound for Kambalnoye Lake.
The helicopter was loaded mainly with wood to ensure that we would
destroy no more of the local dwarf alder. The majority of my gear was left
behind in PK, pending Vitaly's decision about our project.

On the flight I was as amazed as ever by the accumulation of snow.
When we got to Kambalnoye, it was a basin of contoured white, and the
cabin itself was in a hole surrounded by drifts. We landed, unloaded, and
got busy preparing the cabin to be lived in.

I should take a moment to describe my companions. Vitaly was a stocky
man, about to turn sixty. He had a pleasant face and eyes that really
sparkled. He wore a neatly trimmed, grey-brown beard. Stas, his interpreter, was an art student. He was slight of build but very fit. He had a
problem seeing, which may only have been that his glasses were the wrong
prescription. He was forever squinting and either rubbing his glasses with
a cloth or his eyes with his fists. He was a smiley fellow who considered
himself a radical. Radical at this time in Russia meant preferring a return
to Communism.

The moment we were inside the cabin, with a fire made and a kettle heating for tea, Vitaly started to talk non-stop. I kept hearing the word for bear,
medved, and a word roughly the same as the English word "program." The
fact that I didn't understand more than that didn't slow him down. Stas did
not translate per se, but gave me a sentence or two of explanation every
five minutes, which I learned was plenty to keep up with the gist of Vitaly's
prattle. One of these summaries was that Vitaly was sure we would never
find the cubs, that they probably had been killed and eaten by adult predator males. Or, if they had by some miracle survived, they would have departed
for the east coast upon leaving the den, there being nothing here to eat.

In the busy work of unpacking and opening up the cabin, I had hardly
taken time to look around. I did so now and immediately spotted two

bears across the lake. One was going east, the other west. I excused myself and climbed from the snow to the roof for a better view. I saw a bear on a knoll about half a mile away, in the direction of the pass. When I focused the binoculars, I could make out two bears. So much hope surged through my brain right then that my eyes lost focus. When I could see again, there were three bears, one darker than the other two. They moved a bit and my recognition was assured. It was Rosie, Biscuit, and Chico, lighter in colour than six months ago but unmistakably themselves. They had made it.

Meanwhile, Vitaly was rattling on, no doubt about how the bears were dead meat. I called to Stas and told him to tell Vitaly that the cubs were alive, and I was going to see them.

I walked up Char Creek, or at least in that direction. The creek itself was far under the sculpted snow. The drifts were set enough that my boots hardly sank. Slivers of afternoon sun shone through holes in the cloud, and the scene before me was shadow broken by pools of brilliance. The knoll the cubs were on happened to be one of the spots of dazzling light.

Stas caught up with me on his skis. Vitaly was 200 yards back, yelling for me to wait. I did wait, and all the way, he kept up a monologue about something. It turned out he was saying we could not go farther. He wanted to watch the bears for a few days without their seeing us. I couldn't even begin to take that suggestion seriously, with the cubs right there. Obviously it hadn't sunk in all the way that Vitaly was calling the shots now; that this was becoming his study more than Maureen's and mine.

I looked back at the cubs. They had seen us and were starting to run away. By automatic reflex, I called to them.

I was in turmoil. Tatiana's caution and my own common sense were telling me various sage things about the importance of the moment and not blowing things with Vitaly. But I was desperate to go to the cubs. When I looked again, they were climbing a steep slope beyond the ridge. They stopped, sat down, and stared at us. By their actions, I knew they had recognized my voice. I asked Stas to tell Vitaly that I had to go and say hello. They were welcome to come along. I started out, and all kinds of abusive-sounding Russian came bouncing along the snow at my back.

Vitaly was out of my head the moment he was out of earshot. I began to chat to the bears, with all manner of questions about what they'd done since

I last saw them. They looked in pretty good shape, not fat but not skinny. I noticed their colour change even more close up. Biscuit and Rosie, blonds to begin with, were paler than they had been in the fall. Chico, being dark, was more noticeably lighter. I guessed it was bleaching from the sun's reflection off the snow. It meant they had been out of the den for some time.

The bears watched me approach until I was at the foot of the steep snow slope they had climbed. As soon as I started up, Chico stood. Then she dropped back onto all four paws and raced straight at me. With twenty-five feet to go, she lay down and rolled onto her back. Head first, feet waving, beady eyes locked on mine, she barrelled down and thumped against my shins. Her feet were still in the air and I placed my hands on the pads of her forepaws.

I looked up and Rosie and Biscuit were coming full speed, sliding and rolling. They rode down onto my tracks and began to roll in my footprints the way they would if the prints were full of a scent they wanted on themselves. Since I was in rubber boots, I couldn't imagine that there was much scent there, but all three kept rolling and rubbing their faces in any snow that I had touched. Then they sat down with me, and we looked at the valley together, out to the black Sea of Okhotsk with the snowy cone of the Kuril Island volcano, Alaid, rising 7,000 feet out of it.

Looking down, I could see Vitaly steaming off on his skis towards the cabin. The distance suggested he had started off about the time the cubs and I were greeting one another. Whatever was bugging him, I would find out soon enough. I wasn't about to leave the cubs right away.

I wanted to see what the cubs had been up to on the knoll, so I walked back along their tracks to the top. They stuck right with me. Up above, it was pretty easy to figure out what they had been doing and how they had been surviving. In this white world, so lacking in visible vegetation, they were able to smell pine cones under the snow. The knolls were where the snow was shallowest, and they were digging down to find last year's cones and eat the nuts. It was a lot of work, and I couldn't imagine it being energy efficient, but the cubs were sustained by it. That was the main thing.

Finally, I started back to the cabin, so I could make supper for the crew. I thought maybe the cubs would come along in hopes of some sunflower seeds, but they did not. They just kept on digging.

18

Befriending the Enemy

I hope I am not what the world would call a control freak, but faced with a man who had the authority and the desire to take over the project that I regarded as the most important work of my life, I was pushed to the outer limits of my patience. If I failed to get along peacefully with Vitaly Nikolaenko that May of 1998, it could very well mean the end of the Russia project. Given Vitaly's belief that we had converted our bears into dangerous time bombs by feeding and befriending them, the cubs might even be killed as part of closing the book on us.

That risk had been there from the start, but it was far more personal now.

I also had to remind myself of the simple truth that Maureen and I were guests here, relying on the generosity of the Russians for a place to work. After what we had done to get the cubs in the first place, and considering the direction our coexistence research was taking us, it *was* logical that officials would want us to have an overseer.

Determined to make a success of things with Vitaly, I utilized my most reliable befriending technique for any animal, which is to take an interest in them. It worked wonders with bears and was about to meet its most severe test among my own species.

I tried to imagine, and sympathize with, Vitaly's position. For twenty-five years, he had studied the social structure of bears. Except for a bit of notoriety, he had known few rewards. Now, two foreigners had entered his territory with an interesting bear study. His instinct was to destroy it. Or, if it seemed viable and valuable, he might hijack it and take credit for it instead.

My challenge was to persuade him that it was a good study, even though that amounted to coaxing him to take authority over it. If in so doing I could assure him that I was an able and co-operative type, we might be able to stay involved. That was assuming Vitaly was rational, and, with people, that assumption is sometimes a mistake.

In practice, what it meant was sitting across the table from Vitaly in our cabin asking what must have amounted to hundreds of questions, which Stas, the intermediary, translated. Vitaly loved to talk and virtually never stopped. Nor did he ask many questions in return. If he did, it was inevitably a ruse, a trick in this ridiculously one-sided game, by which to one-up me. Nevertheless, I learned a lot. He had seen some fascinating things in bear society.

Over several evenings, he outlined what he wanted me to do with "our" study. He had developed over the years a set of tables for charting dozens of kinds of observations. Maureen and I were to keep a chart on every bear we saw, noting what it was eating, what it was doing when it wasn't eating, how long it slept and where. There was a particularly large and detailed area of the tables devoted to sexual activity. We were to draw each bear and assign it a letter code for what shape it was (fat, skinny, etc.). Even the pattern by which it shed its winter hair was deemed worthy of note. If we complied, we would be doing nothing else but keeping Vitaly's charts all summer.

Ever the optimist, I imagined that once Vitaly saw what I was doing with the bears, and how it was at least as interesting as what he had in mind, he would change his thinking and let me get on with it.

As to our domestic assignments and arrangements in this forced togetherness, I did the cooking and most of the chores. Vitaly criticized the North American techniques we had used to build the cabin and took on the challenge of stopping some of the drafts. He and Stas split wood and kept the fire burning. My greatest challenge was getting three more weeks of service out of the disintegrating tin stove without burning the cabin down. Our new oil stove would arrive with Maureen, at which time this decrepit fire box could be retired. My solution for the interim was to take a bit of extra tin and shape it to the inside contours of the box. And because the annex was unheated, Vitaly slept on the darkroom bench and Stas on an army cot in the middle of the floor.

The first days of our three weeks together were cloudy, cold, and windy. It was miserable weather and Vitaly did not budge from the fire. Stas and I went out on skis, and I led the way to Chico Basin to see if the cubs could be found. On the day after our reunion, I spotted a big male bear in the basin, sniffing a fresh set of tracks. He followed the tracks to the base of a cliff. Even though it was a bigger cliff than the cubs had used for protection in the fall, I guessed it was their new haven.

I glassed the cliff carefully, and finally, through the mist and swirling snow, I made out the three bears lying on a high ledge. They were watching the big male but seemed secure in the knowledge that he could not get up the steep wall to where they were. I guessed that they had spent a lot of time on this perch since coming out of their den. The male bear stared up at them for a time, then gave up and went back down the valley.

I took off my skis and climbed alone to where the big male had just been. I walked in his footprints because they made a solid track. The cliff was coated in ice, which stopped me where it had stopped the bear. The cubs raised their heads to acknowledge me but, beyond that, they seemed almost in a trance. Biscuit and Rosie lay curled together while Chico sat on her haunches. Her head hung down and her eyes were almost closed. They did not move for a full fifteen minutes, the length of time I could stand to stay dug into a little hole in the wind-exposed snow. It seemed likely to me that the bears' state was a way of conserving energy, of burning up their remaining reserves of fat as slowly as possible.

The first day that Vitaly came out any distance from the cabin was May 15. I led him and Stas to Chico Basin. While trying to locate our trio of bears, I found a track I couldn't make sense of. It came straight down the mountain in big bounds or bounces. I was aghast to see a patch of blood in the final depression to which those strange tracks led. My interpretation was that one of our cubs had fallen and hurt herself. But just as I was gearing up to a panic, Chico led Biscuit and Rosie around a corner at the clifftop into view. They were obviously fine.

Even Vitaly took an interest. He glassed the scene at a thousand yards for an intense five minutes. Then he started talking into his tape recorder. I asked Stas to tell me what he was saying. Vitaly's interpretation of the event on the mountain was that an adult bear had been chasing down a young cub. From the eastern edge of the cliff, in five big bounds, the adult bear had caught the cub, eating it whole on the spot.

This analysis flabbergasted me—to be able to know all that at such a distance! The more I considered what I was seeing, the more I was sure it was true. I had missed that interpretation because I had preferred it not to be true. I was impressed, and I let Vitaly know I was. But that wasn't good enough for him. He invited me to go with him to the actual spot, as if I were arguing against his interpretation, which I was not. When we got there, we found part of the jawbone of a cub and a bit of hair in addition to the blood. Metaphorically, Vitaly was rubbing my face in it, and Stas seemed very pleased to see his boss win this round.

I hadn't seen much bear cannibalism before, but I certainly knew from reading and from conversation with other bear watchers that some adult males did hunt cubs as a survival strategy. A great deal of our work with the cubs the first year had been designed to prevent such a fate. The killed and eaten cub was proof that we had done the right thing. It occurred to me that this male bear was probably the same one who had been checking on our cubs two days before.

On the way back to the cabin, I began thinking about food. There were nine sacks of sunflower seeds left at the cabin from the previous year. I was wondering if now wouldn't be a good time to feed them to the cubs. Their slow movement and trancelike state might be an efficient way of killing time until new food was available, but it seemed likely to make them vulnerable to the predator male. Food energy from the seeds would translate into more alertness and strength in the face of that threat. I also had a pretty good idea Vitaly would be dead set against it.

I have seen for myself that hand-fed bears are usually big trouble, but our first year with the cubs had persuaded me that feeding bears wasn't as cut and dried an issue as people like Vitaly thought. We had been proving for most of a year that what was most important was *how you fed the bears*. The use of bowls made some difference, though we did not yet know what. Trust was another important factor. My feeling was that the "no feeding" principle was a commonly held belief more than a tried and tested proposition, but I also wanted to make sure that my strategy on feeding came out of the facts and not just out of my affection for the bears and my desire to make life easier for them.

By the time my ruminations were complete, I was certain it was only a matter of time until the predator bear picked off at least one of the cubs. Affection aside, without the cubs, there was no study. At that moment, our goal of changing world attitudes towards grizzly bears meant finding a way to feed the cubs, with or without Vitaly's permission.

That day, I watched Vitaly work. He measured every track, studied every bear, talked incessantly into his tape recorder. Later, in the cabin, he listened to the tapes and wrote his observations onto his charts. His hard work and apparently upbeat mood emboldened me to ask what he thought of feeding the cubs. He flatly refused.

I went ahead and made my argument anyway. He did listen, and in a way that suggested he wasn't as sure of his position as he said. My guess was that he had by now seen the value in the cubs, and though even their deaths might serve some purpose for him scientifically, they were undeniably more valuable alive, especially if they lived to be adults. Maybe there was an echo of his own work at Kronotskiy Preserve, where he had also befriended bears, though he said he never completely trusted them.

Whatever the motivation, he finally relented—with conditions attached, of course. I was not to feed them at the cabin, which was by far my preference, and I must surreptitiously leave the food where they could find it without finding me.

Of the two conditions, I could only agree to feed them away from the cabin. I knew I had to be open about feeding them; they were too smart to be fooled that way. It would take the cubs no time at all to figure out that the seeds were in the pack. My only question was whether I could do this without them becoming demanding and impatient while I was getting the food out. We would be out in the open without any electric fence between us, so it changed the whole ball game. In short, Vitaly's plan would put a lot more pressure on the relationship between us. I would have to trust the cubs much further than I had ever needed to before.

One of the things that gave me the confidence to try it (though I didn't mention this to Vitaly) was an unforgettable scene from Grizzly Adams's book about living with grizzlies. One of his grizzlies, Ben, a five-year-old, had been a long time without food when Adams shot an antelope:

> [Ben] sat himself down on his haunches in front of me as I began to skin the antelope. The noble fellow was already so well trained that he never presumed to touch anything till I gave it to him; but he had a way of grumbling for food when hungry, that was irresistible. I shall never forget how he sat there wistfully eyeing my carving, looking into my face and remonstrating about my strictness with him. His perquisites were generally the entrails of game, of which he was remarkably fond; but as he now had to wait until they were removed, his impatience at last assumed such a pitch, that he got excited, and grumbled more than ordinary. I resolved to try to tempt him; but the faithful fellow continued true to his training and the meat remained inviolate. Seeing this, I threw his portion to him and he ate—devouring the entrails and lapping up the liquid of the antelope's stomach, which to his palate seemed as sweet as honey.

It had never been my intention to "train" our bears in any way. All I wanted them to be was their own wild selves. But discipline is part of every bear's life. Mother bears demand it of their cubs, and they punish the bears physically to enforce it, giving them a good swat when they misbehave. Now, out in the open without any fence, I would have to make the bears wait politely while I took the seeds out of the pack and measured them into their bowls. Although I was worried about the outcome, it also struck me what a valuable addition to the study it would be if the cubs accepted this innovation without making problems.

It was close to blizzard conditions on May 16 when I first set out to feed the bears. I measured sunflower seeds into three zip-lock bags and started towards Chico Mountain on skis. Vitaly had agreed to give this name to the cubs' new home and to call the mountain to the south of the cabin Rosie Mountain. Since there was already a Biscuit Mountain, no one was left out. (Such are the luxuries of being the first people to live in a place in modern times.)

It was awkward skiing with a pack and three big bowls—and an aneurysm—and I resolved to leave the bowls at the base of the cliff from now on. After I was underway, I heard a call. It was Stas, coming to join me. By fluke, in the heavily falling snow, we happened onto three sets of tracks I was pretty sure were the cubs'. They led up Biscuit Mountain, and, at its base, we took off our skis and climbed. The wind was blowing towards the bears, and when we found them, dug into the side of a cornice and almost drifted over, they were well aware of us. Even when they saw the bowls, they were slow to react. I had plenty of time to kick out three level spots and dole out the seeds. When they finally did come, I was surprised by what difficulty they had eating. They would eat some, then vomit it all up, then try again. Chico never finished her portion, though it was quite small, much smaller than the amount they had been polishing off back in the fall. I was convinced I was giving them their first square meal in six months, and I knew how important it was that I was doing so. They weren't skinny yet, and I'm sure they could have survived a lot longer without my intervention, but I'm also sure the lack of quick energy would have reduced their chances in the lethal game of hide-and-seek with the predator male.

After their second feeding the next day, the cubs started to play and chase. That was the first day that Vitaly came out to meet them. He was obviously a bit afraid, but their manners around him were excellent and soon set him at ease. It was at about that time that Vitaly asked me to write a proposal for my study. It would be a proposal to the preserve, and he was offering to coach me through it so it would be acceptable. I assumed a major turning point in his thinking had occurred, and I sat down and began writing that very night. I turned myself inside out in those pages, trying to be reasonable and non-threatening. By now I was hyper-aware that everything I was and wanted to do seemed to threaten science in one way or another. Though I knew he would drive me crazy with objections, I was also glad to have Vitaly review it.

The weather took a turn for the better about then, and Vitaly and Stas skied off in various directions to explore. One day when they were headed north I took the cubs for a trip out to Itelman Point. The cubs amazed me with their ability to sniff out green shoots through as much as a foot of wet snow. In this place of short summers and severe climate, the plants get a jump-start under the snow, and the cubs had learned to exploit that opportunity. Some of the pines were also melting out, and before the cones could dry and the nuts rattle out in the wind onto the ground, there was a brief chance for the bears to feed on them.

Vitaly began taking a big interest in the cubs. As a photographer of bears, his work had appeared in many international magazines, and he was quick to shoot slides and videos of such willing subjects. At the same time, I was nervous about leaving him alone with the cubs. For all his experience, I had already seen him run from the cubs a few times when they were only coming over to say hello. He insisted that running was a good form of defence that had saved him many times. I really had to stifle a laugh at this, as I was just as sure that bears have a strong chase instinct, triggered by the sight of anything running from them. I didn't know how to tell him that he could run from any bears in the world *except these three*. I didn't want my bears chasing him, as he said his friendly bears at Kronotskiy had done. He said he'd been knocked down from behind several times. That definitely sounded like bear play to me, but it was a kind of play that would get a bear labelled dangerous and aggressive.

Another of his suspect practices concerned bear spray. The previous year, we had given a gift of ten canisters of bear spray to the Kronotskiy Preserve, so the rangers could try it. Vitaly had already gone through three of them. At five long shots per can, that's a lot of spray. Maureen and I had a problem with our cans going stale because we never had any call to use them. I begged Vitaly not to spray our bears, but I didn't trust him not to. He was a jumpy type, and because of that I had to stay with him whenever he was around the cubs. It would be maddening to have their behaviour change in a negative way as the result of his interference.

When Stas translated my proposal for Vitaly, his response was that everything I had written was wrong. Given that my aneurysm demanded I keep a cool head, I had to head straight for a blood pressure pill once he got going on his objections. I will not write out what he had to say. I found it haywire, vindictive and above all, boring—a manifestation of his inexhaustible capacity for competition. Even holding all the cards, he had to differ with me and best me on every point.

May 28, 1998, was the cubs' first anniversary at Kambalnoye Lake. They celebrated by completely outwitting and outclimbing the predator bear. I watched him track them all the way to their place of rest for the day, a steep cliff, but still one that he could climb. They let him come so close I was having an anxiety attack. When he made his rush, his great weight wallowed him down in the snow. The cubs ran up the hill so fast he was out of the race in no time. I couldn't believe how quickly they got up and down that mountain. They had great judgment too when selecting places to slide, managing to pick chutes that bypassed cliffs and pinnacle rocks. Now that they had had something to eat, they were much more confident and skilled.

As for the worry that they would get rough when I put out seeds for them, it never became a problem. Only Biscuit was a little impatient. I had to speak to her sternly and whack her a few times as well, until she learned to back off and wait. A more difficult situation was that another young bear, a three-year-old, had taken to hanging around with them. He also used the cliff as a safe place to sleep, and they permitted it. I had to be very careful to keep this new bear out of the feeding ritual.

A few days before Vitaly's scheduled departure, he demanded that I stop feeding the cubs. I knew what he wanted, and that was to see how they would react when deprived. I hated this demand because the pine nuts were gone and the plentiful greens still a long way off. If the bears had come equipped with a mother bear, they wouldn't even have been at Kambalnoye; she would have long ago removed them to the coast, where the season was further advanced. But our bears did not know about the coast; they only knew Kambalnoye. The seeds were obviously tiding them over that blank spot in their knowledge, and it was a shame to take the food away.

Vitaly was counting on the bears becoming aggressive if their food was withheld. Then he would have something negative to report about them, and it seemed clear he wanted that. I fretted about it, but finally had no choice but to do it. If the cubs didn't become aggressive in demanding their food, it might be the difference between our being able to continue and our being chucked out of there. It might also result in our being given a new cub to raise.

Vitaly decreed May 30 as the day feeding must stop. I had hoped for good weather, so climate would not pressure the situation, but it turned out to be a day of heavy rain. Inside the cabin, we sat waiting to see what the cubs would do. It was maddening, listening to another of Vitaly's non-stop discourses. I had lost all interest in having his words translated. When the day ended, and silence finally overtook the cabin, I lay in bed with his voice echoing on inside my head. The cubs had stayed away.

The next day the cubs again stayed away from the cabin. We went to where we could look into Chico Basin with binoculars, and there they were, playing with their new acquaintance, whom Vitaly had dubbed Podrosky. They ended up going over a ridge, in the opposite direction from the cabin. If this stupid ordeal was a competition, the cubs and I had just won. I was elated, and proud of the bears. Over the next few days, with Vitaly still present, the cubs did come around to the cabin a couple of times, but only to visit. They never made any indication of wanting food.

By now, Maureen had been in Petropavlovsk for a few days, and I often wondered what was going on there. I imagined her proceeding with the familiar drill of clearing our stuff through customs. I imagined her meeting Tatiana and the two of them discussing political strategy. I wondered what progress they were making in the city while Vitaly stood over me here, reciting his theories and chewing up my proposal. He planned for me to return to PK with him in a few days, where we would work out with the science committee how (if) we were to proceed.

On June 5, the helicopter finally showed up, but with a major surprise aboard. Maureen had managed the customs clearance in record time, and there she was, along with Tatiana, a season's worth of sunflower seeds, premium gas for the Kolb, the oil stove, sheets of tin for a leak-proof roof, lots of food, my computer and, to my amazement, a satellite phone and a digital camera!

In a very quick conversation (the pilot was anxious to get going), I was apprised of the plan. Tatiana had been working hard to soften up Vladimir

Mosolov, who was still the temporary director of the Kronotskiy Preserve (and in charge, therefore, of the South Kamchatka Sanctuary). Once we were back in PK, Tatiana would help me draft an agreement for the continuation of our work. Vitaly would still be involved, so I could look forward to the sound of his voice for some time still to come. Igor Revenko had told Tatiana about an orphaned cub somewhere out in the boonies, and she thought there was some hope of our getting the cub for rehabilitation.

In these few hurried moments, it was very clear that Vitaly hated Tatiana, and that the feeling was mutual. He was very resentful that discussions, and even decisions, had been taking place before his report had been submitted.

For Maureen and me, hello was quickly goodbye. Her plan was to stay at Kambalnoye alone while we all departed for PK. In about a week, I would return in the Kolb, hopefully with a new cub in my trusty green canvas sack. If so, I would let the cub poke his head out of the drawstring, so it could enjoy a view not too many bears ever experience.

19

Survival Strategies

For the next nine days, Maureen lived alone at Kambalnoye while I was in Petropavlovsk. Tatiana and I had worked out a strategy whereby we offered to pay Vitaly for his summer and fall fieldwork at the Kronotskiy Preserve, using money out of an emergency fund. If it kept him out of our hair, it was worth it. Tatiana shepherded me through the permit process as well.

Sadly, I did not get permission to take the orphaned cub. It had survived this long because a circus in Khabarovsk had wanted it. The only reason we were brought into the picture was that the deal with the circus had fallen through. Then we were refused without explanation. In the end, the cub went to a woman in a mountain village. It lived there for a year, became dangerous, and was killed.

My stay in PK also played out against a backdrop of deepening economic crisis. The Russian government had stopped paying its employees, including many of our Russian friends. The power was off more often than it was on. There was a sense that the worst was yet to come, and no one knew how bad it might get or how long it might last.

Finally, I was able to leave. On June 14, I got the Kolb into the air for another summer, heading south with a bag of food on the passenger seat in case I was forced down into the snow between PK and Kambalnoye Lake. Despite some heavy wind, I made it home without mishap to find that Maureen was thriving on her own.

Part of her achievement was making sense of the mountain of hand-written notes she'd gleaned from her various gurus back home concerning the new communications system. She already had mini-essays and compressed photos beaming off the satellite to San Francisco. I set about trying to catch up, spending my nights with Mavis Beacon, my virtual typing instructor.

The computer, satellite phone, and digital camera weren't the only new toys. I had a wonderful new electric gadget that would allow me to protect my plane wherever it was moored. Powered by flashlight batteries, it had a spike for grounding that I pushed into the tundra beside the plane and an alligator clip that attached to anything metal on the body. The float acted as an isolator, keeping the system from shorting out. With this device, enough electricity could be circulated through the plane to give anyone who touched it a jolt.

The new system solved the problem of protecting my trusty steed from prowlers, bears, and foxes, but it did nothing for the other dilemma of finding solid ground to tie it down to. As usual in spring, the ground with the root matrix anchors was deep under snow. But I was also getting smarter. I found some solid ground on a steeply pitched hillside above a snowdrift. It was tucked under some pines and had protection against the proven danger of an east wind.

The last of the new technologies was our oil stove. After one last trip to the coast for firewood, we retired the thoroughly rotten wood stove and installed the new oil model. We had three barrels of diesel oil to get us through the season. Not only would this be a safer and more reliable heat source, it also freed up an immense amount of time. Without the regular chore of flying firewood runs, I could restrict my flying to better weather and be safer.

Altogether we were a safer outfit in 1998 than we had been in our first two years—that is, if you didn't factor in my aneurysm, which I often didn't. Most of the time I felt healthy, and the trick was to remember in time before lifting something heavy. Other times, I would scare myself for no reason. Something as simple as a pang of indigestion would have me certain my aorta had sprung a leak.

With Vitaly and the permit process behind us for the year (or so we thought), I was able to relax for the first time in five weeks. The cubs continued to amaze us with their inventive food and survival strategies. The three bears were often out on the lake, navigating around the dark patches of candle ice. It took us a while to understand that they were eating char that had died over winter and were frozen into the ice. It was no bonanza, but they had it largely to themselves, since the rotting ice kept off the bigger bears.

In the latter half of June, when the main lake and the smaller lakes opened up, Biscuit discovered another food source. We saw her along the shore, carefully pulling up stems of grass. Gradually we figured out that attached to those stems were strands of salamander eggs. She either fished with the stems or reached down and gently fetched up the long jelly-like ropes in her claws. The other two cubs watched and quickly learned. Soon, all three were making the rounds of the lakes north of the main lake.

The other cub, Podrosky, had wandered off by now, probably down to the coast, and our bears were associating with others. On June 23, Maureen spotted a pile of bears in Chico Basin who turned out to be our three cubs and two newly-weaned two-year-olds. The new bears drifted away when we came near, and we never saw them with our cubs again. In these brief encounters, we always got the impression that our cubs were in the driver's seat. Their motherless state meant they had to look after their own feeding and protection, which gave them a confidence far greater than other bears their age. Their faces had more expression and character, as if life had already written stories there, while the other bears' faces remained blank.

The second half of June was an idyllic time for Maureen and me, spent visiting and travelling with the bears. Maureen began her season of artistic endeavour, her most ambitious to date.

MAUREEN: I started audiotaping the cubs in their first year with us, 1997, and continued to do so in 1998. Because I was taping their sounds from so close, I was able to hear them better than some of the others who have done this work of listening, taping, and trying to figure out what the different sounds mean. I have heard the popping sound that bears make in times of distress described as "a clashing of teeth," which I soon figured out was wrong. The sound is made deep down in the diaphragm and emerges with a pop. The teeth get involved after the pop when they close. I have also heard it described as a sign of aggression, which it is not. It's about feeling fear and giving warning. When the other bears in the family hear it, they take immediate flight. Similarly, the bears make a "chew, chew" sound that is also about fear. I have learned to imitate this latter sound, but the popping is beyond me.

By 1998, the five themes that I was pursuing in my artwork were clear. I was finishing *The Bear Who Looked for Beauty*, the tableau about bears' nesting sites and their ability to appreciate the view. *Anthropomorphism* was a series of drawings, half complete, derived from my hundreds of black and white photographs of the cubs. The idea was to zero in on the bears' wide range of emotions, some identifiable, others not. I was also trying to make a film called *In Situ*, but here I was floundering. I was gathering plenty of good footage, but was also realizing I am not an avant-garde filmmaker by any stretch. The sound installation I was planning also ran into difficulty in 1998. The year before, the cubs had been nearby most of the time and were easy to tape. Now they were so mobile, I had to run to keep up and be with them as they vocalized. If I timed it right, the wind would blow and carry their voices to me. The fifth grouping was a series of paintings that I loosely titled *Another Dimension*. I wasn't sure what they were yet, except that they were about the world of the bear that I was being allowed to enter so intimately.

The fish had not come into the lake yet, but when we were particularly hungry for one, I would fly over to Kurilskoy and get a sockeye. The sockeye at Kurilskoy were taken where the salmon crossed the weir. They were fresh and silvery, whereas the ones near us were always red and well into the spawning stage. In return for the fish, and all the other help and favours we got from Katya and Alexei, I helped Katya with her zoo plankton study. She was fully aware of my aneurysm but decided she would take the chance and fly with me. The plan was to take zoo plankton samples and related measurements at four mountain lakes in each season for the next four years.

The outside world interrupted our solitude on June 26. We were out walking with our bear trio when a helicopter topped the ridge and headed for the cabin. Tatiana had e-mailed a couple of days before to say she might be coming, but had not told us why. When we reached the cabin, we saw that there was a man with her, who turned out to be Anatoly Yephemenko, the Director of the Environmental State Committee.

We made tea for them, and the news that emerged was excellent. Anatoly Yephemenko's Environmental State Committee was planning a takeover of the South Kamchatka Sanctuary. Currently, the committee had jurisdiction over environmental protection in all of Kamchatka, but was below the Kronotskiy Preserve director in power with regard to the preserve system. But now, with Sergei Alexeev fired and no one having taken his place, the Kronotskiy Preserve was floating rudderless. Anatoly saw an opportunity to seize control of the South Kamchatka Sanctuary, an island of power that could be expanded later.

The entire plan sounded alluringly positive. Anatoly's committee (on which Tatiana was an officer) was much more receptive to our project than were the bureaucrats of the Kronotskiy Preserve. If Anatoly's plan won out, it would be goodbye to Vitaly's meddling, which alone was a pleasing possibility.

Anatoly was going to Moscow soon to put his proposal forward. With Kronotskiy's current record of mismanagement and possible graft, he was optimistic about his success.

One of the best things about this new deal was that the committee promised to curb poaching in the South Kamchatka Sanctuary as soon as they had authority. Rangers would be posted to the area as early as this fall. For Maureen and me, this was the best news: that a force would be protecting the local bears, including Chico, Biscuit, and Rosie, in both our presence and absence.

Already this summer, I had seen how much more flighty and paranoid the bears at Kurilskoy were around humans as a result of the blatant poaching going on there. This was a serious regression from the almost model bear-human interaction we had witnessed earlier. The irony was that the Kambalnoye Lake bears, who had been so fearful when we arrived in 1996, were now as fear-free as the Kurilskoy bears used to be.

Maureen and I were feeling pretty good about our prospects as June turned into July, the real heart of Kamchatkan summer. On June 29, we took a big walk to the pass. Our bears smelled us coming and ran to join us after a mile. We witnessed just how confident they felt around other bears when a mother bear and her two cubs came down the trail from the opposite direction. At first they could only smell the bear, not see her, but they advanced along the trail anyway, noses testing the air. Just before the ridge that concealed the other bear, Chico broke into a run and the others followed. When Maureen and I were high enough to see, the bears were going full out, chasing the mother bear and her cubs, chuffing away like mad. They didn't let up, either, but continued the chase up the steep mountain and over the top. The way the wind was blowing, that mother bear couldn't have seen or smelled us, and it would have been easy for our bears to put some safe distance between them. But they hadn't. They had chosen to chase instead. I still don't know what they were up to that day, frankly, or why the adult female chose to run from them.

Proceeding on our own, we were treated to a drama. The mating season had been in full swing for some time, but what we saw, or heard before we saw, was a suitor being spurned. From just over the lip of the pass we heard some really angry roaring. The roaring bear was coming our way, and we got off the path to make way for it. What turned up was an old female in a very cranky mood. She was looking back over her shoulder when a massive male appeared from that direction. She didn't want any part of him and was making it loudly known. The male wisely stopped and went back the other way.

Next day, we were out with the cubs again when Rosie gave us a scare. Suddenly, she began to stagger. At first she tried to lie down, but when the other cubs continued walking, she dragged herself to her feet and tried to go on. She then flopped down, apparently unconscious.

Seeing this, Chico and Biscuit came back and waited beside her. They wrestled for a while, then slept. In about twenty minutes, Rosie woke up, seeming to be her normal self. The only thing we could think of was that she had become so tired that she'd lost control of her limbs. It was one of those events, like yesterday's pursuit of the mother and cubs, that I felt I had better not jump to conclusions about. Better to wait and see if further happenings showed a pattern that was more easily read.

MAUREEN: From the very first, the bears had always walked in the same order: Chico–Biscuit–Rosie. Because Rosie was always the most curious of the three, and the most likely to become lost by virtue of hanging back to investigate something, I had concluded that she was the caravan's trailer by default. While Chico took the lead, supported by Biscuit, Rosie straggled along behind.

In July of 1998, I was following the bears with the wind strong in our faces when I noticed that Rosie was frequently looking back. When the bears walk into the wind, they hardly bother to look up. Their noses are so good, they know what's coming. Surprise can only come from behind.

I walked up close behind Rosie while she was back-checking in this manner, and she gave me a really annoyed look. Acting on a hunch, I moved into the line between Rosie and Biscuit and was at once rewarded when they both relaxed. They liked it better to have me there.

Whatever else it meant, it was clear to me that I had, out of ignorance, misunderstood Rosie's role. She wasn't a straggler, she was a rear guard. With the wind coming from the front, her vigilance was all that stood between them and disaster. The bears all seemed to enjoy my having figured this out. When we stopped for a while so the bears could graze, Rosie showed what a difference my breakthrough in understanding made to her. Always the most standoffish of the bears, she began grazing on sedge grass closer and closer to my feet. Finally she had nibbled the tufts in a semi-circle around each of my boots. Charlie said it was her way of inviting me to trust her.

To complete the story of how the battle between the two bureaucracies played out that summer, in late July Maureen and I received two copies of a beautifully worded and well-thought-out document that had been written by Anatoly Yephemenko and translated by Tatiana. We were called over to the research station at Kurilskoy to sign them, keeping one copy and sending the other back to PK on the next helicopter flight. The document described our project very well, and very much according to our desires for it. Our understanding was that, by signing it, we had replaced and nullified the restrictive agreement we had signed earlier with the Kronotskiy Preserve. That, of course, depended on the successful transfer of power over the South Kamchatka Sanctuary from the old regime to the Environmental State Committee, but that was supposed to be in the bag.

20

The Cubs
Meet Their Public

July in South Kamchatka is a month of unbelievable growth. The snow is still deep in the shadows, but the tundra surges with emerald green. Plants grow and flower as if there is no tomorrow. There aren't any extra tomorrows before winter.

For our bears, July was a frustrating month because they could see and smell the salmon entering the lake to spawn where the springs well up through the gravel, but they couldn't hope to fish them until the salmon had finished spawning and begun to die off. There were other things to eat—flowers, dead flies, birds' eggs, salamander eggs—but not enough on which to fatten. Thin, restless, impatient, and losing last winter's hair in rags and patches, July was not their "beauty month," which concerned us a little, given that reporters and photographers were on their way to further immortalize our bears in world newspapers and magazines. Ian's film would be ready in the fall so it really was the year that the cubs would be unveiled to a largely adoring public.

The writers coming were Rick Paddock, Russia correspondent for the *Los Angeles Times*, based in Moscow, and Paul Rauber from *Sierra* magazine.

Rick was due in late July, and Paul and his wife, Marion, in early August. Rick was bringing a photographer, Yuri Gozyrev, who in the end illustrated both articles. Their interest was due to the wave of publicity produced by our new website. Maureen and I had been posting stories and photos regularly, and James Gosling had reported that the site was getting several thousand hits a day.

With another two visitors scheduled before the end of August, Mike McIntosh, the Ontario black bear rehabilitator, and our friend Dr. Margaret Horne, it was shaping up as a not very private summer. But it was also enjoyable to show off Chico, Biscuit, and Rosie to people who knew how to enjoy them. The best way to counter negative assumptions was to have observers come and record how the bears really were. We needed as much of this kind of publicity as we could get.

My first social occasion was a meeting in PK. The invitation came by e-mail from Jim Thorsell, a Canadian living in Geneva who worked for the World Conservation Union. It was a session between his organization and the Global Environmental Facility, the United Nations Development Program, and the World Bank. The invitation had been extended to both of us, but Maureen was holding fast to her commitment not to fly with me until my medical problem was fixed.

The meeting was at the Hotel Petropavlovsk, the closest thing PK has to a posh establishment. I had no idea why Jim Thorsell wanted me there, and it became no easier to understand as the meeting got underway. The session was about spending us$18 million in Kamchatka on environmental projects, and the first standard of eligibility ruled out Maureen and me. A specific Russian partner was necessary and we had none. In Russian terms, it was a lot of money, and I was pretty sure even a fraction of that amount would touch off a local feeding frenzy. Kamchatka was absolutely cash-starved. Most government employees hadn't seen a paycheque since April. The agencies that employed friends like Tatiana and her husband Volodya, and Katya and Alexei, accomplished much while operating on a shoestring. It would be interesting to see what could be done with a few hundred thousand dollars. All I could do was hope our friends would be among those rewarded. Personally, all I got out of it was a plane ride.

MAUREEN: While Charlie was in Petropavlovsk meeting with Jim Thorsell, I continued to work on a print-casting project. Part of my exhibition plan was to have people walk in the footsteps of the bear as they entered a bear's world. While in Kamchatka, I would cast bear tracks in plaster, then return with them to Canada where I would use the casts to print tracks in a more permanent medium. I would eventually build a pathway into the exhibition covered in these tracks of bears and other animals.

That was the plan, but first I had to get the tracks. Naturally, I assumed our cubs would supply many of them. I wanted their paw prints to be part of the larger story told about them in the exhibition. My first method was to gather mud from the marsh and to place a four-foot-long swatch of it on the path the cubs used most often when entering camp. After the cubs had travelled the path I went to check, and there wasn't a single print on it. Next, I lured them to the mud pie by dragging a stick, a game they could never resist. But when we got to the mud, each bear daintily walked on the outer edges of the path so as to avoid it. Finally, I got it. The mud had my smell all over it. It was "Maureen's mud," and the cubs had been schooled to always avoid anything belonging to Maureen. Once I understood, I walked through the mud myself, and seeing this they decided it was okay for them too.

The track collection proceeded nicely, except that I was short a good sample of the right forepaw. Not long after, I discovered a wonderful mud flat on a major bear trail. I went there daily to collect the prints of a variety of bears. On July 15, I persuaded the cubs to come with me to the mud flat, and to my delight, they fanned out, each one leaving her personal track perfectly across it. After six weeks of trying, I had an identifiable set of prints for each of our bears. An hour later, I went back to examine all the prints and found the biggest set of bear prints I had ever seen. This bear must have come through while I was watching a family of foxes I'd become friendly with, no more than a hundred yards away. I cast this big bear's footprints, as well as a set for each of our cubs. When I finally got back to the cabin, I was able to measure Big Daddy's prints. The hind paw prints were fourteen inches long and nine wide. When Charlie saw them, he pointed out that they were each much larger than my head in diameter.

Rick Paddock and his photographer Yuri Gozyrev arrived at the lake on July 21, about the same time that a layer of smoke darkened our sky. It was drifting in from the west and, on my short wave radio, I found out it was caused by many forest fires on the mainland, across the Sea of Okhotsk. Some of these fires were near Khabarovsk and others in Manchuria. The smoke would trigger fog when humidity attached itself to the smoke particles.

This weather had complications for the photography, and it also mucked up our communication with the outside world. With so little sunlight hitting our solar panels, we didn't have enough power to run our computer much of the time. The electric fence was also down, but even given intermittent power, the bears respected it. Its potential to jolt was now part of the world of the bears of Kambalnoye Lake, and they stayed clear.

Our own bears were very well mannered for the *LA Times* team, and again for Paul Rauber of *Sierra* after August 3. The only unusual incident came one day when Yuri was walking in line with the bears, in the guest spot between Biscuit and Rosie. Looking back, he saw a shot that appealed to him and he turned to get it. It was a shot of Rosie, and Yuri walked backwards to keep the distance between them that he wanted. Just then, Chico and Biscuit came face to face with a strange bear. They stopped dead and Yuri, still backpedalling, fell over Chico, landing heavily right on top of her. The strange bear ran away and the upshot was that Chico was given a double scare, first by the strange bear, then by the strange man.

Later, when we got to the lakeshore, I could see that Chico was watching Yuri very closely. My guess was she was trying to figure out if what had happened was an accident or intentional. I asked Yuri to talk to her, to explain that he was sorry. Yuri thought I was nuts. He could not fathom the notion of communicating with a bear. At the same time, I was sure it was important and insisted he do it. He should tell Chico, in Russian, that he was sorry, and he had to mean it. I told him to say he was "very" sorry, and to stress the "very." He tried it a few times and, by the third attempt, I could tell he was getting some sincerity into it. Chico got the message as well. She turned away from him, and we were able to continue on. From then on, Chico acted as though nothing had occurred, behaving no differently with Yuri than with anyone else.

The visits went well, and both teams seemed satisfied when they left. Their articles and Yuri's photographs would, in time, do our project a lot of good.

As August got underway, we started to notice that the bears passing our cabin were heading west. In even-numbered years, there is an ocean run of pink salmon, usually in August, and we surmised from the migration of bears that the pinks had arrived at the ocean mouth of river. I fired up the Kolb and flew west. Sure enough, the first mile above the ocean was stiff with pinks. Reasoning that it would still be a couple of weeks before the pink salmon would enter our lake and pass through it into Char Creek, where our bears could fish them, I made a major, and perhaps risky, decision: I decided to start feeding our bears again, until the supply of pinks rendered it unnecessary. I decided too that this would be the last time I'd do it.

As mentioned, the collective wisdom of bear experts is that we would have trouble when we stopped feeding. But I had come to doubt it. In any event, the final stoppage would provide a conclusive test. When I stopped the sunflower seeds, my hunch would be weighed against the experts' opinion, and our reputation would hang in the balance.

On August 4, I flew to PK again to have an ultrasound test to see if my aneurysm was expanding. The doctor who had examined me last spring had lined up a specialist to interpret the test. The results showed that the ballooning area of my aorta was holding at two inches. Relatively good news.

The day after, I went to the airport to meet Margaret Horne, a retired psychiatrist from Kamloops whom I had guided in the Khutzeymateen, and Mike McIntosh. Mike had a dozen cubs and three adult black bears in his Ontario rehab facility at the time of his visit, cared for in his absence by his mother.

Mike, Margaret, and I attempted to fly south on August 7. I was in the Kolb, and Mike and Margaret had chartered a helicopter. Although there were no specific hairy moments, my entire flight felt dangerous. The cloud cover was low and dark from the still prevalent smoke. I was clearing the passes by no more than thirty feet. There was also a heavy headwind. It took four hours, often through heavy downpours of rain, to make it home, by which time I was out of daylight and almost out of gas. Margaret and Mike, meanwhile, had been forced back. They didn't arrive for another twenty-four hours.

Mike and Margaret's visit coincided with our making solid friends with an adult female bear we called Brandy. Back in 1996, Brandy had been the first bear at Kambalnoye to decide we were trustworthy. It was she who fed on pine nuts right outside our cabin and slept on the path we took each day to fetch water from the lake. This season, Brandy had three cubs and was again living in the vicinity of our cabin. Maureen named the cubs Gin, Tonic, and Rum.

In early August, the first run of sockeye salmon in the lake finished spawning and began to die off. This was the bears' ideal fishing time. Just prior to Mike and Margaret's arrival, Maureen and I had gone with our bears to the lake to give them encouragement with their fishing. They liked us to go along and still seemed to hold out vestigial hope that we would transform into proper bear mothers and catch them some fish.

When Brandy saw us coming to the stretch of beach she had staked out for herself, she quite politely tried to move us off. Our cubs sat down behind Maureen and me, letting us do the talking. We pleaded with Brandy to let us stay. She came within twenty-five yards of us before deciding we couldn't be intimidated.

Now, a few days later, with Mike and Margaret in tow, we returned to Brandy's beach. This time, the cubs approached Brandy on their own. Without apparent comment, she let them fish for salmon right next to her and her family. In an accepting manner, she sat and watched. When one of our bears caught a fish, she would come to us and parade back and forth with it in her mouth. She would also show off the fish to her sisters. Mike and Margaret had a great time watching our cubs and Brandy's family, and another young dark-haired male whom Mike named Walnut.

On another outing, we went together, humans and bears, to Itelman Bay. On a small beach, our cubs fished in company with about seven other bears. If another bear approached them, the cubs would come in among the humans, where the other bears dared not go. Peering out from behind us, our bears were thumbing their noses at the other bears, and Margaret got a great kick out of that.

Overall, I had trouble that summer making sense of our cubs' reactions to other bears. Sometimes, they would seek refuge among humans. Other times, strange bears would scare them right up the mountain. We could not tell from looking which bears would cause which reaction. It certainly had little to do with the bears being scary-looking, or at least not from our perspective. What I had to remind myself was that, for all our interaction with the cubs, we were still witnessing only ten per cent of their non-hibernating lives. We had no notion of many of their experiences, so it was natural for gaps to exist in our understanding.

I had wondered how Mike would feel around brown bears, given his experience was with the much smaller black bear, but he was relaxed from the start. He never got tired of being around them, and only darkness and hunger could get him into the cabin. In the evening, he and I talked bears until Maureen threatened to go stark raving mad if we didn't stop.

Mike and Margaret were still with us on my birthday, August 19. When the cubs came up the path to say hello that day, Margaret and I went out to greet them. The fence that had given the cubs their protection in year one had long ago been taken down, but their cub house was still standing. I decided to untie the rope latch and swing the door open to see if they might be interested in checking it out. Immediately, all three entered and lay down to roll in the old dry grass that had been their bed when they were small. Then I went in with them, and so did Margaret. With all of us in there, and the cubs so big now, it was cozy. I chatted to them and scratched Chico's head, much as I would have done when they were cubs, and a remarkable thing happened. Chico began to make the "churring" sound that Rosie made when she sucked on Biscuit's fur. Rosie was still inclined to do this, but hadn't been doing it right then. She was lying on the floor with her sisters, waving her feet around and looking happy. Soon Rosie chimed in with Chico on the sing-song, and then, for the first time ever, I heard Biscuit begin the strange "churring" noise as well.

Margaret and I could only laugh at what was going on, one of those infectious good times with the bears that can scarcely be done justice to in a story. Although I try to be careful about giving bear emotions the names of human emotions, I really do think this was pure nostalgia. Chico, Biscuit, and Rosie, all three, were struck by an emotion-laden memory for which Rosie's nursing song was the appropriate hymn.

■   ■   ■

Two days before that magic birthday, some sombre news had come in over the short-wave radio. Russia had undergone an incredible economic collapse. On August 17, the ruble was devalued from six rubles to the U.S. dollar to thirty-five rubles per dollar, literally overnight. Though the devaluation and final meltdown were sudden, the symptoms had been everywhere for some time. In our very limited view of Russia and our limited understanding of economics, Maureen and I had still noted the "bubble" feeling in local finances. Prices of various services (helicopter charters, for example) were ridiculously high. People had been importing various foreign luxuries like TVs and VCRs at a clip that suggested wealth. Now, it was as if a portcullis had fallen, and all of it was history. It didn't take an economist to figure out that the devaluation translated into an extraordinary diminishment of personal savings. The government safety net for the elderly vanished at the same time.

Given this situation, the power shortages and non-payment of government wages that had been going on since spring seemed likely to continue into winter. The suffering that lay ahead was almost unimaginable. There was no way of predicting how any of it would affect our lives and project, but we had made so many close Russian friends that our concern was no longer restricted to ourselves and our bears. Kamchatka was our second home, and it was in serious trouble.

August 23 was the day of Mike and Margaret's departure. We had arranged for a Kuril Island helicopter flight to pick them up on its way through. It gave them a chance to add to their adventure a visit to that mysterious place before they went home. I had never been to the Kurils and was envious.

Though the helicopter arrangement had been made, the weather was bad, and I considered the whole plan uncertain. When the sky did open up on the twenty-third, I didn't wait around to see if the helicopter would arrive. I flew over to Kurilskoy Lake to see if any other flights were scheduled for PK in case the Kuril Island one failed. In this way I missed the actual moment of Mike and Margaret's departure and the totally unexpected and unwanted arrival of Vitaly Nikolaenko and his interpreter Stas.

21

High Noon

MAUREEN: Charlie wasn't there to see Vitaly and Stas climb out of the helicopter. I received the shock alone, and believe me, it was a shock. In our fool's paradise, we had believed we were done with Vitaly the day we signed the new agreement with the Environmental State Committee. The transition of power was a done deal, according to our sources, which meant that Vitaly was out of the loop. But there he was. Almost more unsettling than his presence was the mountain of gear and food he and Stas unloaded. They had enough supplies to stay the winter.

Right from the first minute, Vitaly had a smug, bullying, victorious attitude that made no sense in terms of what I thought I knew. If Vitaly did have the right to be here, it meant something had fallen through in the Environmental State Committee's plan. If that was so, and Vitaly still had authority over us, I was certain he meant to kill our bears.

The arrival angered me on another more practical level. I was working flat out to complete my art exhibition for the fall. I needed all the remaining time and all of my studio space to make that deadline. I did not have time, nor room, for these men in my life. As Vitaly started giving me orders through Stas, I went and got the new agreement. I waved it in his face. That was about the state of things when Charlie floated out of the sky to discover our new and dismal state of affairs.

When I got back from Kurilskoy, I could scarcely believe the change in atmosphere. I had left a good-hearted scene of parting, and I returned to the climax of *High Noon*. Seeing Vitaly and Stas, I was instantly upset. I had so hated my involvement with Vitaly that spring, and had been so relieved to sign the piece of paper that was supposed to free me of him, that it was a wrenching disappointment to see him back. But I tried, against all my strongest instincts, to be civil and diplomatic. Maureen too stepped back onto higher ground, offering to make tea.

If being civil was our approach when the four of us sat down in the cabin to tea, it was soon evident Vitaly was on an opposite course. Sharp, emphatic, downright rude, he scoffed at the agreement that we believed now governed our work. The deal had not gone through, he said. The Environmental State Committee had finished their run one signature short, a signature they could not do without. What a sinking feeling. We had put all our eggs in one basket. The basket was smashed.

Vitaly's power over us was no longer in doubt, so he told us, and he was behaving like the tyrant he surely was. He had come to see our bears, he said, to assess their behaviour. When we told him they had shown not the slightest sign of aggression towards us all summer, he treated it as an obvious lie.

As I sat there listening to the incessant voice that had already persecuted me for three weeks this year, I started to get angry. None of this had to do with science, as Vitaly claimed. Nor did it have to do with Maureen's and my beliefs, abilities, proposal, or findings. It was purely territorial, without the dignifying feature of necessity that animals in nature possess. Vitaly refused to see what was in front of his nose, refused to be moved by evidence or argument. We had nothing to look forward to from him but endless opinions, unfailing rudeness, and treatment as inferiors and slaves. And for what? Where was the hope?

Vitaly then told us that he was going to take his gun and his tent and camp away from our cabin. From this vantage, he would spy on us. Maureen explained that he couldn't do that. Our project policy was that no one should camp outside the electric fence, lest they trigger, through some abusive action, a change in the bears' behaviour toward humans. Any such change, coming from outside the boundaries of our project, could ruin it completely. We said this and it was true, but our fear went beyond that. It was Vitaly's rifle that worried us most. All Vitaly had to do to debunk and undo our project was to shoot the bears. If he claimed the bears were aggressive towards him, that he'd shot them in self-defence, or to protect others from them, our project would be broken. Believing the man was erratic and jealous enough to do such a thing, I grew more and more furious.

When Maureen told him that our rules did not allow him to camp outside the fence, Vitaly pulled out his wallet and thumped it open on the table, revealing his badge of authority from the Kronotskiy Preserve. The action was straight out of a bad American cop show. With maximum arrogance, he spoke in Russian, and Stas proudly translated.

"I have the authority to do anything I want, and you have no say in the matter."

I don't much remember choosing my next action. I grabbed Vitaly by the throat and pressed him down on the bench behind the table. I remember the wideness of his eyes, the disbelief they held. What stopped me was Maureen. If she had said, "Stop! You'll hurt him!" I'm not sure I would have stopped. What she did say was "Stop! You'll kill yourself!" and I knew at once it was true. Whatever Vitaly was doing to us, and to our bears, and to our project, bursting my aorta and dropping dead would only help him. However ruinous the future looked, I had to be alive to try and prevent the worst from happening. So I let him go.

The initial result was that Vitaly and Stas did start out camping outside our compound; that is, until the second night, when their tent blew down in one of the heaviest wind-driven downpours we had ever seen at Kambalnoye. To watch this happen was like observing the Divine Scorekeeper deftly at work. It felt even more so at noon the next day when I answered a knock, and there they were on the porch like two drowned rats, asking to shelter in the studio. Some might have been chastened by such an experience, but Vitaly's resolve to gather evidence against us was only strengthened.

When the rain stopped, he went out and gathered scat samples from our bears, so he could prove by the sunflower seeds that we had been feeding them against his judgment and orders. He had to make do with old scat left in the yard, because Chico, Biscuit, and Rosie, as if sensing his hostility, had chosen to stay away that entire week. Meanwhile, I e-mailed Tatiana and demanded that a helicopter come for Vitaly, immediately. Even knowing that the helicopter might have orders to pick Maureen and me up instead, we decided to force the issue. Diplomacy was wasted on this mess. With our new agreement invalid, forward was the only direction it was possible to go.

On August 31, eight days into Vitaly's unwanted visit, Chico, Biscuit, and Rosie finally showed up in the vicinity of the cabin. Vitaly set out after them immediately, notebook in hand. If he had taken his rifle I would have gone with him, but he did not. I climbed to a knoll to watch. Ignored by the bears, he followed them along Char Creek. They romped and played for a while, and then, as if wanting to demonstrate their independence, they put on an amazing display of fishing. They caught and ate pinks until they were too full to catch more. Watching this made tears come to my eyes.

Later the same day, the helicopter came. Vladimir Mosolov, the acting director of the Kronotskiy Preserve, stepped off it. He was Vitaly's boss and the highest authority in Kamchatka over our project. We had been warned on the satellite phone that he was coming, but had no idea of his purpose. It still seemed possible that he was coming to drag us away. Once he was here, what was more clear was that Vladimir Mosolov had no great liking for Vitaly Nikolaenko. As for our having sided with the Environmental State Committee and, hence, against him, Vladimir didn't seem overly concerned. In Russian terms, that was pretty normal behaviour. We'd attempted a strategic move and failed. It happened every day.

Vitaly and I took turns telling Vladimir our version of what had happened to cause this fuss. Vladimir gave no indication of who he might be siding with while we talked. But when he took his leave, it was Vitaly and Stas who were on board with him.

By now, neither Maureen nor I were naive enough to believe we had won anything permanent in this showdown. But when your expectation is rock bottom, just to be left standing is a victory. As the helicopter topped the ridge, we ran along the lakeshore whooping in wild celebration. If only for the moment, the enemy had been repelled from our gates, and we were roaring like warriors of old.

Eventually, we wound down and nature sounds replaced our noise: the breeze brushing the lake onto the shore, a gull's cry.

By the time Vitaly left, our foreshortened 1998 season in Kamchatka had entered its final stanza. There would be no staying until the bears denned this year, as I had a date with a Canadian surgeon before that would happen.

Mike McIntosh had helped us get started on a re-roofing project for the cabin, and Maureen and I finished putting on the remaining tin during the first two weeks of September. As well, Maureen was working unbelievably hard on her multi-pronged art project. While she worked, I wandered with the many bears who had by this time accepted us as part of normal life at Kambalnoye.

Against the uncertainty that blew through me each day like a cold wind, a more powerful determination held fast: to continue what we had set out to accomplish here. That I didn't know, in any absolute way, what the end goal was didn't bother me. It was the nature of our work not to know, not to force things unnaturally in some hurry to find a conclusion.

I picked September 1 as the day to stop feeding the bears. According to all the experts, our bears were well overdue for becoming dangerous, and this action was supposed to guarantee the aggression.

Nothing happened. Chico, Biscuit, and Rosie did stop in to camp for the next few days, just to verify that there were no more seeds. That was the end of it. In their perception, it was as though a berry crop had dried up. Time to move on to something new. Their behaviour towards us did not change in any way.

Looking back, I haven't any qualms about our decision to feed Chico, Biscuit, and Rosie. Thanks to that feeding, they were much larger than mothered bears their age, a fact that assisted them when it came time to flee bigger bears with malicious intent. In terms of our project, not only did the feeding program give us live bears to study, it provided very important proof that bears can be fed, in a carefully controlled way, without making them dangerous. If you took everything else that we had learned and threw it away, that one point was enough to justify a change in how to deal with natural food shortages among wild bears.

After a wonderful final two weeks of privacy at Kambalnoye, it was time to go. Alexei Maslov's pilot flew in on September 14 with a crew from the research station. Everyone helped us break camp—help given in light of my medical condition. It was done quickly and efficiently, and before I knew it, everyone had hopped onto the helicopter, including Maureen, and I was alone. The weather was good and there was still lots of daylight left for the flight to the city. I was taking apart the electric fence at the spot where I had been tying down the Kolb, the final chore, when who should come ambling along the lakeshore but the cubs.

Chico flopped on her back at my feet and reached out her forepaw. I knitted my fingers through her claws and put my palm to the pads of her foot. Our high five, if you like. I wished all three bears a good winter and promised to come back to do whatever I could to make their lives long and happy. We had our problems with the authorities, and I had a problem with my health, but the pledge to return I made to them was in no way false. I meant it, and it helped me get through the painful winter that lay ahead.

Then I took to the sky.

The weather was so fine that day, and darkness far enough off, that I had complete freedom to visit any area I wished to see. What I chose was the Ksudach Lakes, pockets of water tucked inside a volcanic crater. For a long time, the beauty of those lakes had seemed like a trap to me, a siren call. If I let the lakes seduce me, I might never be able to pull away. The year I challenged that superstition, I was rewarded with a flying experience and a place that are now among my favourites. There is even a hot spring in one of the bays that is the perfect temperature for swimming. The beach sand beside it is hot.

With the day in its last hour of light, I flew the high plateau around the Goryely Volcano—thousands of acres of tundra where black rivers—lava congealed in motion—spill down the grassy terraces that flank the slope to the cone. I was close to Petropavlovsk now, and I rounded the volcano to its east side, where a road leads to a thermal power plant under construction. All along the road in the autumn twilight were camps, people cooking their suppers over open fires as their children climbed the volcanic boulders. They were mushroom pickers, granted this glorious night by a new necessity in their lives, the desperate need to take from the land what the city could no longer provide.

Their faces lifted to the sound of the Kolb's engine as I flew slowly by. I was close enough to see their smiles. It is an image whose golden light and joy unfolds in my mind each time I think of Kamchatka, a picture synonymous with a country I have come to love.

Before we could get out of PK to return to Canada, we were told that all U.S. dollar accounts at the bank, including our own $7,000 emergency fund, were frozen and inaccessible. The economic crisis became personal in a hurry when we were told that we would likely never see the money again.

By now we had learned not to be panicked by every categorical statement we heard in Russia. We asked around our circle of friends, and Olga Yefimova thought she might be able to help. Olga worked the systems of Russia with a combination of hard-headed persistence and "woman power." After a couple of days on the phone, she led Maureen to the locked door of the bank and commenced banging on it. When it swung open, a guard pointed a machine gun at them and told them to get lost.

Another unique characteristic of Russians is their seeming nonchalance when faced with loaded weapons. Armed only with her presence and her formidable good looks, Olga smiled forgivingly at the fellow, then hit him with a barrage of dubious facts and threats. She claimed that Maureen and I were important people. Mess with us and there would be trouble. Likewise, Olga conveyed that she herself was not anyone to tangle with unless the guard felt really sure of his power.

They were soon inside, walking the dark corridors to the inner sanctum of the bank president's office. After a long speech from Olga, again stressing our importance, the matter was settled. We got the original $7,000 back, forfeiting only the interest. And when Olga and Maureen were leaving the bank, the guard asked, "Would you like me to escort you to the bus?"

During the remainder of our time in PK, there was no electricity, no hot water, no heat. There was simply no money to pay for tankers of coal and oil. What little fuel remained was being hoarded for the coming winter.

While there, we learned that Sergei, the helicopter pilot who had flown in the *LA Times* crew, had been badly hurt in a crash. His engine had failed and his chopper had ploughed into a potato field by the flying school. Three mining officials travelling with him had been killed. Sergei was the only survivor. Now he was in hospital in Yelizovo, and we visited him there.

The ward looked like a '50s *Saturday Evening Post* cartoon full of men with bulky casts—arms, legs, heads—and a maze of pulleys and cables holding their busted limbs aloft. Typical of local ingenuity, Sergei's traction system for his broken leg was counterweighted with a pan of rounded river rocks.

Knowing I would soon be in a Canadian hospital, I looked on this scene of unpainted walls and rusting welds with different eyes. I felt sympathy for what was going on, and I felt fortunate to be heading somewhere that still had good equipment and the money to feed me and heat my room.

We flew out on October 18.

When I got back to Canada, morbid thoughts translated into a strong urge to get on with this book. In case I didn't make it, I was desperate that there should be a record of what we had discovered. Already, we had a pile of evidence that contradicted what scientists and wildlife officials believed to be true about brown bears. With our orphan cub project and our travels with other bears in Kamchatka, and with our electric fence project at Kurilskoy Lake, we had all but proven that humans and brown bears can interact safely, given observance of certain rules of etiquette by the humans. Perhaps most important, we felt we were well on our way to proving that the problems humans have with bears are all created on the human side. If brown bears really were the unpredictable, dangerous beasts people assumed they were, Maureen and I wouldn't have survived a week at Kambalnoye, let alone years. To get all this across, I wrote as fast as possible every day until my operation.

Events in Canada were also providing an incentive. During 1998, British Columbia and parts of Alberta had been hit with a serious drought that caused an almost total failure of the wild berry crop. Black bears in particular were forced by starvation into the valley bottoms, where most of the humans live. If backyards and orchards solved the bears' food problem, the solution was not acceptable to the humans, and thirteen hundred bears were shot by wildlife officials and members of the public. Knowing no other approach, they kept shooting until hibernation stopped the carnage.

When I tried to talk to Canadian biologists that fall about preventing such disasters by supplementary feeding, or even about the possibility of studying supplementary feeding as a future possibility, I got a resounding no.

So I kept writing to the last minute on November 4, when Maureen drove me to the hospital.

Some people can write engagingly about their experience of sickness or surgery. I both cannot and don't want to. It is part of this story only insofar as it represented a major obstacle in my ability to continue with our bear project. It would have been more than that if I hadn't pulled through.

But I did make it, albeit feeling like a wreck. A full month later, I could not imagine getting back to Kamchatka in 1999. As I struggled with my recovery, I would fire up my computer and see incredible stories pouring in by e-mail from Russia. Fedor Farberov, a mountain guide with whom we were friendly, told of his knee operation. He had to take his own bedding, food, and even drugs to the hospital. The room was so cold the pipes froze.

Our friends wrote of how they had rigged up wood-burning stoves in their apartments. There were crazy right-angled stovepipes sticking out of windows all over PK's high-rises. The price of kerosene heaters, butane bottles, and candles had gone through the roof. The jerry-rigged heating systems and the inexperience of those running them led to frequent fires. At one point, four boats charged with ferrying scarce fuel from an offshore tanker stood icebound while Petropavlovsk froze. We sent care packages, and pathetically inadequate though we felt them to be, our friends were hugely grateful for such items as fleece pants, gloves with no fingertips to be worn while typing, and vitamins.

There is no doubt that the stories of the Kamchatkans' courage and endurance in these hard times helped me with my convalescence. Just when I was thinking I was hard done by, I would hear about people in PK, old and young, shivering through their dark, cold winter, showing pluck and even humour. I would accept my good fortune and move on.

PART FIVE

(1999)

22

A Hard Discovery

While I suffered through a season of surgery and recovery, the project itself had been doing rather well. It enjoyed its biggest wave of publicity yet when Ian Herring's film appeared on the PBS series *Nature* in the U.S. and then on Discovery Canada. The *Los Angeles Times* ran its piece on the front page with a photo of me asleep with my head on Chico. *Sierra* magazine published its article, packed with controversial photos that showed Maureen and me doing things with bears that were regarded as foolish and lunatic by the wildlife management and scientific communities. All this drew attention to our work, and, because the website address figured somewhere in most press releases and write-ups, the number of hits spiked upward.

Of course, not everything was positive. The bear gurus who had refused us permission to do our study in North America were now upset with me. I had not taken their advice about the inappropriateness of my study. What's more, by conducting the work in Russia, I had placed myself beyond the pressure they could apply to somebody like Timothy Treadwell. After simply walking into the wilderness in his first year in

Alaska, Timothy went legal thereafter, securing permission from the U.S. Parks Service. Lately, they had told him they would refuse further permits if he were ever seen again on TV befriending Alaskan bears.

The main difference between my ideas and those of my severest critics comes down to whether people can adjust their attitudes enough to allow grizzlies to share a little of their space, and whether they can change their behaviour enough not to cause trouble with bears in that shared space. I remain optimistic that a better understanding of grizzlies will benefit them, just as it has gorillas, elephants, and killer whales. But what a gigantic job: big enough with the support of the wildlife scientists, bigger without it.

Because of my condition and Maureen's usual teaching and painting workload, we were terribly behind in our preparations for year four. Several friends came to the rescue by taking over the fundraising. I started work on the book again in January, somewhat tentatively. The length of time I had spent under general anaesthetic during surgery had caused a depression that could not be quite overcome by my pleasure at being alive.

In February, I started to exercise. Such a long time doing nothing had left me in terrible shape, and I was anxious to get myself fit enough for the rigours of Kamchatka. Too damned anxious, it proved. I overdid it and wound up back in hospital having my entire abdominal incision implanted with reinforcing mesh. Frankly, this second surgery was more painful than the first.

I was so weak when I got out of the hospital that I was shuffling around like a very old man. I have to be careful what I say here because my father, at eighty-five, was moving better than I was. I slept most of the time. Getting over this surgery was the most difficult physical hardship I have ever endured.

Somehow, though, I got it together to leave home for Great Falls, Montana with a truck full of stuff in early May. There, it was loaded onto a commercial truck headed for Seattle. Everything, including a store of fresh gasoline went into a container and onto a ship for Petropavlovsk.

On May 14, I put myself aboard a Reeve Aleutian plane and headed west to the Far East once again.

So began year four of our project in South Kamchatka. Every year to date, we had entered Russia not knowing if we would be allowed to proceed. The arrangements for 1999 were no more secure, but at least we had built an extra two weeks into our plan for negotiation. This was the headstart I had before Maureen would join me in Russia.

By that spring, the Kronotskiy Preserve finally had its new director. He was Valery Komerov, a well-educated hunter by background who had lived in Kamchatka most of his life. We did not know him, but Tatiana had warned us by e-mail to expect more resistance and hostility. Vitaly had spent the winter doing his best to poison the well. A talented writer, he had published several articles about our preposterous ideas, our mistaken project, and our dangerous bears. He arranged talks and showed slides of Chico, Biscuit, and Rosie, with a carefully concocted commentary portraying every aspect of our project as faulty. Alexei Maslov attended one of these events, at the Science Library, and spoke up in our defence. It was all propaganda, of course, but we didn't know how much of it the new director and the rest of Kronotskiy officialdom might believe.

Surviving the surgeries had the effect of making me more cheerful about the bureaucratic hassles to come. When I thought about meeting the new director, for example, I had no trouble feeling generous towards him. I was happy to be alive. I was also confident that our bears would not have changed towards us, even with another eight months of maturity. Compared to my desire to get back to them and to continue our study, Vitaly's mischief didn't rate very high. All in all, when the jet powered back and slid down into Petropavlovsk, I was elated. I felt very much like I was coming home.

Jennya and Tatiana were waiting. Before long, I was in Jennya and Viktor's apartment with Tatiana, basking in the warmth of their family. People were reluctant to talk about how hard the winter had been, and again I saw a parallel between their trials and mine. All of us were more keen to go forward than to look back.

Tatiana had a schedule of meetings set up for me, scattered over the next several days. What came of them was that Vladimir Mosolov, Kronotskiy's head scientist, was going to accompany me to Kambalnoye for a week. He would assess what was going on with the bears, particularly their aggressiveness towards humans. He would then write a report, by which it would be decided whether Maureen and I could continue.

The new director, Valery Komerov, was a tall, thin man with a craggy, troubled face, but quick smile. I was surprised by how sympathetic he was to the conservation aspect of his job. Not being a scientist, he was having difficulties working with the preserve scientists. Welcome aboard, I thought.

I listened to a lot of things in these meetings that were hard to swallow. Perhaps the toughest realization was that the Russians, after all this time, were still choosing to ignore the main thrust of our project. After three years, they refused to acknowledge that it was about discovering the potential for long-term trust between humans and bears. They preferred to view it as an experiment in restoring orphaned brown bear cubs to the wild. They probably thought this was charitable. If they described our project as it really was, they might feel obliged to get rid of us immediately.

In terms of aggression, the cubs, according to their age, were approaching another danger point. The few authorities on the subject seemed to agree that the age for a change from benign behaviour to aggression was two and a half years. Born in their den in early 1997, Chico, Biscuit, and Rosie were already two and a half and would be well past that magic number by the time we left this fall. Therefore, the experts were sure the cubs would become dangerous this summer. Maureen and I were just as sure they would stay the same, provided humans kept on treating them with respect. If given a chance, the bears themselves would determine who was right.

I was supposed to be long gone to Kambalnoye by the time Maureen arrived, but I hadn't moved an inch. What I had been able to accomplish was the clearing of our container through customs. Maureen arrived on June 1, but did not stick around for long. She and Tatiana boarded another plane for Moscow the next day, where they would meet Vsevolod Stepanitsky, the head of all Russian environmental preserves. He was the highest power in the system that ruled us, and to visit him was a gamble. If he said no to our future in Kamchatka, it really would mean no. On the other hand, a positive word from him would go a long way in ending our bureaucratic woes.

While waiting for the weather to break, I went to the zoo and took several photos for the website of an orphaned bear cub who was there awaiting his fate. The cub was being treated reasonably well by a female handler, but the little fellow was constantly pestered to be entertaining. He was

expected to chase and play with every child who showed up. Bear cubs
certainly pester each other, but I worried that the cub wasn't getting enough
downtime. Anatoly Shevlyagin, the zoo owner, was again keen to have
Maureen and me take the cub, and we were certainly willing. But in order not
to lose the three cubs we already had, we had to rule out another cub-napping.

On June 3, I boarded a helicopter for the trip south, accompanied by
Vladimir Mosolov and our mutual friend, mountain guide Fedor Farberov,
as interpreter. Fedia, as his friends called him, was still walking very
gingerly, as he was convalescing from his knee operation. As we lowered
into the snowy basin at Kambalnoye, I slid open the side door to watch
the countryside while the pilot made his approach. The first two bears I
saw in 1999 were running in the direction of the cabin from about a mile
away. That alone made me think they must be two of our three. I lost sight
of them as we turned to land.

We were on the ground, already carrying gear and removing door and
window shutters, when Chico and Biscuit walked up to the cabin and lay
down on a drift. I was in turmoil at the sight of them. Naturally, I wanted
to go to them and say a proper hello, but one of the conditions set by
Vladimir was that I would show no friendship towards the bears during
this trial week. Most of all, I was distressed by the number. Why two bears
and not three? Where was Rosie? I kept waiting for her to appear. Rosie
was often, because of her curiosity, the one left behind, the one who got
lost, but this was different. If Rosie were lost or left behind, Chico and
Biscuit would have been concerned. They would have been looking around
for her. In their calmness, I read the terrible truth that Rosie was gone for
good. She was almost certainly dead.

To have that knowledge and not be able to visit with Biscuit and Chico
about it was an agony. Worse still, Vladimir ordered us into the cabin. He
watched out the window, holding his gun, and I had no doubt that he
would shoot the bears if they came too close.

Earlier, Vladimir had told me what he expected to find at Kambalnoye.
He described scenes of the bears ripping at the cabin, determined to crack
it open for the food they had been taught was within. In fact, there was
not a single rip in the tarpaper covering the annex where the leftover bags

of shelled sunflower seeds had been stored in the rafters all winter. What he saw out the cabin window were two bears turning over a bit of sod, picking at some roots in the small area kept free of snow by the wind swirlling around the cabin. After half an hour, the cubs wandered out onto the frozen lake and made their way down its north side into Itelman Bay. I have no doubt they were puzzled by my behaviour, the distance I was keeping from them. But seeing that I was not approachable for whatever reason, they accepted it calmly and went away.

That day, I followed Vladimir on a walk to observe the available bear food. At each step, I sank into the soft spring snow. The two operations and the long recovery time had left me terribly weak and out of shape, and I was paying for it in pain and exhaustion. I resolved to borrow skis from Fedia for all future trips out.

As for what food was available, I had hoped there would be pine nuts from last year's crop, but they had long fallen off. The majority of bears we saw were heading over the mountains to the east coast, where spring came earlier. Our bears had not learned to make this migration and had to struggle for their survival here at Kambalnoye, the only home they knew. They were relying on their remaining fat while they waited for the emergence of new green. However, their energy level appeared to be much higher than it had been a year before, when they had often sat in a kind of stupor.

That night, while I tried to get to sleep, I spent a long time thinking about Rosie and what might have caused her death. Vladimir insisted she had simply gone her own way, but having watched the three of them together for two seasons, and seeing that Chico and Biscuit were as close as ever, I knew this wasn't true.

Naturally, I was sad, but I tried to remember as well that our intervention in her life had probably given Rosie two joyous years that she otherwise would have missed. Rosie had always refused to take life's hazards as seriously as the other two cubs, and perhaps that was her final undoing. Whatever had happened, there was a hole now that would not be filled by another. She had been very special.

I thought back to the last walk the five of us had taken. The previous fall, the cubs had been away for a week and we were not sure they would return before we had to go. With a couple days left, they showed up, fat and fluffy in their new winter fur. Rosie was quite a sight, almost white in the slanting fall sunlight, and no longer the littlest of the three. She had finally caught up in size to her sisters, but it hadn't changed her approach to life. She was still the most curious and inventive.

Going on these walks occasionally felt like a nostalgia junket, something planned by the cubs to please us. That particular day, Rosie took the lead, and first on her agenda of places to visit was a side branch of Char Creek that was brilliantly carpeted with moss. It was a favourite place for us because of its elegance. Maureen had never questioned a bear's capacity to enjoy beauty.

When we got to the mossy gulch the bears wanted a rest, but were careful not to disturb the pristine carpet of green. They spent ten minutes carefully carving out three beds from the eroding hardpan on a ledge over-looking a pond. All around them was velvety moss and late-blooming wildflowers. They fell asleep, each in her newly-sculpted depression. Later, when I visited those beds, they would look as if freshly made. The extra one, the empty one, always hurt a little.

After the nap, Rosie took the lead again, something she seldom did, and this time her destination had nothing to do with elegance or beauty. Recently, she had found a hollow in an alder grove that was filled with gooey mud the colour of charcoal and the viscosity of axle grease. Maureen and I saw her heading there and said goodbye to the bears' fluffy, clean appearance. Rosie was supremely delighted to have her sisters join her for a rambunctious mud bath.

These were my thoughts the night I arrived back at Kambalnoye in the spring of 1999 and found Rosie gone.

23

The Chase

On the second day at Kambalnoye Lake that spring, I borrowed Fedia's skis, and the difference they made was a great relief. I felt like I could go forever. Essential confidence in my body was regained that day. Vladimir Mosolov and I travelled on the ice to Itelman Bay, where I could see Chico and Biscuit on a bare piece of tundra high up near the rim of the basin. I sat down on a rock to watch as Vladimir forged ahead. He continued at a good clip until he was out of sight around the shoulder of the bay. Then he came hustling back because a big male out on the ice was wandering towards us. There is nothing wrong with brown bear eyesight. They see at least as well as humans, but, like people, they aren't always looking. This bear didn't see us until the breeze gave him our scent. In response, he ran across to the south side of the lake and continued along that shore. He was a big-shouldered male with a skinny hind end, and I was to get to know him well in the next few days.

As the week progressed, the cubs behaved as if they knew they were on trial, as if they knew precisely what fears and doubts Vladimir had, and were dedicated to proving him wrong. The cubs only bothered to visit twice during the week. They seemed to be just passing through and never stayed longer than fifteen minutes, nor did they act in any way like they were seeking food—all this when they hadn't eaten their fill in half a year.

I finally got a chance to ski up the valley alone. I went to a place that was out of sight of the cabin but within view of the high place where the cubs were sleeping. I called to them, and both jumped out of their beds and came sliding down towards me. Just like the year before, the first thing they did was rub their faces in my tracks. To give them something stronger to smell, I put my hands in the snow. They rubbed even more excitedly in my handprints. Then they started running circles around me and sliding down the snow at me, coming close but never actually wiping me out. Chico started digging a hole beside me. She dug herself practically out of sight, so just her hind feet were showing. It was a quite a reception.

I would have stayed for hours, but I didn't want Vladimir to figure out what I was up to. He was starting to admit to Fedia that the situation here was far from what he had expected. This was good news, and I didn't want to jeopardize our relationship by pushing him too fast, too soon.

The male bear that had gone by us on the lake the second day turned out to be the cannibal we had observed the year before. Though I had seen leftover evidence of such a bear, I had never watched one at work. I was about to have that experience. In the two previous years, female bears (not ours) had used Rosie Mountain as a place of refuge, a means of keeping their cubs out of the main traffic and danger below. There seems to be a time in early spring when cubs are most vulnerable to a male cannibal. If the mother can get her cubs through that time, she has a good chance of raising them.

This year, we watched as the newest female on Rosie Mountain scented the predator male before he saw either her or her three cubs. She looped around the top of the peak, then she and her cubs slid halfway down a steep drift. She took them on a complicated route over the cliffs and back to the top of the mountain. The predator followed their scent, but got carried away on the slide, slipping past her point of departure and sliding right to the bottom. He was too lazy to climb back up.

Next day, Fedia spotted one of the three cubs sliding down the same drift. Glassing to the top, he saw the other two cubs alone. No mother. Knowing the mother would not leave her cubs without strong cause, we guessed she was fighting with the male on the other side of the summit.

Just as the lone cub was climbing back to its two siblings, the mother appeared suddenly over the ridge. The cubs spooked at the sudden sight of their mother and took flight up the hill away from her. The cannibal male topped the ridge above them, and they ran straight into him. The mother was pursuing hard by now, and she tackled the male at the same time as he grabbed a cub. The three of them tumbled together into a ravine. By the time they got to the bottom, the cub was dead and the mother probably hurt, since she did not leave the area the whole time the male bear was eating her cub.

That afternoon, the predator caught a second of her cubs. Clouds were rolling over Rosie Mountain and we saw the mother bear run out of a cloud and then disappear again. When the cloud lifted higher, it revealed the predator male eating the cub.

Two days later, we were sitting on the porch on a sunny evening watching a number of bears, when one of them, a male, walked on the ice towards the bay that was Chico and Biscuit's current haunt and disappeared around the corner. Next, we saw three bears running across the lake. Through binoculars, I could see that it was Chico and Biscuit being chased hard by a male bear. I was certain it was the same predator that had been killing cubs.

The male singled out Biscuit as his target. Chico was able to veer off and get away. I was onto my skis by now, trying to get launched in the direction of the chase. I was shocked and terrified at how close the pursuit was. With each great lunge, the male's forepaws were literally fanning Biscuit's behind. The chase inscribed a big arc around the lake, and then I saw Chico closing in on them. She had got herself free and clear, but then had chosen to cut straight across the neck of the arc on a line that brought her shoulder to shoulder with Biscuit again. She must have thought she could help in some way, or else couldn't stand to see her sister in such desperate trouble without getting back into the chase and sharing the peril.

Together now, Chico and Biscuit ran, disappearing from view into Itelman Bay. I crossed the lake in record time and entered the bay, greatly fearing what I might see. But somehow our bears had lengthened their lead, and were just disappearing over the ridge that would drop them into Chico Basin. Knowing how well they knew the terrain there, I relaxed a bit. When I came to their tracks, I studied them, trying to understand how the chase had proceeded beyond my view. First, Chico and Biscuit had gone up a snow-filled coulee, a strategy that nearly cost at least one of them her life. Since the last time they'd gone that way, a wall of pines had melted out of the snow and risen. They were forced to turn downhill again and the male was able to gain on them by putting his long stride to work. This time they crossed the valley going north, and running uphill gave them the advantage again, though it meant several additional miles of running around the rim of the basin before they were on safer ground. The race was still not over.

I skied back the way I'd come until I could see into Chico Basin. By then, the chase was over. The big male had quit as soon as he had crossed the ridge. He was lying in the snow at the top. Chico and Biscuit were already down in the basin and were coming back out onto the west side of the lake. They raced over and skidded to a halt next to my skis.

What amazed me in that moment was how calm they were. I had expected terror. They showed little sign of being tired even though they had covered at least five miles during the chase. What it told me was that the lethal game of tag was not unique to this day. Likely they had been through it many times, including the time Rosie had not run fast enough.

After a quick hello, Chico and Biscuit continued along the lake, and I went with them. Chico led, I followed, and Biscuit went last, watching the back trail in case the predator male decided to try again. Though not hurrying, Chico made a beeline back into Itelman Bay. Once there, she and Biscuit methodically reviewed the chase they had been through. They followed the trail back to where they had met the male. They sniffed often in the tracks. It seemed to be pure study, aimed at learning for future reference everything they could about how the male bear was able to surprise them. It was obviously an important part of their strategy for staying alive. How they had managed to outrun a full-grown male on a high-protein diet when they themselves hadn't had a square meal in at least six months, I do not know.

Finally, I pried myself away and skied home. It was hard to leave them.

■   ■   ■

The following day, the helicopter returned to take us back to the city. We loaded the remaining sunflower seeds onto the chopper, to be stored in PK as per Vladimir's instructions. The implication was that he didn't trust me, but it didn't matter in that I was no longer planning to feed Chico and Biscuit. The only reason we would need the seeds is if we had a new cub to raise, and I would just bring them back if that were the case.

I was certain that Vladimir had watched the chase the previous day, including me walking in line with the cubs back into Itelman Bay, but he made no mention of it in the conversations before our departure. Maureen and I had made a pact to co-operate with the Russian authorities, playing by all the rules, at least when we were being watched. I had already acted in a few ways contrary to that resolve, but I also couldn't imagine having done otherwise: watching the cubs in a potentially fatal chase and doing nothing. Though we didn't talk about that event, something between the lines of what Vladimir was saying suggested that he might not be as sure of his position as he had been on the way to Kambalnoye a week ago.

As we flew north, I was full of resolve to get back to the cubs as soon as possible, to at least see and try to understand the forces of threat and flight and survival that were playing out at Kambalnoye that spring.

By the time I got back to Petropavlovsk on June 10, Maureen was already back from Moscow. The first thing she was interested in was the health of the cubs and so, within minutes of our reunion, she was dealing with the news that Rosie was almost certainly dead.

When she felt like talking again, she told me about the official letter of support and permission she and Tatiana had coaxed out of Vsevolod Stepanitsky, the highest authority over the Russian preserve system. We were still in business, albeit with two bears instead of three. Maureen had also made progress in her quest to have a major exhibition of her art in Moscow. She had obtained the support of Anne Leahy, Canada's ambassador to Russia.

Even with the letter from Moscow, it took two more weeks out of the month of June to get the final papers signed so that we could actually leave for the south. While waiting, I got on with a new anti-poaching initiative for

South Kamchatka. Ever since the ATV debacle of 1997, we had been determined to get some form of protection against poaching up and running. Last
fall, I had put the idea to Bill Leacock, and he and I had left Russia with an
understanding that we would both seek funds for the anti-poaching program
through the winter. Maureen and I had managed to find US$10,000, and Bill
had one-upped us by finding US$15,000. Together, it made a war chest of
respectable size, and got the Russian officials to pay attention.

In a deal separate from our bear project, Valery Komerov agreed to
accept and administer the money and to provide detailed documentation
of how it was used. The many changes the money funded that summer
actually amazed me. It paid for the construction of a new ranger's cabin at
Kurilskoy Lake and the restoration of the old cabin at the mouth of the
Kambalnoye River. It paid the wages of four rangers to live in those cabins
and patrol from there. It bought an outboard motor and helicopter time.
In my view, the money was well spent and the documentation by
Kronotskiy was impeccable. I kept track of the developments with my plane
so I knew that everything listed on the documentation actually happened.

Despite our long wait in PK, Valery Komerov really did seem to be
doing what he could to help us. The only new stipulations were that we
must have a ranger with us at all times at Kambalnoye and that we should
invite the famous bear biologist and brown bear rehabilitator Dr. Pazhetnov
to visit us for a week, at our expense, to assess the scientific element of our
work. This scientific assessment was the key to getting more cubs, if they
became available.

On June 24, we were at last able to get away. It was the dawn of a new
age—and for more reasons than the loss of Rosie. After convincing us to
agree to have a ranger with us constantly, no such ranger showed up for
the trip: not then, not ever. Maybe it was obvious to Vladimir Mosolov
from our earlier trip that we had no room for such a person. Maybe it was
the letter from Moscow, or the anti-poaching initiative, or a change of
heart by Vladimir based on his meeting the cubs. Or maybe it was a
combination of everything. But whatever the cause, we left Petropavlovsk
feeling that we were over a hump and might not have to put up with much
interference in future.

■ ■ ■

I went to the flying club the night before we left so that I could take off on the morning dew. With the wheels off and the float back on the plane, the dew was slippery enough to allow a takeoff—or it usually was. Almost no dew formed that night, so my flying year got off to a somewhat stuttering start next morning.

I arrived at Kambalnoye ahead of Maureen's chopper and guided them down to an "X" I had stomped in the snow. The snow was so unstable the pilot would not land, but hovered while we unloaded. This meant dropping five barrels of aviation fuel and one of diesel into the snow.

Maureen had a Petropavlovsk TV crew with her to do a news profile on the start of our fourth year. It was much-needed positive local press. She put the crew to work hauling boxes, while I flew to Kurilskoy to fetch the goods we had stored there over winter.

Next day, we went looking for our cubs, but the first bears we located were the members of the Cocktail family: Brandy and her two remaining cubs, Gin and Tonic. The cub we called Rum was gone, likely taken by the same predator that had killed the two cubs this spring, and maybe Rosie too. The Cocktail family seemed to recognize us, and remained totally calm as we passed by.

Then we found Chico and Biscuit, feeding on sedges among the alder trees. When they saw us, they came barrelling down a snowdrift and acted out their full, enthusiastic greeting ritual. Biscuit sniffed and rolled in Maureen's tracks, then slid down them delightedly. Chico came to me and rolled on her back, putting her big paws up in the air towards me. I placed my palms on hers, and knitted my fingers through her claws. It delighted me that she remembered. Her feet had grown so they felt twice as big as my hands. Both Maureen and I noticed that the bears seemed to be getting gentler with us as they grew larger, and they certainly had got big. I could tell how pulled apart inside Maureen was by this greeting, so joyful, but with such an absence in every aspect.

MAUREEN: I don't think anyone can really imagine how sad I was to learn that Rosie was gone. I had always thought of Rosie as the artist of the trio. She was the cub who needed the most love and attention of the three, and was always the first to stop and gaze at something interesting. It was a terrific blow for me to realize my bear alter-ego was gone. Not only did I miss her gentle company, but I felt I had lost a part of myself.

For the first few days at Kambalnoye, it seemed like the cannibal bear danger was over. Then one day, when Maureen was crossing the big bear trail on her way back from the outhouse, Biscuit came running by at high speed and disappeared into the dip south of the cabin. Before Maureen could figure out what her hurry was, a large bear came pounding down the same trail. He skidded to halt as Maureen shouted at him to stop and then stepped over the fence into the security of our yard.

I was inside when Maureen yelled to me that Biscuit was being chased. I came out and ran up the ladder onto the roof. By then, the cannibal male, who looked like the same one as before, had changed both direction and target, and was chasing Chico. Chico was well ahead, and the male soon gave up and evaporated into the landscape. I watched as our bears made two wide loops and met back on Char Creek. Again, the manoeuvre looked like a practiced one, perfected after many such chases. Had Biscuit deliberately taken her pursuer by the cabin, hoping we might intervene?

Soon after this chase, the killer-bear drama ended. We saw the male occasionally, but he seemed to have reverted to vegetarianism, at least until the salmon came to the river. It was interesting to me that a bear who was such an obvious killer seemed to have no interest in us as food. However, the lingering memory of those nerve-racking attempts on the lives of our cubs kept us more watchful that season.

Although obviously it was not enough to make up for missing Rosie, Maureen was cheered up somewhat when a fox she had befriended the previous summer, a male she had named Squint, came calling. Squint rolled around in the snow in front of Maureen and basked in the attention she gave him, and in the squeaky high voice which she put on for his enjoyment. Squint enticed Biscuit and Chico into a few half-hearted chases but must have been wondering where the really fun bear had gone.

■   ■   ■

Now that the danger from the predator male had passed, I felt more free to go off and explore. One of my unfulfilled flying desires was a trip to Lopatka Cape, the southern tip of the Kamchatka peninsula. Though only twenty-five miles south, I had only attempted it once before, and failed. The lighthouse at the point was one of the places off limits to me for security reasons, but that wasn't the reason I hadn't tried again. The real cause was the weather, the southern point being one of the windiest places on earth. On my previous attempt in 1998, my plane and I had been beaten back by severe wind, even though there hadn't been a breath of a breeze at Kambalnoye when I had left.

For my second try, I selected a day of record heat. On July 20, the temperature at the cabin rose to eighty-four degrees Fahrenheit, shattering our previous Kambalnoye record of seventy-two degrees Fahrenheit. That sort of heat usually produces calm air, so I decided to give the cape a try.

As I flew south, the air remained calm but I still approached the last twenty miles of naked tundra with great caution. When I was well out on the treeless tundra, I was hit by a side wind that quickly rose beyond the limits of safety for landing. Closer to the peninsula's tip, I was having to crab along at a severe angle. The air, though moving fast, was smooth and predictable. Between the wrecked boats littering both shores of the point, I set the Kolb down on a small lake less than a mile from the lighthouse.

Having moored the plane at the correct angle to the wind, I made for the lighthouse on foot, asking myself all the windy way what kind of reception I might receive there. In South Kamchatka, you hear stories of people going mad from the incessant gales, especially in winter when an inhabitant can't even go for a walk for fear of being blown away. The manager of the lighthouse came to the door and greeted me happily enough, with no strange gleam in his eye. He invited me in for tea, and we tried to make a conversation out of our couple of dozen shared words. I saw about six people in total around the lighthouse, two of them women, and all but the manager were very chilly towards me for reasons I didn't understand.

Our conversation was interrupted by the manager's need to send out a weather report. I followed him into a room filled with vintage equipment. His barometer was a three-foot-long tube closed at the top and filled with mercury, and open on the bottom end, which was inserted in a bowl also containing mercury. The level of mercury in the vacuum at the top end of the tube gave an accurate measure of barometric pressure. Next, we went into the radio room where he fired up a telegraph and gave a fine display of the lost art of keying Morse code. He could really send fast.

The walls of the buildings were four feet thick, another testament to the wind. In the course of our conversation the manager told me that the local record for wind was 210 kilometres (130 miles) per hour. He also told me matter-of-factly that they'd had to eat one of their horses during a stretch of bad weather last winter.

Taking off from the lake, I flew over two bears, probably three-year-old cubs, in dunes up from the beach. They were fat and looked a bit like Biscuit and Chico. I wondered if they would grow up to be the kind who live off sea otters. Unlike North American sea otters that spend their lives at sea, the otters of this locale come ashore, where bears hunt them. Flying the coast, I saw a few of the giant otters loping along.

The bears are very exposed on this naked point, and take quite a risk to come here and hunt. But even in this place of no cover, they have learned a way of hiding. Cruising along the coast on my first visit, where the land began to narrow and define the cape, I had seen a bear ahead of me along the beach. Making a turn, I lost sight of him. When I came back to where I had been, he seemed to have vanished. I stuck with the search and finally found the bear, crouching in the rough water. Amazingly effective camouflage.

Flying away from Lopatka Cape, I remembered a story that Igor Revenko had told me. He had studied the otter-eating bears here when he was the sanctuary's biologist, and one time he saw a bear enter the waves right at the point and begin to swim. As far out as Igor could see with binoculars, the bear was still swimming out to sea. He had heard ship's captains talk of seeing bears swimming between Lopatka and the nearest Kuril Island, a distance of thirteen miles. Having reached the point and observed the formidable cross-currents in that strait, I could hardly imagine a bear choosing that trip or surviving it, but the brown bear populations on the Kuril Islands did not lie. Bears so often exceed what humans can imagine for them.

24

Where Rosie's Last Trail Led

July was a good weather month. About half the days had been calm enough to fly the Kolb (my standard of weather) and there had been no big storms. Nature promptly intervened to correct the imbalance.

A storm blew in on July 22, and Maureen and I endured forty-eight solid hours of dense fog and heavy rain, trapped in the cabin with all the claustrophobia that entails. Our reward for trying to take a short walk was a revisitation of the downdraft problem. I hadn't latched the door properly, so when the wind and rain swung around to the north, the door blew open, causing the chimney to downdraft—into a diesel stove this time rather than a wood-burner. The olfactory and pyrotechnical results were entirely different. From outside, we heard a booming sound. We rushed back, and from the door could see the stove backfiring jets of flame. Smoke was pouring out the flue into the cabin, and the air was already rank with diesel. Maureen crawled in along the floor to turn the fuel stopcock off. After that, in the surging wind and rain, we had to leave the door wide open and position ourselves near it so as not to suffocate. Our bedding smelled like diesel smoke until the weather turned sunny and we could wash it.

When the sky cleared, we might have believed we were destined for a return of good weather, except that the barometer continued to plunge. We braced ourselves, and soon after, an incredible windstorm began. The base wind was 100 miles per hour, with gusts well above that.

MAUREEN: The cabin rocked on its pilings. Its metal skin buckled and banged. The new floor-covering of insulated linoleum lifted and rolled with the wind blowing underneath. My kayak, which I had just repaired for the season, was picked up and hurled against the electric fence. Charlie was up several times during the night, securing the plane.

From time to time, the storm let up and we would strike off to see what was happening with the Cocktail family. I was trying to sort out Brandy's territory and how it overlapped with Chico and Biscuit's. Some of Brandy's range spilled over onto the east side of the peninsular divide, and she would repeat an anti-clockwise circuit around it that took about a week. She would disappear over the pass at the head of Itelman Bay and then a couple of days later would come back with her cubs into our watershed through the pass northeast of the cabin. From there, they would work their way down the creek and spend a day or two in the area around the cabin, before heading east along the lake to complete the circuit. About half of that territory was also used by Chico and Biscuit. Our cubs would keep out of Brandy's way most of the time inside the area of overlap, but occasionally they would get careless or ambitious, and she would put the run on them.

The world over, female grizzlies with cubs are viewed as the most dangerous of all bears. Obviously, this can be true. Bear mothers are, as a rule, very good mothers and will risk their lives over and over to protect their own. But like all across-the-board dogmas where bears are concerned, I wanted to see if this behaviour was as extreme and as automatic as people thought. Brandy was a female with cubs who had made a leap of faith where Maureen and I were concerned. She had decided to trust us, and as we observed her that summer of 1999, Brandy pushed that trust to a height many would find hard to believe.

I first noticed that Brandy had crossed a frontier with Maureen and me when, during a visit with the Cocktail family, one of the cubs ran around so that I was right in between the cub and her mother. It's the situation we are all told to avoid, right? An almost sure trigger for a bear attack. But Brandy did not turn a hair. She was completely at ease.

Then she started to show that she liked our company on walks, much as Chico, Biscuit, and Rosie always had. If we lagged, she would wait for us. We went on walks with Brandy and her family quite often that summer, and, eventually, I inserted myself into the line of bears, taking the position behind Brandy and ahead of her cubs. If anything, Brandy seemed to like the arrangement, and encouraged it by making a point not to leave me behind.

But the really incredible breakthrough—behaviour I have never read or heard about in the lore about grizzlies—was when Brandy began to use us as a babysitting service. In general, bear mothers hate to leave their young for any reason, and will only do so because of an absolute threat or emergency. But one day, Brandy left her cubs with Maureen and me while she wandered off to eat, going as far as a mile away. This was real trust and we felt honoured to have earned it.

Another demonstration of Brandy's trust happened at Itelman Bay when she brought her cubs about thirty yards from us. When the cubs starting moaning, the sound they make when they want to nurse, she moved to a spot even closer to us, where there was a spectacular view of the bay. There she sat, letting her cubs come to suckle. They were right beside us, and the "churring" sound they were making brought back warm memories of the song Rosie used to hum while sucking Biscuit's fur.

I want to stress the distinction between our cubs' trust for us and the trust that Brandy showed that summer. It can be argued that Chico, Biscuit, and Rosie trusted us because we had raised them, although I think it's clear that it had a great deal more to do with how we had done it. Brandy, on the other hand, had chosen us in a way that our own cubs had not. With all the space and freedom in the world, Brandy had befriended two humans at the same time as she was raising a litter of cubs. It was all her idea; it was obviously not instinct. It appeared to be a swift and accurately reasoned adaptation, made possible because of her keen intelligence.

She had simply decided to take advantage of a situation not normally part of the everyday life of a wild bear.

In Brandy's behaviour that summer, I saw many similarities to the way the Mouse Creek Bear had felt towards me in the Khutzeymateen. I wouldn't say either bear started out trusting me, but eventually they decided to. It is quite remarkable how quickly this can happen once a bear understands that your actions are predictably courteous. It was not my intention to explore what it might take to break trust with a bear, but a couple of events, caused by carelessness that summer, show both the annoyance a bear will express when you've failed to take into consideration the urgency of their search for food, and how much of a break they'll give you if you are a human they trust.

One day, I was feeling rushed on a Web entry that was late. It was well into the evening when I finished writing the passage and, with a storm brewing, I decided to run out and take some digital photos of the cubs eating pine nuts. I went to where I had seen them earlier and, sure enough, found them just as it was turning dark. Chico was in the middle of a patch of pine on a small knoll and I began by taking a flash picture of her from a fair distance away. She made no sign of being annoyed, so I moved in and took a couple more. Finally, I was right in front of her, peering through the dim viewfinder, trying to get a final close-up that showed how she balanced the cone on the back of her paw. The camera was suddenly jerked from my hand. She had moved so fast, I didn't even see it. Her claws had deftly hooked the neck strap that, instead of being around my neck, was dangling below the camera. I watched the camera arc out into the brush, where it landed softly. When I glanced back at Chico, she had picked out another cone and was calmly dissecting it as though nothing had happened. I told her I was sorry, retrieved the camera, and sheepishly went home.

Brandy gave me a similar message that same fall. She had a particular routine for fishing on the east shore in a place where there was a steep drop into the lake. She would patrol a section of shore over and over, moving between vantage points that allowed her to look down into the lake from above. When she saw a salmon venture into shallow water, she would make a dash down the slope and try to jump on the fish. She was very good at this. Her cubs were close at hand, ready to take their share of the catch.

One day, I was sitting on a big boulder that several other bears, but not Brandy, often stood on while fishing. It was a few steps out in the water from shore and about sixty feet from one of Brandy's lookouts. I watched her climb to that place and I draped myself over the rock to be more inconspicuous, so I wouldn't scare off any of the fish she was trying to catch. My plan was to photograph her flying descent and the splash when she leapt on the fish in front of me.

She was shifting her weight from one front foot to the other, studying the water on both sides of my rock. Finally, she must have decided I was keeping the salmon from entering the spot where she wanted them. She stopped looking for fish and looked at me. I should have taken the hint right then, but still imagining great photos, I stayed put. She gave me a few more seconds to understand her problem, then walked very deliberately down her runway. When she was about thirty feet away, she made a short rush at me, stopping at the edge of the water.

By then, I had the message and was climbing off the rock, insisting out loud that I was sorry. "I get it, Brandy. I'll move." She leaned out over the water as I circled her to get back to shore. She watched carefully until it was clear I was leaving. There was no malice that I could see, only sternness.

These were two of the lessons that taught me that there was room for mistakes in the trust between a bear and a human, in the bear's point of view. If a human could learn not to be belligerent after making a mistake, the two could go on having an enjoyable relationship.

By year four, our project covered a lot more territory than the basin in which we lived, and it had many facets beyond raising orphans and watching local bears. I was often out monitoring bear activity at Kurilskoy Lake, along the Kambalnoye River, and down both coasts. The anti-poaching initiative was underway and apparently working. During extensive flying in July, I had spotted no signs of bear or salmon caviar poachers at work in the South Kamchatka Sanctuary.

Then there was the electric fencing mission. Maureen and I kept trying to find new ways to let electricity do the police work along the boundary between people and bears. The electric fence around the Kurilskoy salmon research station had been in place now for three years and was a fantastic success. The station and its associated village are the best example in the world of people and bears going about their separate business in close proximity without conflict: a model worth copying. The research station workers and their families were happy not to have bears wandering their streets and paths any more, and were no longer at risk of tripping over a sleeping bear at night. The bears respected the electric fence and did not try to cross it. As a result, they could relax too.

Before the fence went up, the weir had been a centre of conflict, with the bears regularly breaking it by accident as they took advantage of the way the gates concentrated the flow of salmon. Fencing the weir meant the bears had to take a step back from it while fishing. No more breakage, no more conflict.

What prevents the Kurilskoy research station electric fence project from being a total success are the local dogs, the ones belonging to research station employees and families. The dogs get a sense of security from the electric fence and take advantage of it, becoming bold and obnoxious. When the bears fish beside the weir, the dogs get up on it, protected by the fence, and bark furiously. The turmoil upsets what would otherwise be a peaceful scene.

When people leave the fenced perimeter, the dogs go with them, which again produces a tension that otherwise would not exist. Though I think the situation could be improved if the dogs left, I have to respect that the dogs are to these people what bear spray is to us. Just as we feel protected by bear spray when we go into bear country, these Russians feel protected by their dogs.

In the U.S. and Canada, Karelian bear dogs are now used by special handlers to teach bears to stay away from campgrounds and other places where they are not wanted. Perhaps if grizzly bears are to be harassed, this is a good way to do it, because they are less likely to attach blame to the humans who are really behind the disturbance.

In August, we tried another electric fence project: one for backcountry camping. We set up a tent beside a major bear highway along the south shore of Kambalnoye Lake, a place we could watch from the cabin. As a further incentive to get bears to investigate the tent, we built a wooden box, put some dead fish in it, and placed it beside the tent. (The box was to keep birds from taking the fish.) Finally, we put a solar-powered electric fence around this simulated campsite. The electric fence was the Gallagher from New Zealand, developed for sheep and goats. It runs off six "C" batteries that will last up to three months, providing the fence is kept from shorting out on vegetation.

All through August, we kept the tent site powered up and stinking of fish, and not one of the many bears who travelled that deeply worn bear road past the tent tried to cross the fence. This research should prove useful for anyone trying to come up with a practical way for bears and outdoor enthusiasts to share the same landscape.

Even our outhouse was a fence experiment. For three years, all we had around our toilet was one wire about ten inches above the ground. Not a single bear ever got inside that flimsy barrier.

There have already been a great many attempts to develop something that could protect campers from bears in the backcountry. One of the more promising is the development of bear-proof food containers in California. I suppose you could also add Troy James Hurtubise's rubber and titanium suit of bear-proof armour, which he pioneered in a National Film Board film called *Project Grizzly*. After firing guns at the suit, having himself assaulted by baseball-bat wielding bikers, and jumping off a cliff, he went to Banff and somehow cajoled the wildlife managers to allow him to try and pick a fight with a grizzly while the cameras rolled. Of course there was no attack, and I'm sure if the human audience did not see the funny side of this story, the bears did.

What we had in mind as an end-product was less dramatic: a portable electric fence for backcountry camping. Places in North America where both bears and people love to go could be rendered a whole lot safer by the use of such a fence.

If national parks in Canada and the U.S. would take this idea and expand on it imaginatively, it could be very good for bears. It could cut out the late-night mayhem that develops in a mountain campground when a bear decides to take a stroll through it. It could keep bears from getting into cars and other sources of human food, the most frequent prelude to their deaths.

We hope that the Kurilskoy station experiment, being so successful, will become a model for other settlements in bear country, hopefully all over the world. In British Columbia and Alberta, the bear death toll in the drought year of 1998 (bears killed by wildlife officials and others) peaked at 2,000, which, as far as I'm concerned, is totally unacceptable if we want to consider ourselves civilized—especially when a viable alternative exists.

In late August, I got a sharp reminder of what can happen with a bear who had no previous experience of our electrical gadgetry. The idea that all the local bears had long ago been educated about the fencing had caused me to become lax about checking that the fences were actually carrying power.

You could tell if the electric fence immediately surrounding the cabin was powered up because of the amount of static electricity that gathered inside the cabin when it was working. The electronic pulses in the fence gave us regular shocks when we were on the computer. Even weirder, we could take a fluorescent tube in hand and have it pulse light in tune with the pulsation in the fence. In one of the sideshows of my childhood, a woman with a name like "Zoriana, the High Voltage Queen" did this fluorescent tube trick to the amazement of the passing rubes, including me. In our case, perhaps part of the reason it happened was because our house was covered in tin. Knowing if the remote fences (around the toilet and the plane) were working was not as obvious.

The reminder came when a strange bear visited our camp. She wandered by the cabin and left without testing the fence. Though this behaviour is typical of a fence-educated bear, my instinct led me to follow the bear when it wandered in the direction of the lake and my plane. I kept out of sight and I saw the bear sniffing the fence around the Kolb, then calmly walking through it. The boat was also inside the fence and the bear went to it and started rubbing heavily on it. Then she started biting it. The boat is made of tough stuff, so I let her go to it. But when she tired of that and headed towards the tail of my plane, I jumped from cover and yelled until she was frightened away.

Needless to say, if I hadn't obeyed the urge to follow the bear, my next trip to the plane would have yielded a nasty surprise. The problem with the electric fence? Four years without incident had made me careless. I had forgotten to reconnect the wires the day before after taking the Kolb out for a spin.

Maureen's 1999 season at Kambalnoye was scheduled to end early because of a major exhibition of her art that was set to open that winter in Canada. The plan was that she would go and I would stay on for a couple of weeks. The main reason for my staying was that we were expecting a visit from Dr. Valentine Pazhetnov, the bear biologist. He was supposed to scientif- ically assess our project, the results of which would determine if we could ever have more cubs. The visit was supposed to have happened earlier in the summer, but Dr. Pazhetnov's busy life kept getting in the way of his coming east.

During the summer, Tatiana had been to Moscow on business regard- ing falcons, and had travelled 400 additional miles by train, on her and our behalf, to visit Dr. Pazhetnov at his rehabilitation center. That was how the September visit had been arranged. It was supposed to be my chance to explain our work to him and to show him Chico, Biscuit, and the other bears who had learned to trust us.

Vladimir Mosolov came for a visit in late August, four days before Maureen was to leave. They were planning to share a helicopter out. He was going to be in Moscow himself during September, and this was his only chance to see how the summer had gone for us. His questions: had the cubs, now very close to three years old, become dangerous toward us as collective world bear wisdom said they must? Were they truly inde- pendent of us when it came to food?

I had hoped Vladimir's visit would coincide with a time of food plenty, but, in fact, the reverse was true. Since it was an odd-numbered year, there were no pinks in Char Creek. At the lake, the salmon were spawning but still had a week or two to go before they started to die off, which is when Chico and Biscuit would begin the big feed that would fatten them up for winter. If there was ever a time when they were pressed for food, it was now. Vladimir would have his test of their resourcefulness, independence, and aggression when they were thin and frustrated—and looking scruffy to boot.

Vladimir may have shared a lot of opinions about bears with Vitaly Nikolaenko, but at least he had already demonstrated a willingness to see and be influenced by what went on before his eyes. I was counting on him to do so again. At the same time, I counted on Chico and Biscuit to be well mannered, even in the direst circumstances.

Vladimir seemed to believe that cubs were only marginally capable of survival. One of the things he wanted to see, therefore, was if Chico and Biscuit could catch fish. The first night of his visit, we were walking along the lakeshore to where we had seen the bears on the mountainside above the lake. I was no doubt brooding on the fact that the really good fishing scenes would not happen until well after Vladimir was gone. Suddenly, Chico ran down the steep slope, plunged into the lake, and started chasing a big salmon through the shallows. This was not a salmon on the verge of death but one with lots of vigour, and Chico, looking marvellously athletic and skilful, nailed it. What an amazing fluke. I hadn't seen her catch a salmon in ages, and she suddenly managed to do so right under Vladimir Mosolov's nose.

The other half of Vladimir's mission was to ascertain the bears' aggressiveness, especially their behaviour around strangers. That same day, after Chico and Biscuit had shared the big salmon, they came walking towards us along the beach. When I say "us" I mean Vladimir, his new interpreter, Yuri, and me. We were at a spot where the beach margin was narrow, hemmed in by a bench of tundra just the right height for sitting. I asked Vladimir and Yuri to sit there, and I sat beside them.

The bears kept coming, with Chico in the lead. Chico was walking the water's edge, and she went by us with only the slightest glance at me, and paid no attention to the others. Biscuit was about fifty feet behind and was walking a line that was much closer to the tundra bench than to the water's edge. If she maintained her line, she was going to pass right in front of our noses.

Biscuit did not change course at all. When she was no more than a foot from Vladimir, she stopped. Her closest paw was inches from his foot. What had stopped her was a sound out on the lake, the splash of a salmon. She looked out to the water, away from the two strange humans whom she was almost on top of, and then, without once looking at the people, continued on.

Vladimir's eyes were like saucers. He really made me laugh by turning to me and pronouncing the English word "indifferent." We all laughed. I have to hand it to both of the men for following my instructions to the letter. They had not moved.

As for me, I had been secretly holding my breath the whole time. I was praying that Chico wouldn't choose this moment to have one of her goofy inspirations. All I needed was for her to break into a lope and fling herself on her back in front of me, embracing my legs or some fool thing, with Russians no doubt flying right and left. I blew out that held breath in pure grateful relief when she passed, maintaining her most dignified attitude.

The next day Vladimir wanted to have a look at the area from the air. Flying was something I rarely suggested myself, partly because of the liability aspect. But if someone asked for a ride, and the weather was good, I enjoyed taking them. Vladimir soon had his notebook out and was tallying the numbers of animals we saw. Knowing that his area of academic study was snow sheep, I headed for a place where I had recently seen a group of rams. They were there, and we counted eight on their usual haunt, a cliff high above the crashing surf.

We landed back at the cabin after about an hour. Vladimir counted his pencil marks; the number of bears was eighty-seven. I could tell by the tone of his voice as he talked to Yuri that he was impressed. We made the flight in the middle of the day, and I knew the number would have been much higher had we gone at evening. On the day that everyone left for the city, I took an evening flight that lasted about as long and counted 131 bears.

The day before Maureen left Kambalnoye, she made a discovery that was both sad and fitting, one that would allow her to go home with fewer doubts about the demise of her favourite, her artist, Rosie.

MAUREEN: I had gone on a hike to say goodbye to the bears, and one of the places I looked for them was a spot we hadn't been to all year: a bench beside a small lake, less than a mile north of the cabin. We had spent many enjoyable times there in past years with the three cubs. Crossing it, I found a mound of debris with a lot of bear hair in it and some bones. Something—maybe that Chico and Biscuit had seemingly avoided the place all summer—made me think almost immediately that it was Rosie. I went back to the cabin and told Charlie. He and the others came out, and we all examined the area. The skull was gone, and, though we examined all the scat in the vicinity, we could find no teeth. The colour of the hair and the size of the few bones kept on suggesting Rosie.

I knew that grizzly bears often cover their kills by scraping up whatever they find nearby. Here, the predator had scratched up a bunch of berry plants from about a twenty-foot radius. That proved to us the season of her death. It could not have been spring because the area would have been deep under snow. It had to have been between the time we left in September and late October, before the snow had come and stayed.

As I collected hair samples, certain it was Rosie, I felt a terrible sadness and horror at the thought of how she may have been ambushed. Perhaps she had straggled behind Chico and Biscuit to admire a bird or to play inquisitively with whatever was underfoot. Like the other two, I have continued to avoid the site of her death.

There was a scientific doubt of course about the bear's identity, but we both felt certain that it was Rosie, mainly because the cubs had always loved that place before this year. All the same, I collected hair samples at the kill site and vowed to get blood or hair samples off the cubs that I could take back to Canada for DNA analysis.

With that knowledge, Maureen left, sharing the helicopter with Vladimir back to Petropavlovsk.

On my own for another two weeks, I packed up the camp and observed the pressing rituals of early fall among the bears. In August, there had already been frost, and with the colder weather came a new intensity in the bears. Chico and Biscuit were all business, packing on flesh that would see them through not only winter but the even more risky Kambalnoye spring. Salmon, pine nuts, and berries were the foods that really counted, and the salmon, though beginning to look plentiful, were very late this year.

Something we noticed that summer was that the siblings were no longer inseparable. On a few occasions we had seen them split up for the day and patrol different areas for food. Watching them, I suddenly understood the solitary nature of bears. The most important truths are often the ones that are obvious, but only in hindsight. Much as Chico and Biscuit enjoyed one another's company, now that they were so big it made no sense for them to feed on the same thing in the same place. Being together meant they would be sharing food that a solitary bear could have to itself. If they split up, they could cover twice the area and eat the whole of whatever they found. It was more efficient. When a food supply was plentiful, like pine nuts or salmon, they could come back together to feed.

This occasional separation was the first step apart, and a major moment in their development into adult bears.

In the last few days, as I waited for Dr. Pazhetnov, I went after the samples that would allow the DNA comparison between the dead bear and Chico and Biscuit. Since Chico liked for me to brush mosquitoes off her eyes and nose, I easily captured several mosquitoes full of her blood for the purpose. But an e-mail message from my scientist brother, John, suggested that I set up a rubbing post on a path they liked and get hair samples instead, so that Chico's DNA would not get confused with that of the mosquitoes.

I put a steel plate on the post with several hair snags on it, but at first the bears wouldn't go near it. To lure them, I applied two attractants. I sprayed it with pepper spray and I dabbed it with used oil from my plane. Soon they were both rubbing away like mad on the post and the plate, and I had all the samples I could possibly need. (Pepper spray is only repugnant to bears when sprayed at them from close range, when it hurts their eyes and noses. Otherwise, they like the stuff. So don't do as many have done and start spraying it around your campsite as a preventive measure.)

The last thing I did was to try and assess the effectiveness of our new anti-poaching initiative across the South Kamchatka Sanctuary. Over several days, in the last possible light, I flew to the places, like Kurilskoy Lake, where poaching was most likely, and I looked for the poachers' campfire smoke rising from the trees. It would be dark along the ground by now and the weather was cold enough to warrant a fire. On daylight flights, I examined sixteen rivers for the telltale piles of netted dead salmon, and often landed to examine sandbars for human tracks. But I saw nothing.

The new rangers paid for by the anti-poaching fund were at work in the sanctuary and, though it sounded as though they were ill-equipped and ill-trained, they must have been serving as some deterrent. I have found that it does not take much of an obstacle to make these local poachers change what they are doing. In this case, it was simply easier to move out of the sanctuary than to bother evading or confronting the new rangers. Although the poaching undoubtedly had not completely stopped, we had come a long way towards breaking the long-standing practice of poaching in this locale. I felt very happy about that. Chico, Biscuit, and all the other bears were much safer as a result.

Dr. Pazhetnov never did come to Kambalnoye Lake. He never saw Chico and Biscuit. When it came time for the September visit, he had an eye accident and was told by his doctor not to risk the long trip from Moscow. Vsevolod Stepanitsky, the head of all the preserves, was going to come in his place, but cancelled on account of weather. He wanted me to meet him in PK, but the weather ended up being an obstacle in both directions. I was no more able to come to him than he to me.

The sad part of all this is that, without meeting us or seeing Chico or Biscuit, Dr. Pazhetnov went ahead and reported on our project to Moscow anyway. The report went to his boss, Vsevolod Stepanitsky, in Moscow, and eventually back to Vladimir Mosolov in PK. It was a terribly disappointing restatement of all the standard dogmatic beliefs. Here are some of his words:

> Brown bears and men have always been enemies to each other. The bear is a large, strong predator. This animal is and has always been a danger to humans. Bears stay away from people because of a well-founded fear of people. This is supported by hunting (there is no other way yet). Animals that are not afraid of people die first. Wounded ones, if they survive, are extremely afraid of people, and anything they find that smells of people. The fear reaction is fixed in bears genetically. One may expect (and this has been proven many times) that bears who are not afraid of humans by the age of 2.5, and especially over 4 years, will become dangerous to people. We must not forget that a bear's life in the wilderness is a permanent struggle to survive. When supplementary

feeding occurs, bears soon get accustomed to "easy food" and it is very difficult for an animal to go back. There exist many examples of this, but it is enough to look at the "bear-human" problem in Yellowstone Park. The problem is over a hundred years old, but it is still there.

That Maureen and I had never had anything but respect, affection and even, at times, protection from Chico, Biscuit, and Rosie didn't enter into the picture. What the report meant, no doubt about it, was that we would not be getting new orphaned cubs. Not now and probably not ever. There seemd to be an insinuation that we had already gone beyond the bounds of what should have been allowed in the first place, and that with the bears we had now we were creating an ongoing, dangerous situation for ourselves and others who visited the area.

The chopper came for the remainder of our gear on September 17, late in the day. By the time the helicopter was loaded and gone, it was after 5 p.m. I needed to make haste and get away myself. Staying another night was out of the question because the weather, already iffy, was supposed to get worse.

The cubs' sense of timing was once again perfect. When it was time to go, Chico and Biscuit just happened to be munching pine nuts nearby. We had a brief but satisfying farewell—as always, it was a melancholy moment for me.

When I took off into the evening, the wind was already close to the limit of what I could handle. Through the ridges and valleys, under the clouds, I zigged and zagged, trying to avoid the lee side of the peaks where the air came tumbling down. Along the way, I caught glimpses of many pretty places, and I had to fight the urge to set the plane down and stay a while: my annual resistance to the return to civilization. The remote life at Kambalnoye is wonderful to me and I always hate to leave it.

While we were away in the summer of 1999, something very important happened with regard to the management of black bears in North America. A non-lethal bear management technique was adopted for black bears in many places in Canada and the U.S., a method developed by Steve Searles of Mammoth Lakes, California. Following is a description of the new system from a Vancouver newspaper:

An innovative new concept in bear management has come into use in North America. This cutting-edge technique is more promising than any other method that has been utilized to date. It offers wildlife managers a much needed alternative to destroying the animal.

Steve Searles, better known as the Mammoth Bear Man, uses a variety of non-lethal tools combined with aggressive "alpha" male posturing to send black bears a clear message of who's boss. With his arsenal of rubber bullets, pyrotechnics and pepper spray, problem black bears are taught to stay away from people and non-natural food sources.

Searles' approach requires a new way of thinking for humans. Using his dominance, and demonstrating a body posture and vocalizations that speak the language of the bear, Searles commands the bear's respect and reinstills its natural fear of humans. Currently, the most widely used method for control of nuisance bears is to destroy the animal.

Readers of this book can probably guess my mixed feelings about this development. First of all, let me say in no uncertain terms that I was ecstatic that wildlife managers throughout British Columbia and in the western U.S. were adopting a different method of dealing with bear-human frictions than shooting the bears. All people who love wildlife, and bears in particular, had to be very thankful for this long-overdue change. But in my opinion, it was more of a step in a better direction than a totally satisfactory destination.

I can't say more than that about Searles's non-lethal technique. Though it provides an alternative to killing the animal, thank goodness, it still functions by domination through fear. Domination is hardly a new idea, certainly not to human males. Therefore, while I was encouraged by the change, I couldn't be delighted by it.

The newspaper piece spoke of "commanding a bear's respect." The cliché "commanding respect" has always seemed haywire to me, whether applied to humans or to animals. Can you really command anybody's respect, or are you really just making them fear you? In my dictionary, fear is defined as "a painful emotion caused by impending danger or evil, a state of alarm." Respect is defined as "deferential esteem felt or shown towards (a) person." I doubt anybody earns the esteem of a bear by shooting it in the face with pepper spray or in the rear with a rubber bullet.

Respect from bears should be the goal, but our work indicates that you have to be willing to earn a bear's respect to get it. Once you have a bear's respect and trust, you're not apt to lose it.

The non-lethal technique was also restricted to black bears on the assumption that they are easier to dominate than grizzlies. Obviously, Maureen and I could not wholeheartedly applaud a solution that left the brown bear in the solution-by-gunfire zone.

When bear managers are ready to look beyond that system to the next step, I hope to be in a position to work with them. To my way of thinking, that next step would be for humans to relax in the presence of bears, enough to become the students of bears, rather than their would-be dominators. Maureen and I had proven that it was not a pipe dream, but a question of how high people are willing to set the bar.

A final footnote to year four is that the comparisons of the dead bear's DNA samples to those from Chico and Biscuit did show a family connection. We had definitely found Rosie.

PART SIX

(2000)

25

A Grand Unveiling

Almost from the beginning of our Kamchatka bear project, Maureen and I had considered how it should end. When the cubs were still the size of badgers, and I could pick them up one-handed by the scruff of their necks, we talked of going on until those little females were bear mothers, and Maureen and I were grandparents. It started out as a joke, but became a sincere target for us, and remained so year after year. As any such blessed events were unlikely until Chico and Biscuit were five or six years of age, we had a lot of project ahead of us as we completed year four and headed into year five.

There was also a feeling of things coming to maturity and fruition. Our real goal, above and beyond anything that would happen in our lives or the lives of Chico and Biscuit, was to cause real positive change in how the world regards bears and responds to them. In metaphorical terms, we had put our shoulders to a boulder many times our size. After four years of pushing, it suddenly felt different. It wasn't exactly rolling down the hill, but it had perhaps begun to give a little. The act of pushing the stone seemed less lunatic.

The feeling that we were progressing towards our biggest goals also helped us accept those things that were never going to be. Around the millennium New Year, we received an e-mail from Vladimir Mosolov saying that, once again, his committee was refusing us more cubs for Kambalnoye Lake. Given Dr. Pazhetnov's sight-unseen negative report in the fall, this wasn't much of a surprise, but it still caused a dramatic change. We had tried and failed so often to get more cubs that being told no yet again should not have stopped us—but it did. Somehow, Maureen and I accepted that this decision was final. We would not try for new cubs again. Instead, we decided that watching Chico and Biscuit mature into parents and putting the anti-poaching program for South Kamchatka Sanctuary into top-notch working order were projects enough to fulfill us.

As we moved into year five, Maureen was putting the finishing touches on the powerful manifestation of what the bears of Kamchatka had drawn out of her as an artist: an exhibition of the substantial body of art that she had created since the beginning of our project. Immediately upon returning from Russia in the fall of 1999 she began creating a sculpture in the form of a concrete pathway of bear tracks, the ones she had cast in Russia, a "bearway" on which people would walk when entering the exhibition.

The exhibition was called *Through the Eyes of the Bear* and it was the inaugural event at Alberta's new Art Gallery of Calgary. It was a huge success. And it was only the beginning of what was going to be an amazing year for Maureen. Components of *Through the Eyes of the Bear* were scheduled to travel to the city of Ljubljana in Slovenia, then to the Camac Art Centre in Marnay, near Paris, and on again the next fall to the Contemporary Art Centre in Moscow. For years I had watched Maureen struggle in a totally committed way. Now the world was going to experience what I had long enjoyed in private. There was little doubt of how much good these exhibitions would do for our project and its primary goal of a more balanced and benign view of bears.

Interest in the Calgary presentation was enormous, and there was some controversy, as some of the professional art community thought Muareen was popularizing her art too much. But rather than worry about that or bask in the glory, we had to pack ourselves up, along with the travelling version of the exhibition, and head for Slovenia. While the travelling edition went up in Ljubljana, I was scheduled to give four slide talks in the region. Then Maureen would be off to France, I to Canada, and somehow we would be ready for Kamchatka in May and June.

The trip Maureen and I took to Slovenia in the spring of 2000 is off the beaten track of this story, but worth mentioning for several reasons. Slovenia is situated between Hungary and the Adriatic Sea, and we arrived in the city of Ljubljana smack in the middle of a brown-bear controversy.

Local farmers had been having bear trouble, and, recently, one of them had been badly injured by a bear. This situation had touched off a reactionary fury and a demand that 200 of the country's remaining 300 to 500 bears be destroyed. On the other side, Slovenia boasts a wildlife bio-diversity second only to Albania in all of Europe, and conservation advocates were fighting to see that bears stayed part of it. Tensions were high, and our arrival, obviously on the side of bears, may not have seemed as accidental as it was.

While Maureen prepared for her opening, I got the lowdown on the bear attack. It was a typical scenario. The farmer and his dog, walking in the woods, had come upon a female bear with her cubs. The dog ran ahead and barked at the bear. The bear took a run at the dog, who retreated and stood behind the farmer. The bear attacked the farmer, who was hurt badly enough to keep him in hospital for ten days. As in Canada, the tolerance in Slovenia is zero where bear attacks are concerned, despite the fact that such incidents are much rarer than, say, car accidents.

I had all this in mind when we did our slide lectures. One group we talked to were farmers. Their interest picked up when I said I had ranched in Alberta's grizzly country for eighteen years. I showed them a video taken by a rancher friend on various ranches around Waterton Lakes National Park. At one point, a grizzly and her yearling cub are shown eating a cow that had died of natural causes. Other cows and calves graze calmly within feet of them. The Slovenian farmers watched with interest, though I knew they did not fully trust what they were seeing.

Another audience consisted largely of hunters. Again, I was able to win their attention by telling them I grew up in a hunting family. What I found out was that legislation compelled the hunters to do their bear hunting from a high stand over bait. Once again, I was very disappointed in the people who make a sport of killing. Shouldn't a hunter have the honour of assuming some small share of the risk? Isn't a high-power rifle advantage enough?

We were taken to one of these stands by a man who controlled a large hunting territory. We saw bear tracks, but the bears themselves were shy and nocturnal because of the hunting. The hunter was feeding the bears, because warm weather and a lack of snow had kept them from hibernating over the winter. I grilled him about whether the bears had shown any aggression as a result of the feeding. He said no. He claimed it had prevented the bears from going into nearby populated areas and from eating farmers' crops. Non-hunters told me the practice was designed to control bear movement and increase the hunters' advantage even more. I took it as more evidence that feeding bears, if done correctly, could become a way of preventing rather than causing bear-human scrapes.

One of our slide presentations was followed by a 70-minute TV debate with a local wildlife expert and a university professor. After watching an excerpt of Ian Herring's film, the wildlife man called the story of our Kamchatka project "a fairy tale." For this, he got a blast from Maureen. When she was through with him, he was more careful with his choice of words.

I couldn't quite understand why these people were so incredulous when confronted with what we were saying and what they saw in our slides and videos. It seemed that, despite a long history of living with bears, the Slovenians were nonetheless persuaded by the idea of bear as unpredictable killer. At the same time, it was an education for us to see how well their bears did living in such a densely populated place. I saw a bear-crossing marked on a highway not far from several villages, and we were told that the bears made a habit of winding their way unobtrusively through these towns to get across the valley to the mountains on the other side. They had been doing it for hundreds of years. Slovenia has also made a considerable effort to keep their bears from having to cross major highways by creating over- and underpasses for them.

If the credibility gap between us could be bridged, there was a lot we could learn from one another. The best thing was that the Slovenians were willing to listen and share, and that their country had gone to the trouble and expense of bringing us in, which was really all we could ask. (To add a happy ending to the Slovenia story, the 200 threatened bears were saved when a more bear-friendly minister was installed.)

MAUREEN: As if continuing the theme from Slovenia my exhibition at Marnay, France, went up at the same time that a bear controversy was being aired between conservationists and the sheep and cattle farmers of the Pyrenees. The farmers wanted the few remaining brown bears to be removed, while the conservationists were arguing for them to stay and for the farmers to live with them in peace as their forefathers had known how to do. In France, I was often asked how farmers and grizzlies could ever possibly share the same country, and it helped to be able to trot out my central British Columbia ranch upbringing: a ranch where bears, cattlemen and cattle had coexisted for a long time.

After some frantic preparation back in Canada, I headed for Russia in May. Maureen stayed at home to complete a big sculpture commission—another bearway—and hoped to join me in late June.

When I arrived in Petropavlovsk to begin year five, the city was deep in snow and more storms were on the way. Naturally, my strongest urge was to get south to Chico and Biscuit. The shock of Rosie's absence last spring was still reverberating in me somewhere, as was the scene of Biscuit running flat out, inches beyond the claws of the cannibal male. Chico and Biscuit were probably a hundred pounds bigger now, and much stronger and faster, but I knew that food conditions would determine the energy they would have to fight back if a cannibal happened to be operating in the valley again this spring. What kept me from getting south as quickly as I wanted was not bureaucracy, for a change, but weather. Due to a long storm, I didn't get to Kambalnoye until June 2.

The flight south began the now-annual, one-week prelude to our project year: the reconnoitring of Chico and Biscuit's behaviour that the administrators needed to satisfy themselves that our bears had not become dangerous. This time, the party included Tatiana, a new ranger named Igor Kuleshov, and me. We flew in by helicopter.

The young ranger's recent life story provides some insight into the ranger system in Russia. Very recently, Igor had come from Moscow, where he had been a bus driver and a businessman's bodyguard. He flew the 7,000 miles to Kamchatka on a one-way ticket, paid for by himself, with no job waiting. He had been lucky enough to get on as a ranger with the Kronotskiy Preserve. When he realized the job would take him deep into the wilderness, he asked the director for some equipment: an axe, a knife, a backpack. He was told no. He asked for an advance against his 450 rubles monthly salary (US$16) so he could buy some of it himself and was again refused. While he waited for the helicopter to take him south, he ran out of money altogether and spent the last couple of nights of rain and snow sleeping in the streets.

Igor had never seen a bear in his life. He had no formal training as a ranger. But he did have a dream of living self-sufficiently in the wild. After our week at Kambalnoye, he would be dropped off at the ranger cabin at Kurilskoy Lake for the summer.

The helicopter I had rented was small. Having emptied the cabin last fall, we had to take enough gear back in to support ourselves for the week. It was a squeeze, and the pilot had a little trouble getting the chopper off the ground. Flying south, my thoughts were mostly about Chico and Biscuit, but I did think about the bigger picture too. If the cubs had survived, and if they were as good-natured towards us as they had always been, would it finally make a difference to how grizzlies were perceived in the parts of the world lucky enough to still have them? Would the fact that they were unaggressive to humans, despite having been fed in their first and second years, affect the perception that feeding a bear always leads to danger? One of the stories I had heard at home was about eighteen starving grizzlies being shot at Rivers Inlet, British Columbia, because the salmon had failed to come to their river and they had gone, in their hunger, to the nearest town. If these bears could have been given corn or seeds to get them through, could they have stayed among the living?

As soon as the helicopter landed at Kambalnoye Lake, I knew the cabin had been broken into. A few shutters were off, and the door to the studio/storage annex stood open. I was under the impression that a ranger had been posted for the winter to the river-mouth cabin, and my first thought, or hope, was that he had skied upriver to Kambalnoye during the winter and stayed a while. But, as I looked around at the mess, in and outside the cabin, I couldn't believe it. Everything was strewn around, not by bears but definitely by people. The linoleum had been hacked by an axe when the interloper had split wood indoors and missed. The place was really dirty. Two jerry cans of aircraft gas hidden in Maureen's dark room were empty. Surely, a ranger would have more respect.

But, if it wasn't a ranger, then who? The possibility I hated most was poachers on snow machines. This was more consistent with the state of the cabin and also fit the fact that there were almost no bears around. That day, with the spotting scope, we saw only one bear, on a distant ridge.

That night, I had a hard time sleeping. The wind was lashing the cabin. I still didn't know what had happened to Chico and Biscuit. I kept imagining them coming out of their den, so innocent of humankind's darker side. Everyone was afraid of the danger bears posed to people because of their lack of fear. I knew damn well that bears were the ones who were in danger.

But I had also seen evidence of a happier possibility. Outside the cabin on a bit of tundra that had melted out were signs of fresh digging, where a bear had been after roots. Near the cub house was a fresh track in the mud. Last year, I had seen the same signs in almost the same places. Given that the bit of tundra could only have melted within the last week or so, and that the damage in the cabin looked older than that, I persuaded myself that the cubs were probably still alive and maybe not far away. Clinging to that interpretation, I fell asleep.

By morning, the wind had dropped and the sun was shining. The three of us headed out after breakfast along the lake towards Itelman Bay. There is a sun-facing slope above that bay that melts early and supports a good growth of grass. Given how much time the cubs had spent in that vicinity last year, I chose it as our first objective. We travelled on the lake ice, which was all blown clear, watching carefully for the dark, rotten spots of candle ice. I was also watching the shore for bear carcasses.

Rounding the corner into Itelman Bay, I saw a raven about 400 yards away land and start pecking at something that looked like a bone. I searched higher and thought I saw motion in a dense thicket of alder. Looking carefully, I made out the shape of a bear. Then I spotted a second bear. It took some time for the two to move to where I could see more. Once they were in the open, I could see they were both light-coloured, one more than the other. I was sure it was Chico and Biscuit.

When they spotted us, they started to run away. We were standing close together and may have looked like one very large animal. I cupped my hands around my mouth and called as loud as I could, "Hey, little bears!" the same thing Maureen and I had been calling since they *were* little bears. They stopped, and Chico sat down. I called again, and they started down the mountain. I kept walking in their direction, but Tatiana and Igor stayed back. Watching two grizzlies plunging and sliding towards him was probably a bit much for Igor, who had never seen a bear before. Tatiana had seen our bears, but only when they were small.

The bears and I met where the raven had been pecking. I saw a bear skull, a couple of other bones, and some hair. It looked to me like the remains of a poached bear. It was an odd place to be dealing with the joy of seeing Chico and Biscuit so wonderfully alive. They had really grown, and Chico especially was fat. Biscuit was thinner but not unhealthy. Chico came right to me and I ran my hand down the length of her back. She lay down beside the bear skull. Biscuit sniffed my tracks and then rolled on the pieces of fur in the snow.

I signalled for Tatiana and Igor to come and they did, tentatively. The bears checked out these strange humans, and everything was soon fine. I was struck again by how quickly humans can understand by a bear's reaction that everything is okay.

Chico was chewing on the skull by now, which looked like it had been dug out of the snow that same day. It still had some meat on it, and she must have considered it quite a prize. While she was chewing on it, I decided to ask to look at it for signs of a bullet hole. It occurred to me that she would let me do this even though grizzlies can be very dangerous to a passerby when they have claimed a dead animal as theirs. When I first reached for the skull, Chico swatted gently at my hand. Then she lay on the skull and pressed it into the snow. Finally on the fourth try, she let me take it. I examined it and gave it back. It had been 261 days since I'd last seen her, but the trust between us held. There was no bullet hole in the skull.

All of us, bears included, eventually walked back along the lakeshore to the cabin. Back on the cabin porch, we sat and watched the bears continue their rounds until they disappeared back into Itelman Bay. The more I considered the skull and remains, the less sure I was that the bear had been poached. It was the skull of an old female, who could have died as a result of not denning. An ancient or injured bear, who can't put on enough weight to survive the winter, might not dig a den. Such a bear will wander until the cold and snow overtakes them and they die. As far as there being so few other bears, they could have already decamped for the east coast. All of which brought me around to the notion that the cabin had been occupied by rangers, very messy rangers.

As for Chico and Biscuit, our bears had passed another enormous threshold and test. It seemed like all bear watchers had been in agreement that the bears would turn on us eventually, but they ascribed different dates to that event. As of this peaceful reunion, most of those "best before" dates had been surpassed. We were getting into territory where even the worst doubters had to admit that something was happening here beyond what they understood.

If the bears were failing to provide drama that week, I managed to inject a little myself. Tatiana, Igor, and I were out with Chico and Biscuit on a sun-facing mountainside above the lake. The bears were eating early greens on a steep ledge. Wanting to get some pictures of them from such an elevated perspective, I followed. Holding onto a rock on the ledge above me, I took a step out to some grass and slipped. Off balance, I put more pressure on the rock above, and it pulled out. That was enough to propel me off the ledge.

The drop was six feet to another ledge. It was steeply tilted, and it felt like landing on a ski slope. I catapulted off and dropped again. In this fashion, I went off three ledges until the last one cartwheeled me onto a nearly vertical snow slope headed for open water at the lake edge. On my third flip down the snow, I got my feet planted and stopped.

When all this began, I had the digital camera and my binoculars hanging from my neck. I had the thirty-five-millimetre camera gripped in my hand. The centrifugal force of going arse over teakettle threw off the binoculars and the digital camera and sent them hurtling towards the lake.

There was a five-foot-wide crevasse in the snow near the bottom and the waterproof binoculars fell into it. The not-waterproof digital camera bounced over the crevasse into the lake.

Seeing the camera briefly afloat, I raced down and plunged in to grab it. By then it had sunk in two feet of water and was about as wet as it was going to get. Through the 100-foot fall, I had held onto the thirty-five millimetre camera, and it seemed to be all right. (When I processed the roll of film later, there was a great shot of Biscuit on a ledge followed by eight frames of the world from various angles. I must have had my finger on the release button and on each bounce down the mountain taken a picture.)

Once the commotion ended, I looked up and saw three sets of eyes keenly upon me: Tatiana's, Igor's, and Biscuit's. Biscuit was peering over the edge of the ledge I had first fallen from, and she was studying me carefully. Chico had wandered off up the mountain and missed the excitement.

The fact that I was good and shaken is evidenced by how long it took me to notice that I had no glasses. Without them, I wasn't much good at looking for them either. It took twenty minutes for Igor to spot them in the bottom of the crevasse. He squeezed down and got them.

Back at the cabin, I drained the digital camera and rigged up something so that it could hang over the oil stove and dry slowly at low heat. It made no difference. I put out a call to Maureen as soon as I could, asking her to bring another.

Then there was my physical state. I had definitely done something to a rib, but it wasn't hurting much. I assumed it was only cracked. Two mornings later, I was reaching to light the stove when I sneezed. There was a sudden, severe pain. The cracked rib must have been one attached to the diaphragm, and the sneeze was enough to break it.

For a couple of days, I was flat on my back and very uncomfortable. In a message to the website, I wrote: "Please don't worry. It's not about to break loose and stab my lung or anything like that." My greatest fear was the hiccups. After two days, I could tell I was on the mend, and by the end of the second day I was able to walk, much to the relief of Tatiana and Igor.

By that time, the weather was bad and the helicopter was overdue by two days. We took advantage of an opening in the fog to walk around the lake. After a couple of miles, we rounded a corner and saw a big female with two big cubs coming towards us. The bears were on the lake ice, and they didn't run when they saw us. They all stopped, put their noses up, had a good sniff, and kept coming.

Tatiana was not used to facing such a situation without a rifle, and she didn't like it. I asked her to relax because I could tell it was Brandy, Gin, and Tonic. Brandy came right up and I stepped out to say hello. The cubs were two years old by now. They were curious and a bit shy at first but soon seemed comfortable with us.

I was talking away to Brandy during this greeting, and Chico and Biscuit must have heard my voice. They came over the hill to see what was going on, and Brandy promptly decided to run them off, leaving her cubs with us humans while she did so. It was a nearly exact scenario as several occasions last summer. Tatiana thought we were in terrible trouble now, to be so much closer to Brandy's cubs than she was, and I had to talk fast to settle her down about the situation. After chasing off Chico and Biscuit, Brandy came leaping and sliding down the drifts back to us. She never showed the slightest concern about who had been minding her cubs.

26

Extreme Trust

On June 24, Maureen arrived to meet me in PK, exhausted but glad to be back in Kamchatka. She had been able to get another digital camera and had with her all the components of the travelling art exhibition slated for Moscow in September. Three days later, on June 25, I flew south in the Kolb and Maureen followed by helicopter.

The bears weren't around when we got to Kambalnoye Lake, and the weather was deteriorating fast. We had two extra people aboard the helicopter to help carry our two tons of gear and supplies to the cabin, but the ground was soggy and the load had to be dumped hurriedly while the pilot held some of the weight off the ground. Then the pilot and all the crew flew away, leaving Maureen and me alone to get everything under cover.

Before we knew it, we were into a gruelling five-day storm. As we sat it out, we experienced more than the average amount of frustration. Maureen hadn't seen the bears yet, and I couldn't fly. While in PK, I'd been told about two whales washed up on the southwest coast of Kamchatka, one south of Ozernovskiy and the other only a mile south of the mouth of Kambalnoye River. This one, the closer one, was said to be a blue whale.

I know a beached whale may not sound like something most people would want to see, but I had never seen a blue whale, dead or alive. An average blue whale is seventy to eighty feet long and weighs around 110 tons, with a really large one weighing 150 tons. I wanted to see what happened when such a huge food source arrived for the bears, virtually overnight. It was only ten miles away but the weather was keeping me from it.

MAUREEN: Finally the weather did clear and Charlie and I were able to hike into Chico Basin. We had spotted Chico and Biscuit grazing on some lush new green at the top of the basin the night before. I came over a small hill and, suddenly, there were both bears ahead of me. I called out the now ridiculous greeting, "Hey, little bears!" and they both looked up from their feeding and watched with interest as we came forward. I set my pack down and Biscuit nuzzled it. Then she put her face up, inviting me to touch noses with her, the intimate greeting between bears. Her face was so huge now. I brought my face to within a foot of hers and we stared into each other's eyes for awhile. Her gentle, gentle eyes. She seemed happy with that. The two bears felt very much like family to me. I was delighted to be with them again.

That summer had the worst weather of them all, including our first. I won't say Maureen and I were becoming cheerfully indifferent to bad weather, but we were certainly much more adept at ignoring it. Often, we would strike off into the wet, unless the fog was so dense that we were afraid we'd abruptly pop into visibility and scare the bears.

When the first storm let up on July 3, I jumped into the Kolb and flew to the coast. I found the enormous blue whale, but it was in a precarious place where I could not land. There were bears on it, and I watched for some time from the air. I left sooner than I wanted to for fear I would scare them away.

The weather stayed sour, and the next time I made it back was on July 5. I counted a dozen bears feeding on the carcass. Again, I couldn't land.

The weather got even more miserable after that, and it wasn't until July 13 that I returned again. The bad weather had broken the blue whale apart. I headed up to the second whale near Ozernovskiy, which turned out to be a fin whale about sixty-five feet long. Caught in the rocks below a set of cliffs, where the waves had been smashing at it for weeks, it was also broken up. There were no bears, probably because the salmon had arrived in the creeks and rivers by this time. The area was also poaching country. Bill Leacock later told me of finding two slaughtered bears not far from there, both with their stomachs full of blubber.

On the July 5 trip, although I could not land near the blue whale, I was able to land above the Kambalnoye River mouth and check out the cabin the anti-poaching fund had paid to refurbish into a ranger's cabin. Two men were living there, a fairly rough-looking but pleasant father and son. The father, Nikolai, and the boy, Sasha, invited me in for tea. Though we didn't have a lot of verbal currency between us, they managed to convey that they had spent the winter here. I asked if they had been up to Kambalnoye Lake and Sasha readily told me that he had gone up with a snow machine and stayed for a while around April 4. When I left, Sasha gave me a little tea strainer, which I recognized as ours. In a demonstration of honesty, he told me to give it to my wife.

Back at Kambalnoye, Maureen had been touring the lake in her kayak and had scouted out many of the trends in our end of the basin. The big news was that Brandy had weaned Gin and Tonic, and was in breeding mode with a big male. To wean her cubs, she would run them off, but not too far. Then she would stay within a certain distance of them to make sure they were all right. Gin and Tonic hung around for the duration of the breeding, hoping to be accepted back when it was over.

While breeding and weaning, Brandy managed to continue her turf war with our cubs—mainly with Chico. One day, we watched Chico lead Brandy on an impressively long chase up and down a snowy mountainside. That evening, Brandy, Chico, and Biscuit all grazed the same basin, apparently at peace.

A couple of days later, Maureen and I were watching Chico and Biscuit grazing in a small coulee not far from Gin and Tonic. Coming from downwind, and not visible to Chico or Biscuit, Brandy came creeping through the alders. We didn't know how serious this territorial battle might get and felt increasingly uneasy. Finally, she was no more than thirty feet away, still undetected. She could have easily pounced on one of them, but what she did instead was step out and stare at them. She waited for them to feel her presence and to start to run. Only then did she give chase, pursuing them into the alder thicket.

When we next caught sight of them, it was near the lakeshore. Brandy was hard on Biscuit's heels. We didn't like what might happen if Biscuit lost the race. Chico came into view on a cliff above Gin and Tonic, and the three of them stood and watched. Biscuit had a good lead by the time she reached the cliffs. She and Chico had used these cliffs as a refuge when they were small, but she had lost the manoeuvring advantage of a cub. Awkwardly, Biscuit climbed to the top of the steepest part anyway. Brandy climbed up even higher and approached from above. Then Biscuit took a step towards Brandy, stretched up, and roared in the older bear's face. Their heads were inches apart, their jaws fully open.

We were nervous about the precarious footing. If either slipped, they could easily fall 200 feet. Then Brandy stepped back and walked away slowly. Biscuit found a more secure spot to stand, ate a few greens on a ledge and fell asleep. In the spot from which she had watched it all, Chico had a nap as well. Just before dark, we saw Biscuit heading south in the direction of Itelman Bay. She had left her sister behind.

We wondered that night if Biscuit might be hurt, and we went out early in the morning to look for her. Chico saw us coming and walked with us. Maureen went ahead as we approached Itelman Bay, calling. Biscuit finally emerged from the alder above us. She was fine.

Chico and Biscuit moved towards each other, rubbed heads and touched noses. Chico rolled in Biscuit's scent in the snow. The cubs were doing exactly what they did when they met us after a separation, and of course it made perfect sense. It was just that we had not seen it before. As long as the cubs had been inseparable, it never happened. Now that they were more independent, it did. Maureen could see a change in Biscuit's face—something of the cub had left it. More confidence had emerged.

My interpretation of the squabble between Brandy and Chico and Biscuit was that Brandy wanted to have that end of the valley to herself, especially during the low-food time of early spring. When food became more plentiful, during the salmon and pine nut seasons, she seemed more at ease.

The other change that Maureen and I noticed that summer was that there were no foxes. This was sad for both of us but more for Maureen, who had spent a lot of time getting to know the three fox families and individuals like Squint. Now, they simply weren't there, and neither of us could come up with a reason.

That rainy July, I rigged up a windmill. The stormy weather interfered with our power supply and our ability to contact the outside world. Wind, unlike sunlight, was never in short supply. The windmill was an immediate and lasting success. We were never short of power again.

When the weather started to improve around the end of the month, I got out and did more flying. I took some plankton samples for Katya, and, flying them over to her, I saw that the sockeye salmon numbers were much higher than in a normal year. I took a spin down the river where the run of pinks entering the river was massive, the most I'd ever seen. Chico and Biscuit were destined for a feast. Something else that I noticed from the air were two female bears with four cubs each.

While I was at Kurilskoy, I went over to visit with the rangers at the new cabin. It was there I learned the startling truth about the "rangers" I had visited at the Kambalnoye River mouth. Nikolai and Sasha weren't rangers at all, but trappers who had been told they could use the cabin for the winter. Because the Sanctuary could not afford an actual ranger to live there in the winter, despite our funding, the two trappers were theoretically better than nothing. As payment for protecting the cabin and its contents throughout the harsh winter, they were granted permission to trap foxes.

Sasha had been quite open about his use of our cabin, as well as the ranger cabin, and it probably never occurred to him that we would be upset if he trapped the foxes there, since our interest was bears. As well, he probably didn't see his deal with the authorities as any of our business. It was a ridiculous situation. Even if I bought the logic, it still didn't explain why the trappers had stayed on into summer. Bill, Maureen, and I had raised the funds for the refurbishment of that cabin so it could be used by rangers, not trappers.

Whatever fuss I raised about this at Kurilskoy was absolutely meek compared to the conflagration when I told Maureen what had happened to her foxes. She was very close to marching down the river and settling the score with the trappers herself. She had loved those foxes and couldn't bear to think of what had happened to them.

I didn't like it either, but I knew that it wasn't really Nikolai and Sasha's fault. They did what they were told they could do. It was just one of those frustrating things that happen in Russia, and as usual, the cause was money, or rather the insufficiency of it. I vowed that before I left that year, I would get together with the people in charge and hash out a deal whereby real rangers could be posted to all the cabins for the winter. We would find the money to pay for it, somehow.

In early August, I went back and visited the blue whale one more time. By now, the wind and the weather and the bears and the ravens had picked the whale clean. I was able to land this time, and I walked the length of the vast skeleton. The skull alone was fifteen feet long. I picked up a vertebra, which I later weighed at fifty-two pounds. The fins of the vertebra were so wide that, in order to fly home with it, I had to stick one side in the small of my back while the other held the passenger door open. I wanted to show it to Maureen, and to Chico and Biscuit.

The whale vertebra was a huge success with the bears. They studied it intently. It was pretty smelly, and I stored it on the roof of the outdoor toilet, which was inside an electric fence. When the bears were around camp, Chico especially used to stare at the vertebra wistfully, the great smelly prize of it.

Since Chico and Biscuit were now approaching four, and both weighed at least 400 pounds, everything we did with them had more significance scientifically than it had earlier in their lives. The doubters had predicted that the bears would turn on us when they were yearlings. Others said it would be as late as age two or three. The bears were beyond all those predictions now, and the trust between them and Maureen and me stood fast. Because we were now into the zone of the supposedly impossible, I felt I should widen and deepen that trust, and test it as much as I could.

Though Biscuit and I certainly trusted each other, I chose Chico for most of these experiments. She was the one who always seemed to want to go further in our friendship than I had allowed to date.

One of those experiments happened on August 4. I had carried the pails over to Char Creek to get water and, when I got there, I set them down and hiked along the creek a ways. When I got to where the stream began to wind lazily across a meadow before falling into the lake, I saw Chico enter the canyon upstream and lie down on a grassy bench with her paws hanging over the edge. Biscuit was not with her. They had split up for the day to investigate different stretches of shoreline. Chico stayed where she was, watching me intently.

I knew what she was waiting for. She wanted me to look for some salmon, which sometimes enter the creek from the lake. There weren't a lot of fish available yet to Chico that season, and she had decided to save her energy—unless I signalled that I had found something worth her while. I looked around and spotted a large male salmon, about ten pounds. The fish was half-spent, and, though currently in deep water where Chico would have trouble landing it, it was headed into a shallower stretch. Chico was about 200 yards away, still on her perch, still staring at me.

When the salmon moved into water only a foot deep, I raised my hand. Chico leapt up, ran down the slope, and came across the flat like an express train, straight at me. Anyone watching would have thought I was experiencing the last seconds of my life. Chico had her ears up and her mouth partway open. Her look was very intense. When she was within twenty feet, I concentrated very hard on the salmon so she would know where to look. She skidded to a stop beside me, and I pointed at the salmon, which had a convenient white patch on its back where some skin was already dying.

As soon as Chico saw the fish, she leapt into the creek. In three bounds, she belly-flopped on top of it. The salmon must have squirted out from under her, and with the silt all stirred up she lost track of it. From high on the bank, I spotted it heading down stream. I ran along the top after it. When I was opposite the fish again, I pointed. Chico came bounding down the middle of the creek until she saw it too, then took another mighty leap and caught it.

Chico brought the salmon to where I stood and I praised her. It's hard to describe the look Chico gave me right then. I have come to know it as an appreciation of something I have done. She was proud of our team-work, and so was I.

Later, I found a dead salmon on the beach. I called her. She came pounding down the shore, right at me as usual. This time, I picked up the dead fish and waited for her. When she saw that it was dead and that I was holding it, she slowed and sauntered up to me, then carefully took it from my hand.

In all these things, there was a method that I had been evolving. Bears are very serious about finding food in the half of their life when they're not asleep. The intensity of that seriousness rises as the season grows late and they know they have to pack on weight for winter. They won't toler-ate interference in that pursuit of food, but, by the same token, because they trusted us, our bears welcomed our assistance if we chose to give it, and if it was genuine assistance. Each time we helped them, it made the trust between us stronger.

It is important to say that I was not really doing anything for Chico that she badly needed. She would have found those fish on her own; her survival was not influenced by anything I did. Chico only relied on me when I indicated to her that I wanted to team up and help. Otherwise, she demanded nothing.

Not long after that fishing expedition, Maureen and I saw that the massive runs of pinks and sockeye were choking the river. There were huge numbers of them just below the lake. Because Chico and Biscuit were still patrolling the lake edge looking for dead sockeye, and because they never went below the place where the river drains the lake, we decided to see if we could take them there. I called Chico, and Biscuit decided she wanted to come too.

We led them to the lake's outflow, and, from that mouth, they could see the salmon teeming below. But it wasn't a good fishing place for them. Their enthusiasm to find where this rush of fish was coming from led them farther down, to a place where the water was shallower. When they real-ized what a bonanza we had shown them, they were beside themselves with joy. Chico was shaking with excitement. These were not the spawned-out weaklings they were used to in the lake and Char Creek, but a big, strong batch of sockeye intent on going forward. The bottom of the river was stony and jagged with no stretches of sand between the stones. In short, it was hard fishing, but plentiful too. It was a real circus of flying water and leaping salmon. At one point, Chico was so excited she suddenly jumped up on the small rock I was standing on. I am still puzzled about why. There was no room for us both, and she curled her forepaw completely around my legs and hugged them. Any bump and I would have been off the rock and into the boulders. I try to stay calm in those kinds of situations, but finally I had to yell "Chico!" She carefully unwrapped her paw from around me and plopped back into the water. I'm pretty sure she was trying to thank me for the good fishing spot.

In four years, we had seen our bears near this section of river only once. We had never seen Brandy here. It shows how rigidly their sense of territory is defined. Interestingly, once Chico found this place, she would not leave, perhaps having added it to her home range. But after that first day below the lake, Biscuit went back to Char Creek, where she and Brandy were soon gorging on pinks, with not the slightest sign of wariness between them.

The fact that Chico wouldn't leave the new fishing hole led to our next adventure together. I was beginning to wonder if I had done her any favours. The main surge of salmon had by now passed into the lake, and Chico's feet were getting awfully sore from plunging and running on the jagged rocks. Brandy and Biscuit were having a much better time of it on Char Creek, so I decided to try to lead Chico there.

I have a special way of calling Chico's name when I really want her to pay attention. When I found her at her fishing hole, I used that call and suggested she follow me. It took two false starts before she figured out I was serious and came along. We had about two miles to go, and it was by far shorter to leave the river and cut across the tundra. At one point, I had to crawl on my hands and knees through some really twisted and bent-over alder, and Chico was right behind me, her big canines not a foot from my butt. I decided, given Chico's sudden urges to playfulness, this was trust carried too far. I rolled aside and asked her to take the lead. She stepped over my legs, then rushed through to the clearing ahead. There she waited for me to extricate myself. We continued across the tundra.

Chico was starting to get charged up. She trusted me not to lead her this far unless there was something really good ahead. She couldn't stand the suspense and rushed off ahead several times towards the lakeshore or a creek. Each time, I called her back and we continued. Finally, we came to the stream that was full of pinks. Chico could see them, but the water was deep and I asked her to come with me farther upstream. We continued to where a shallow riffle was loaded with spawning fish. Chico's ears were up, and she was looking at me with that wonderful "What a friend!" expression. Then she jumped in and began her feast. Before I left I watched her eat six salmon in a matter of minutes.

Making Chico understand the difference between serious food-finding and play did cause a few tense moments. On the rare occasions when it was calm and clear for several days in a row, the small lake north of the cabin would warm up enough to swim. Maureen and I used these occurrences as opportunities to bathe. It was inevitable that one day Chico and Biscuit would come along to investigate. When it finally did happen, Maureen was on shore and I was in the water. I called to Chico and I'm sure she thought I had spotted a fish for her. In a few big bounds, she made it into the deep water and started swimming straight for me. I must confess my nakedness made me feel very vulnerable, especially when she got within a few yards and put her face underwater. She was looking for the dead salmon she expected to be on the lake bottom beneath me. What she saw were my white feet treading water, and, for a moment, she must have thought they were the fish I had called her about. Luckily for me, as she lunged forward her visibility improved enough that she saw my feet as feet. She calmed down and we swam together across the lake. I was lucky enough to swim with both cubs once, later that year.

This trust was not exclusive to our relationship with Chico and Biscuit. It existed with other bears, most notably Brandy, but also her cubs, Gin and Tonic, who continued to trust us after they were weaned. The male we called Walnut, whom we had met in 1998 during Mike McIntosh and Margaret Horne's visit, also trusted us, even though he only visited the area every August. Because of the difference in the kind of relationship we had with these other bears, the trust was expressed at a slightly greater remove, which allowed us to share the same area without being distracted by one another's activities. This was the level of trust I felt could realistically be achieved between people and bears who needed to share any area of mutual interest.

In late August, when the pinks were still spawning in the creek above the cabin, Brandy was catching them among the big boulders in the canyon. I was walking upstream and went right up to a little waterfall without realizing that Brandy had wedged herself into the rocks there. She was right under the waterfall, with just a little of her bum showing. I didn't notice and was only a few feet away when she suddenly backed out. We surprised each other completely. The sudden sizzle of fear at the sight of the bear so close and backing right at me dissipated when I recognized Brandy. I could tell that the same up-and-down pattern of emotion was happening in her. She took a deep breath and resumed fishing.

That this was not a blanket trust, bestowed on all humans, was illustrated one day when I flew Bill in from Kurilskoy for a visit. Maureen and I took him on a walk that led to Brandy. Brandy was fishing, and she wouldn't let us get within forty yards of her. If we tried to come any closer, she would leave the creek. Obviously, she did not trust the stranger. Bill was only there for the day so we couldn't experiment to see how long it would take for her to gain some trust with him.

MAUREEN: In mid-August that year, Biscuit and I were walking down the creek from the upper canyon, nearing a bend where the creek enters a second, lower canyon. Biscuit was on the other side of the creek from me, and I could see, before Biscuit could, that Brandy had emerged from the lower canyon and was heading up on Biscuit's side. Biscuit was intent on her fishing and didn't see Brandy until she was just fifty feet away. Biscuit glanced at me, then turned and walked upriver. I thought Brandy would chase Biscuit, but she didn't. I lost track of Biscuit for a little while in the tall grass, and I watched Brandy fish her way along the stream until she and I were opposite each other. Just then, I realized that Biscuit was back at my side. She was looking back and forth from Brandy to me and making the chuffing sound that is a bear's way of warning another bear of danger. I talked to Brandy then, and Biscuit walked away out onto the tundra, but not far. Biscuit looked worried, and she kept on looking at me, looking at Brandy, and chuffing.

I can't be certain that Biscuit was trying to get me to follow her away from Brandy, but I'm fairly sure that was her intention. I don't think she could understand the trust Charlie and I had with this bear who was her competitor. When I finally turned northward and walked away from Brandy, Biscuit walked parallel to me out on the tundra. Finally satisfied that I was on my way, she went out farther onto the tundra and had a rest.

August 25 wound up being a major day in the life of our project, though we didn't know it at the time. We noticed that Chico was gone and that Biscuit was upset and looking for her. But that was all. The bears were quite independent of one another by then, and often split up for the day to fish. But Biscuit did seem worried.

A few days later, Chico still had not returned. Biscuit continued to look around and sniff the air. She could not seem to figure out where her sibling had gone. We could see that the bears were in a migration to the east, flowing over the mountain and probably headed for the coast. These kinds of migrations happened every year, but our bears had never been tempted to go along. Now, it seemed that whatever was on the wind had enticed Chico away. As the days whittled down between the time of her disappearance and the time of our scheduled departure, we began to realize that we might not see her again that year.

27

Sanctuary

I had decided that I would go with Maureen to Moscow in September. Until we left, my focus was on the anti-poaching program. When Chico left bountiful food behind to answer some higher calling, it told me loudly that the time had passed when I could do much good for our bears in the old on-the-ground day-to-day way. To help them now, and to help all the bears of the South Kamchatka Sanctuary, my best bet was to get the anti-poaching system working. Then perhaps we could expand its funding to include all of the Kronotskiy Preserve.

To that end, we had contributed more money this year to the anti-poaching program, above what we paid for our daily use of the sanctuary (about US$60 a day). The payment-for-use system had been revised under the new leadership so that everyone paid the same amount. I was all for it. No more playing favourites. An easily documentable system was less open to bribery.

Beyond contributing financially, the other thing I could do was continue my surveys from the air. As the only regular flyer in the area, I could monitor poaching with my Kolb better than anyone on the ground. That is, if I could stay in the air.

I had been after Maureen for ages to take pictures of me flying the Kolb. To get dramatic shots, with an air-to-air look, she needed to be way up high, which was a problem because Maureen is no fan of heights. On August 26, the day after Chico departed, I had cajoled her high enough up the mountain, and I had been flying by her and her camera at all angles.

At last, I was satisfied. I landed on a little lake beside the cliff she had been perched on, and she climbed down. We were having a nice visit when a helicopter roared by, heading up the valley, and then appeared to land. I jumped in the Kolb and flew upstream to see what was happening.

When I saw the helicopter again, it had landed near another lake, and its crew of two had a tool box out beside it. With another pilot watching me, I was immediately intent on making some kind of flashy landing. Because of the wind direction, I had to do a steep approach down a hill. My first mistake was to descend with half-flaps rather than with flaps full on, which would have been more sensible considering the trick required that I keep my speed down to just over stall. The really conservative thing to do would have been to land at a bigger lake and walk the quarter-mile back. But where's the glory in that?

As the plane touched down on the water, instead of staying there, it bounced up in the air again. I coasted along, hoping to lose speed, trying to get back onto the water, but ran out of space. Much too late, I put on full power, but by then I was stalling and the plane wouldn't climb. Almost any other aircraft would have just crashed right there, but the forgiving Kolb kept mushing along at the same height. The end of the lake was ringed by boulders. Above them was a mass of alders. I knew right then I was heading into the trees. I kept the power full on with the stick all the way back. I hit at the lowest possible speed.

The plane stopped in five feet. I was absolutely encased in alder branches and leaves, such that I couldn't see out, or open my cockpit door. I suppose I thanked goodness that I wasn't dead or busted up, but I wasn't exactly jumping for joy. The moment I hit, I said to myself, that'll the end of my flying days in Kamchatka. Likely, the plane was bent beyond repair.

Just then, the dense leaves against the door-panel window parted and the face of a pilot who had often flown gear for Maureen and me peered through, looking mighty scared. He thought for sure I was dead. I signed for him to haul back on the branches, and I got the door open wide enough to crawl out.

Sure of the worst, I sighted down the wing on that side. I could barely believe it, but, if my eyes were seeing right, both wings were straight. I ran my hand down both struts and they were straight too. All I could see for damage were a couple of fabric tears and that one sponson was knocked off. The sponsons are the small outrigger floats that hang from the tip of each wing. I knock them off regularly, so it was no big deal.

I got the radio out and called Maureen. I told her I had crashed but was okay, and so apparently was the plane.

I asked the pilot and his helper if they would give me a hand getting the plane out of the bush. In ten minutes, we had the wings off and set flat on the ground. The tail had to be lifted out of a depression and, using the shovel like an axe, we chopped the tail-wheel free. I folded the elevators and the stabilizer up against the rudder.

My next brainwave was to start the motor. I thought we could use the propeller's power to move the plane out. We first broke any branches the propeller would hit. Then I powered up and we guided the propeller-driven fuselage out of the bush and down to the lake. From there we kept going, finding a way through the boulders and up a steep hillside onto the tundra, near where they had landed the chopper.

Then we started putting the plane back together. It took maybe an hour to complete the assembly. I duct-taped the biggest rips and also taped the fibreglass nose cone away from the rudder pedals.

As for how I would take off, I'd had enough of that particular lake as an airstrip. On the other side of the tundra was a swampy area I liked better. I tried to persuade my pilot friend and his helper to let us feed them dinner, but they were supposed to be picking up a couple of rangers at the coast. They had only stopped to cool their oil, which was well and truly cooled by now. With one guy running alongside to balance the sponson-less wing, I took off and was soon home.

The helicopter flew over our camp just as I was tying down the plane. I knew the story would be all over the flying club within days.

I had been lucky beyond belief. The float beneath my plane was leading when the Kolb hit. Because of the way I came in with full power on, with the plane's failed effort to climb slowing me down, the float went straight into the crotch of some sturdy alder branches and stuck fast. The alders pressed down, then sprang back. No damage done.

The only thing that was really a mess was my fibreglass nose cone. With a few tubes of slow-set epoxy, I rebuilt it. The plexiglass door panels were scratched up badly, but I had two brand new spares to put on. By the time I had the nose cone rebuilt, sanded, and repainted, the plane was looking better than ever.

What looked like the end of my flying days in Kamchatka turned out to be about a day and a half's interruption. Soon, I was back in the air, and a trip to the west brought on the next adventure. Between the mouth of Kambalnoye River and Lopatka Point, where the tundra rolls without a tree to be seen, I spotted two caviar poachers, probably wishing they had somewhere to hide. They had driven an old Russian 4x4 along the rut track that winds along that coast from Ozernovskiy to the Lopatka lighthouse.

I took a little loop south and could easily tell by their tracks that they were from the lighthouse. The people there hadn't liked me much when I visited, and I had been told since it was because my presence interfered with their tradition of making extra income from illegal salmon caviar, bear gall, and sea otter skins. Here I was about to do it again. Once I ascertaind they didn't have a gun pointed at me, I tried to get a digital photo of them sitting among the piles of dead salmon, but it turned out I had the wrong chip in the camera.

I flew back to the cabin and gassed up. After a discussion of tactics with Maureen, I flew to Kurilskoy to get the ranger who was posted there. It was getting late, but I found Misha out on the lake in a boat with Bill. They were with a CNN crew filming a documentary on conservation. The crew wanted to interview me about poaching, but I told them I was too busy trying to stop it!

It was going to be dark soon, and I laid it on the line to Misha, the young ranger. I wanted him to come with me, and we would fly out and confront the culprits. He hemmed and hawed, then asked me if I'd seen any tracks.

"Dammit, Misha! I saw a hell of a lot more than tracks!"

It was not Misha's happiest day. A whole mess of things he was afraid of were confronting him at once, not the least of which was getting into my plane. When he knew he had stalled long enough that we couldn't reach the poachers by dark, he agreed to come, but only as far as the Kambalnoye River cabin.

There was actually a helicopter at the Kurilskoy ranger station that by rights should have taken over from me. But the pilot's best offer was that he would pick up Misha at the cabin tomorrow and take him to arrest the poachers then. Of course, we all knew they'd be long gone. It was 10:30 at night by the time Misha and I flew over the east shoulder of the Kambalnoye volcano and across the flats to the ranger cabin.

That flight was an incredibly beautiful one. Stringers of mist rose into the cool of evening off all the lakes, which made it look as if they were boiling. The sun had set but the sky was full of fiery remnants. Bears parted right and left as I set the Kolb down among them.

I had to get home, so I urged Misha out into the river with his big gun, and untied his radio-heavy pack from the side of the plane. He looked forlorn, but I couldn't stay to calm him. I'm sure it was the sight of so many bears that scared him, or the idea that he might actually see a poacher. There wasn't much chance of his seeing anybody, unless it was the two trappers, but he didn't know that. I guess I wasn't really expecting a lot of law enforcement out of Misha, not when he was so green and only being paid $25 a month. I was proud of him for coming at all.

Next morning, I flew high over the scene of the crime. The creek was too small to land on but the tundra beside it looked wet. When I knew the poachers were gone, I landed by their mess of slaughtered salmon, just to make sure that I could repeat the process with Misha aboard. Then I flew to the cabin and picked him up.

I showed him the pile of caviar-gutted salmon on the creek bank and the 4x4 tracks leading south. We followed them to where they disappeared into the fog about three miles from the lighthouse. He was happy to see all this evidence, and to be able to photograph it, without having to confront an actual poacher.

I knew that enough fuss had now been made that everyone would know about it. Part of what everybody knew was that the people at the lighthouse were responsible for the poaching. Now, something would be said to them. The effect would be to remind them that this was a sanctuary and that the old rules had been replaced by new ones.

For me, the whole exercise had been about letting everyone know that someone was watching. The rivers were thick with salmon that year. The amount the poachers were taking was not critical. I knew as well how hard up everyone was. All I really wanted was for them to take their caviar business somewhere else—to show that they respected the boundaries of the sanctuary. That it was fish and not bears didn't make it right. I knew that if they were allowed to take salmon caviar now, the likelihood of bear poaching later would increase.

Before I left Kamchatka that September, I raised some more fuss about the trappers at the Kambalnoye River cabin. Though I liked them well enough as people, the cabin hadn't been repaired for their use. In meetings with the South Kamchatka Sanctuary director, we agreed that the trappers would be removed and that rangers would be posted for the winter to both the Kurilskoy and the coastal ranger cabins, and perhaps even one at Lopatka Point where the lighthouse stood. Money from our anti-poaching fund would pay for it. We also began to talk about a future plan to increase the rangers' pay to $150 a month, a very decent wage in Russian terms, enough to make the job respectable and to recompense the rangers for sticking their necks out against poachers. The director was definitely listening. I was confident that there would be no repeat of what happened last winter, when the foxes had been the ones to pay for any poaching deterrent that had existed at Kambalnoye.

With three days to go before our scheduled flight to Moscow, Maureen and I were still at Kambalnoye Lake and the weather was socked in. On the night of September 5, Tatiana e-mailed to say she would be down with a helicopter next day by noon. September 6 did not look good either, but around 5:00 p.m., we heard the helicopter coming. It descended through a tiny gap in the fog and landed. Everybody on board was in a hurry to leave, so we had lots of help with the loading. The sun was slightly visible when it was time to go and, towards that light, the helicopter rose. Maureen was away on her journey.

As for me and the Kolb, I taxied until I found my famous Hole, up through which I flew. The Kolb sprang free into the light and I flew north.

We had to leave Kambalnoye without seeing Chico again. For days we had been rushing towards every bear her colour, but it was never her. The truth, that she had gone a long way away and wasn't going to be back any time soon, had to be accepted. Although she and Biscuit had denned together last year, they almost certainly wouldn't den together again. There was no way of knowing if or when Chico would return. Meanwhile, Biscuit and Brandy were left in charge of our area. A few days before leaving, Maureen had noticed a fox kit not far from the cabin, a hopeful sign that more foxes would be there upon our return.

When I dropped into the flying school late that night, several fellows came rushing out of the buildings. By the way they examined the Kolb, I knew they'd heard the story of the crash and were looking for the damage. I was pretty proud of their perplexity. They couldn't find a thing.

28

What Chico, Biscuit, and Rosie Taught Us

The closer the time came for the Moscow exhibition, the more I appreciated what a culmination of the project to date it was going to be. By the end of the summer of 2000, the first phase of our bear study was over: the babyhood and adolescence of Chico, Biscuit, and Rosie, and the befriending of Kambalnoye Lake bears like Brandy, Gin, and Tonic. We had established trust and achieved coexistence with all these bears, and had gone further into deep trust with Chico and Biscuit—and certainly with Rosie until the end of her life.

Starting next season, year six and phase two, Chico and Biscuit would be on the near edge of adulthood. No longer the inseparable pair they had been for their first four years, they were branching off into their lives as independent grown-ups. As females, they were preparing for breeding and mothering. Phase two would be our study of those developments.

How fitting then that Maureen's artistic record of phase one should appear that fall in the ancient heart of artistic Russia: Moscow.

MAUREEN: The Moscow exhibition was set to open on September 13, and my biggest problem, the one I will perhaps always have as an artist, was my usual fear that the new work I wanted to include, this summer's work, wasn't any good. Charlie, seeing me in anguish, hearing me pronounce it all garbage, got excited of course, thinking it must be really good. But, living so close to so many bears and feeling comfortable about it had allowed me to overcome another fear: the fear of my artistic peers. My exhibit strove hard to avoid academic loftiness, and to avoid and mock a pretentiousness that has always annoyed me. I felt it was very important that the exhibition address the ability and desire of the audience to understand art.

My decision to go with Maureen to Moscow had to do with a simple desire to see her in her moment of glory—and of course to partake in it. But both of us also knew what a great chance it would be to broadcast the news of what we had accomplished. By the end of year five, we had proven a lot of what we set out to prove, and it was time to tell people about it.

My way of preparing was to make a list of the myths about grizzly bears that harm them most, and to show how, in every single case, our experience with Chico, Biscuit, Rosie, and the other bears at Kambalnoye, contradicted those myths. I also wrote down our protocol: our recommended code of action for people sharing space with grizzly bears.

Myth one: Bears are inherently dangerous.
By all previous understanding of what makes bears dangerous, Chico, Biscuit, and Rosie should have been a nightmare. But, treated as we had treated them, here were three bears, living wild, who had never been a danger to anyone. The last time Chico had hurt me, she weighed twenty pounds and had no idea of her own strength. As the bears got bigger and stronger, they became gentler, knowing somehow that we were fragile and becoming more fragile, relatively, as they grew.

Myth two: The only safe brown bear is one located a long distance away from people.
Not just our own three cubs but all the bears who frequented the Kambalnoye

Lake basin had got used to our living there during five consecutive summers. They had not once harmed us, or come close to harming us. There was also the record of trouble-free bear behaviour at the research station after we built the electric fence.

Myth three: A bear that does not demonstrate fear of humans is dangerous.
I have always believed the opposite. Make a bear fearful of humans and you might also make a dangerous bear. When we came to Kambalnoye, the bears were afraid of us. They ran from us. And I felt we had to be very careful on account of it. Over time, the bears lost their fear of us, and basically, we all relaxed. In the past three years, we had become progressively more confident of our ability to move about the basin in security, precisely because most of the bears are no longer afraid of us. There is also the example of the Itelman people. Before guns, bears had little reason to fear people, and there is good evidence that the Itelman lived reasonable lives among the many bears at that time.

Myth four: Hunting bears is necessary to maintain the appropriate fear level.
The bears at Kambalnoye are no longer hunted, or poached (touch wood), and the population shows no signs of "needing" it. Yet, this remains the favourite excuse for continuing the bear hunt worldwide.

Myth five: Bears are unpredictable.
Maureen's and my safety with Chico, Biscuit, and Rosie was always based on their extreme predictability. All we had to do to be trusted by them was to treat them respectfully and be as predictable as they were. Again, with the other bears at Kambalnoye, their predictability, matched by ours, was what enabled trust to grow. Brandy decided we were predictably trustworthy enough to babysit her cubs.

Myth six: Because it entails feeding them, it is not possible to reintroduce brown bear cubs without making them dangerous to humans.
Chico, Biscuit, and Rosie speak for themselves. They were fed in years one and two, to help make up for their not having a bear mother. They never became dangerous as a result. We certainly believe there's a right and a

wrong way to feed bears (feeding in a bowl being better than feeding from the hand, for example) but providing food in a carefully thought-out way, in times of need, can save a bear's life without causing problems later. The availability of bears' food is always sporadic, so the notion of food being provided and then not provided is something their natural lives prepare them for. The often-repeated statement by bear specialists that "a fed bear is a dead bear" is true mainly because feeding bears or letting them go into garbage causes them to hang out closer than almost anyone wants them to be. It is very difficult to regain a comfortable separation once this happens, and the loss of respect that results from trying to get them to move back causes some bears to be demanding and a few others to become very dangerous.

Myth seven: Grizzly bears need total wilderness to exist because all human interaction is unpleasant for them and invariably leads to conflict.
The fact that we have been able to maintain a cabin for five summers among one of the densest populations of bears anywhere calls this belief into question. At Kurilskoy Lake, a whole community is managing to live in an area of dense bear population without problems, thanks to electric fencing. In both places I see no evidence of bears not enjoying being around people, provided the people respect that what the bear is doing is important. Obviously, this situation could occur anywhere in the bear world.

A further proof is the Mouse Creek Bear, who is now over ten years old and still enjoying the company of people. Jeff and Sue Turner were filming in the Khutzeymateen in the summer of 1999, and Jeff described his meeting with the bear to me in this way:

The Mouse Creek mother and her cub provided us with the most amazing footage [while filming *Grizzly Face to Face* for BBC]. I had the opportunity to work very close to her, usually when the tourists were not there, and I felt that she recognized something of you in me. I don't think she has had the opportunity to really interact with someone on the ground since you left. Slowly, as I got to know her and how she would let me move around her, I really began to see what an amazing animal she is. She was quite curious of me and would come right over to within a couple of feet whenever I showed up. She let me film her and her cub wrestling together from about twenty feet and then came over to me in a very playful and curious mood. She very gently reached out and touched the end of the microphone I was holding and then smelled it with her nose directly on the foam, and then took the whole end very gently in her mouth and held on for a few seconds. Then she turned and went back and tackled her cub and they both wrestled some more.

As for the actions we recommend, our goal was never to have people imitate our level of intimacy with our bears. We went to the extremes we did because we wanted to be sure about what we were finding. No one else would need to be, or should want to be, as close to bears as we chose to be.

A big complex protocol that few people would have the time or the ability to learn would be useless to the goal of improving the relationship between humans and bears through a reduction of fear on both sides. Simple, learnable, easily applicable practices—good manners, really— would get us somewhere, and that's what we aimed for.

And here it is, the simplest of protocols:
- Use electric fencing to keep bears out of where people live and away from toilets, garbage, and anything else bears could eat or damage.
- Always assume that bears' activity is important to them and do your best not to interfere, especially when their need to fatten becomes urgent in late summer and fall.
- In surprise encounters, talk to bears, calmly.
- Carry pepper spray in bear country, to be used only at close range in dangerous encounters.
- A little harder to learn, but very enjoyable for anybody with a love of wild animals, is to appreciate the intelligence, instincts, vulnerabilities, and memory of bears. If you want to go into bear country, you should be willing to learn that too.
- If you live in bear country (this can be a village or the edge of a big city), bears will periodically come calling. Don't assume that this is automatically a dangerous situation. Leave the bear at peace and make sure you and your neighbours keep all attractants where bears

cannot get into them. Meet as a group with your neighbours and the local officials in charge of these matters. Then, as a team, decide whether you want to attempt to live with the bears or not. There is more information available all the time on living with bears, but if you decide not to do so, bears can be encouraged to go elsewhere without having to kill or even transport them. Make sure your official knows how to do this, and, if need be, help research the necessary information.

The buzz for the exhibition started even before we reached Moscow. We landed in PK on the night of September 6, and, thanks to the ongoing nature of the economic problems there, couldn't even have the hot bath we'd been dreaming about for two months. September 9 was the 260th birthday of the city, and when we were invited by the local TV station for a morning interview on that special day, we understood the honour completely.

That night, Maureen packed her artwork and frames, and the next morning Maureen, Tatiana, and I boarded an Aeroflot jet for the nine-hour flight to Moscow.

On the day of the opening, Maureen and I had a TV interview at 3 p.m., a press conference at 4 p.m., and the official opening began at 6:30 p.m. It was a terrific event, and my one contribution to it came out of a conversation I had with a Russian professor, a specialist in Canada-Russia relations. Something he said sparked an idea in me about the bear as a symbol of Russia. It seemed to me that the bear's close symbolic connection to the country could be good or bad in accordance with how the world viewed bears. Through the Cold War, the Russian bear was seen as aggressive and unpredictable, potentially violent at any moment. It was easy for the world to use this portrayal of the bear against Russia, because that's what people thought of bears.

Two minutes after the conversation with the professor, I was thrust into an interview, and I launched the idea that the new vision of a bear espoused by our project and by Maureen's art was as an animal that was reasonable, intelligent, predictable, and sensitive, an animal with whom it was possible to coexist peacefully provided you treated it with respect. It was a popular idea from the get-go. The media jumped on it, and it was part of almost every report and review thereafter.

MAUREEN: The opening was a great success. It wasn't until it was actually happening that somebody told me I was the first Canadian artist ever to mount a solo exhibition in Moscow.

Perhaps it is true that art prepares the ground for change in a different way than other forms of activism. In Moscow and St. Petersburg, we really felt that people were listening, and that they wanted to be persuaded by what we were saying. They were "leaning," you might say. Both Charlie and I felt we had broken through a wall of resistance that we had been hitting against for years. We could only hope that the people in charge of the fate of bears, worldwide, would listen to us and spend less time coming up with reasons for not believing us.

29

Where the Final Fear Resides

The nine-hour Aeroflot flight from Moscow got me into Petropavlovsk at noon on September 23, a Saturday. My flight onward to Canada wasn't until Monday. In my two-week absence from Kamchatka, summer had turned to fall. The leaves on the stone birch trees were golden; the air was crisp. I stood on the tarmac, dizzy with jet lag, but the calm air and the clear sky spoke to me through my fatigue. It was flying weather.

I jumped on a bus, and went out to Nicolayevka to see if my Kolb had been put away for the winter. It had not. A couple of my flying-school friends were there, and I asked if anyone knew where I could find a tank and two jerry can's worth of decent Russian gas. Volodya said he had found a place that sold the best gas he'd used in five years. I left him my two jerry cans and a handful of rubles, and he said the gas would be waiting for me next morning.

I spent the night at Jennya's apartment. She was still in Moscow, defending her doctoral dissertation, but the next morning, her son Misha made me a very early breakfast. I shouldered my pack full of survival gear and got back on the bus for the thirty-mile ride to the flying school. There was still a heavy frost on the ground when I got there, which was what I needed to take off. I pivoted my aircraft so that the rising sun could melt the ice off the wings.

At a quarter to ten, I was ready to "hand-prop" the plane. For the last half of the summer, I had been nursing an old and failing battery. Yesterday, the on-board computer had told me it was flat. My plan was to start the plane by hand-flipping the propeller. If I could do it now with the motor as cold as it was, I reckoned I could do it throughout the day.

Though I just about took the ends off my fingers on some stainless steel tape, the motor caught on the third try. I begged a couple of bandages and was in the air by ten. There wasn't a cloud to be seen. With my flight to Canada leaving the next day, I knew I was taking a risk. But the urge to fly, to go south one more time before the close of the year, was much stronger than common sense.

Whether I would have taken this chance had Chico been around for a farewell two weeks ago is a good question. I felt very much like a father would—or in bear terms, a mother. My bear-child, now almost adult, had left home. I was worried for her safety. I was lonely for her company. Chico and I were as good friends as perhaps a person can be with a wild animal, and I yearned to see her again and to know for sure, going into winter, that she was okay.

I flew the familiar country, the valleys, ridges, and mountains—a living map that I could easily read. The tundra was its richest colour, gold and the red-scarlet of bearberry leaves. When it came time to transfer gas from the jerry can to the tank, I was near the Ksudach Volcano, so I lowered into its crater mouth and landed in a thermal-heated bay of the upper lake. I took off my shoes and socks and stood in the hot water while I poured gas, dreaming of what I didn't have time for today: a dip in the hot water, and sleeping on the hot sand without need of a sleeping bag. The Kolb started without any problem, and soon I was dropping over the final pass into the Kambalnoye basin.

Descending, I could see that the pine nuts must be ripe in their cones and plentiful. Wherever there were mats of wind-dwarfed pine trees, there were bears. In my wishful condition, I was seeing Chico, fat with salmon, bushy with new hair, in too many places. I even landed on a little mirror lake because I was so sure I'd found her. I walked to the place, and it was a different bear.

In making that landing, I created my first flying problem of the day. I needed a beach to run up on so the plane would stay stationary when I turned the propeller. On the water, the second it was propped, the plane would pull itself ahead with me outside. The problem here was there was no beach, just a ring of overhanging alder.

My solution was to tie a rope to the frame and wedge it between a pair of rocks. It would hold the plane long enough for me to get inside. When I put on full throttle, the power would pull the rope free. With the rope trailing in the air, I flew the last mile home.

On the ground, I studied the bears that I could see with the naked eye and with binoculars. Most were seated in pine thickets, munching the sides out of cones. No Biscuit. No Chico. I had done such a thorough job of poacher-proofing the cabin it took me a whole half hour to get inside, where a jerry can of gas I needed in order to get back was stashed.

Then I went for a long walk to all the places where I thought it likely that Chico and Biscuit would go for their own harvest of pine nuts. Again and again I called their names in the voice that was our shared language. I saw many bears, but Chico and Biscuit weren't among them.

I had given myself until 4:30. The days were shorter now, and I couldn't stay much beyond that without risking darkness at the other end. I couldn't believe how fast my watch wound around to that time. I was back near the cabin and prepping the Kolb for takeoff, when above the cliff in Bearskull Bay, Biscuit wandered into view.

I walked up to where she was and I could hardly believe how big and fat she'd become. She had gained at least a hundred pounds in two and a half weeks. She had been sleeping and her eyes would not quite wake up. She was in that final lazy stage before a bear digs her den and goes for the long snooze, and she looked great with her long, beautiful blond fur.

Together, we walked the creek for a while. I still kept hoping that Chico would make an appearance as Biscuit had done. But by five o'clock, it hadn't happened, and I was really out of time. I think I knew that Chico wasn't there to be found, but it was also impossible to give up hoping that the next few steps would reveal her. For the second time that fall, Biscuit and I said our goodbyes.

■   ■   ■

It was a melancholy flight back to Petropavlovsk, though sweeter than if Biscuit hadn't shown up to see me off. The gold and red scenery unfolded in reverse, and I wondered, almost until I ached, where Chico was. How had the voyage into new country gone for her? Was she strong and forceful enough to hold her own, or was she having to use her speed and wiles to flee the territory of older, bigger bears? Would she return to Kambalnoye Lake to den, and would she be there waiting for us, as in any other year, when Maureen and I returned?

It seemed likely that she would return, that a lifetime of learning every cliff ledge and creek shallow would be too much advantage to simply walk away from. I dreamt that she would choose to breed and bring forth young in the places she knew best. I also knew she would be learning the advantages of other places that might be safer for her cubs.

That I did not know any of this for sure was not just frustrating for me; it was also quite wonderful. My not knowing didn't mean that Chico was becoming unpredictable; it just meant that I didn't yet know how to read the subtle logic of landscape and instinct that would rule her and Biscuit as adults.

Within that thought was the most important thing we had accomplished here at Kambalnoye. With the always sensible and patient help of Chico, Biscuit, and Rosie, Maureen and I had proven that the problems between people and bears are not rooted inside bears. If we choose to make ourselves better neighbours, wild bears can be counted on to behave within the ancient code of their wild culture.

As for our Kamchatka bear project, Maureen and I were confident we would enter year six with the usual mix of excitement, suspense, and expectation. The Russians would likely continue to torment us with bureaucracy while being our allies in ways that no North American jurisdiction probably ever would. We owed a tremendous amount to the Russians, without whose curious patience and willingness we would never have even met our three bears, let alone had the honour of raising them and helping them be wild.

If I had any qualm about my end of the project, it was that I might have failed our bears in the way that humans have always failed bears: by not trusting them as far as they could be, and may even want to be, trusted.

Chico had often walked up to me with her eyes alight with goofy, infectious joy, wanting me to come and play some new game that would deepen our friendship. I always gave her a shove away, then stood up to show there was a limit to what I would do. She looked at me with such disappointment. If she had words, I think she would have said, "When have I ever hurt you?"

And it's true—she never has.

Maureen will say that she has never seen me afraid in the presence of a bear, but the ancient fear of bear is in me too. And so there is something left for me to do.

NOTE FOR THE 2003 EDITION

Since the writing and first publication of this book, Maureen and I have continued to go back to Kamchatka to build on our incredible experience. It's not likely that we'll be able to repeat such a study, so we want to continue as long as we can. Each year seems to get more interesting. Brandy will soon wean Lemon and Lime, another set of cubs she has raised and has entrusted to us when she has needed time to herself. And our ranger program has worked wonderfully for five years now, protecting both the bears and the salmon as we had hoped it would.

Although we have not seen Chico again, we have no reason to think she is not alive—other than it seems strange to us that she would not somehow keep in touch. As we learn how young bears disperse and claim far-reaching territories, we feel lucky that Biscuit has made her home at Kambalnoye. She was bred by two different males in June 2002 and will come out of her den with cubs in the spring of 2003. We will be there again to see what delights are in store for us as grandparents.

Acknowledgements

We started this convoluted project on a shoestring, with ideas, but no money. To make it happen, we raised the funds ourselves and came to depend on many corporations who believed in what we were doing. Their financial support and encouragement have made our work with grizzlies possible and we continue to appreciate their much-needed assistance. We thank the following organizations: The Schad Foundation, who have most generously supported our work from day one, Clayoquot Island Preserve, Fanwood Foundation West, Raincoast Conservation Foundation, Craighead Environmental Research Institute, the Great Bear Foundation, Trail of the Great Bear Society, Counter Assault, Development Matters Inc., Parallax Film Productions Inc., Sun Microsystems Ltd. of both Canada and the United States, Mogens F. Smed Fund of the Calgary Foundation, Smed International Ltd., Peter Bush Foundation, the Alberta Foundation for the Arts, the Canada Council, Daymen Photo Marketing Ltd., Lowe Pro U.S.A. Inc., Big Rock Brewery Ltd., Ralph Heddin Associates Ltd., Dr. J. V. Horsely Professional Corporation, Morton H. Wynne Insurance Agency Ltd., Canada Trust Mortgage Company, Conex Management Ltd.,

WSG Benefit Consultants Ltd., Masters Gallery Ltd., the Lynchpin Foundation, Microsoft Corporation, S. M. Blair Family Foundation, Trimac Corporation, Kodak Canada Inc., the Calgary Zoo, and a foundation that wishes to remain anonymous.

As well as the corporate donors, the following individuals were generous with their friendship, time, and money. We are grateful for assistance from Robert and Birgit Bateman, Carol A. Bowker, Tom Ellison and Jenny Broom, Peter McCombs and Debbie Conrad, Roland Dixon, James Gosling, Rod and Lois Greene, Lynne and Rick Grafton, Faith Hall, Mike and Maureen Heffring, N. J. Hewitt, Dr. Margaret Horne, Gayadel Heimbecker, Pat and Rosemarie Keough, Joan A. Martin, Russ McKinnon, Uwe Mummenhoff, John and Barbara Poole, Anne, Peter and Tim Raabe, Signa Reid, Liz and Robert Schad, Joan and Jack Sherman, Nicki and Mogens Smed, Ellen Smith, Neil Smith, Anthony Webb, Doug Williams, Bert Van Bekkum, Gerry Zyphers, and approximately 350 others who either contributed items or made purchases at auction fundraisers.

The support of friends has come in many forms. For seven years we have relied on dozens of people around the world, for everything from looking after our home and all of Maureen's animals while we are away to organizing discussion groups with the livestock producers of Eastern Europe, who were having trouble with bears killing their sheep. We are grateful for the support of Pamela Banting, Nancy Barrios, Walter Bovich, Esther and Michael Brenner, Lance Craighead, Al Crane, Creative Travel Adventures/Ried Morrison, DLS Imaging/Jo Cookson, Wendy Dudley, Rick and Bev Durvin, Ernest Enns and Lynne Woodworth, Pat and Joe Erickson, Bristol Foster, Hal Grainer, Frank Hall, Dr. Bill Hanlon, Nancy Hauser, LeeAnne Havens, Ian Herring, Jeanne Kaufman, Pat Klinck, Helen Kovaks, Bill and Tip Leacock, Matevz Lenarcic, Nik Lopoukhine, Anne Lukey, Sid Marty, Michael Mayzel, Ian and Karen McAllister, Debbie and Tim McDonald, Tom and Elaine McFadden, Mike McIntosh, Kathleen McNally, Linda and Ed McNally, Jeannie Minchin, Pat and Baiba Morrow, Doug Murray, Sybil Palmer, Peter and Nan Poole, Matt Read, Ursula and Rick Reynolds, Andy Russell, Gordon Russell, John Russell, Selena Ronnquist, Clint Scherger, Myrna Shapter, Larry and Christine Smith, Ewa Sniatycka, Reno

Sommerhalder, Hopie and Bob Stevens, Tom Sullivan, David Suzuki, Dave Taylor, Jan Theunisz, Rob Walker, and David Wilkie.

Friends in Russia who have made us feel welcome and helped us to achieve our goals are Fedia Farberov, Elena Gaisina, Allison Grant, Tatiana and Vladimir Gordienko, Alexey Maslov and Ekaterina Lepskaya, Valery Komerov, Viktor Komerov, Anatoly Kovolenkov, Martha Madsen, Vladimir Mosolov, Jennya Ptichkina and her family, Igor and Irina Revenko, Irina Viter, Olga Yefimova, and my remarkable pilot friends—Evgeny, Genna, Viktor, Vladimir, and Peter.

We thank the Canadian Embassy, Moscow, former Canadian ambassador Anne Leahy, and current Canadian ambassador Rodney Irwin for assisting us in presenting our work in Moscow.

The most important outcome of Maureen's and my work in Kamchatka was to be able to tell people about it: Maureen through her art, me through my writing, and both of us through our photographs. From the beginning, I saw this book as the best way I could achieve what I had personally set out to do. I am indebted to several people for making the book happen. My brother Dick got me started on the right foot, and Valerie Haig-Brown directed me, early on. Without Fred Stenson's writing guidance, and his organizational and editorial skills, this book would not read nearly as well as it does. He has been marvellous to work with in so many ways. There were challenges, such as bouncing chapters off a rather antique satellite, from our cabin at Kambalnoye Lake to his office in Calgary. Fred and I also have another, older connection. We were both born and raised with the hamlet of Twin Butte, Alberta, (population: six) as our home address. My agent, Anne McDermid, introduced me to Anne Collins, publisher of Random House Canada. She and Pam Robertson understood what I was trying to do even before they saw the manuscript. We are also appreciative of Nigel Lang and Dawn Saunders-Dahl for the time they have spent scanning approximately 10,000 slides and building our database.

Another way that we have kept in touch with the world about our project is via our website (found at www.cloudline.org). Thanks to Paula Oswald for taking over as our webmaster after James Gosling set up the site and skilfully managed it for three years. Thanks as well to Barb Gosling and Derek Small for their friendship and for insisting we learn about computers.

Naturalist, writer and photographer CHARLIE RUSSELL has lifelong experience working with grizzly bears, and is the author of *Spirit Bear*. Artist and photographer MAUREEN ENNS exhibits her work internationally. In 1997, their work was the subject of the documentary *Walking With Giants: The Grizzlies of Siberia*. Russell and Enns live in Cochrane, Alberta.